ASHEVILLE-BUNCOMBE TECHNICAL INSTITUTE

DISCARDED

JUN 2 4 2025

Plastic Tooling

Plastic Tooling

TECHNIQUES AND APPLICATIONS

William P. Benjamin
The Boeing Company, Seattle, Washington

McGRAW-HILL BOOK COMPANY
New York   St. Louis   San Francisco   Düsseldorf   Johannesburg
Kuala Lumpur   London   Mexico   Montreal   New Delhi
Panama   Rio de Janeiro   Singapore   Sydney   Toronto

Library of Congress Cataloging in Publication Data

Benjamin, William P   1935–
  Plastic tooling; techniques and applications.

  1. Plastic tools. I. Title
TJ1104.B45   621.9   75-39845
ISBN 0-07-004554-2

Copyright © 1972 by McGraw-Hill, Inc. All Rights Reserved. Printed in the United States of America. No part of this publication may be reproduced, stored in a retrieval system, or transmitted, in any form or by any means, electronic, mechanical, photocopying, recording, or otherwise, without the prior written permission of the publisher.

1234567890   MAMM   765432

The editors for this book were William G. Salo, Jr., and Lydia Maiorca, the designer was Naomi Auerbach, and its production was supervised by Teresa F. Leaden. It was set in Caledonia by The Maple Press Company.
  It was printed and bound by The Maple Press Company.

To my lovely wife, Barbara, for her encouragement, assistance, and patience during the writing of this book.

Contents

Preface   ix

1. Tooling Concepts and Materials   1
2. Models and Modelmaking   27
3. Laminated Plastic Tools   68
4. Cast Plastic Tools   100
5. Foundry Applications for Plastic Tooling   125
6. High-temperature Plastic Tools   146
7. Integrally Heated Plastic Tools   169
8. Flexible Plastic Tools and Molds   185
9. Rework and Repair of Plastic Tools   206
10. Safety Precautions in the Use of
    Plastic Tooling Materials   218

Glossary of Tooling Terminology   221
Index   229

Preface

From the time that the first item was produced in quantity, man has required tooling to enable him to maintain uniformity, quality, and economical manufacturing costs for his various products. Tooling has been around for a long time; we know that the early Egyptians used molds to reproduce certain items. Tooling is required by virtually all modern-day industry, whether it be a small mold for casting miniature electronic components or a large assembly fixture for joining sections of our giant commercial aircraft.

The use of plastics for making tools had its greatest impetus during World War II in the aircraft and automotive industry. Prior to that time, the use of plastics in making production tools had been insignificant. However, during World War II, both the limited supply of skilled labor and the shortages of many metals led industry leaders to turn to other materials and production methods. Some of the advantages of plastics were quickly recognized, and plastic tooling was taken seriously for the first time. Since then, not only have plastics been used as an interim substitute for metals in tools, but in many instances they have replaced metal tooling for a number of applications.

Plastic tooling is therefore a new industry, still in its adolescence. However, through trial and error, as well as experimentation in various industries, plastic tooling is now emerging as a science rather than an art. One big problem that still exists is that many plastic tooling techniques as well as data on various plastic tooling materials have never been published, or written down for that matter. The Tooling Resin Formulators Division of the Society of the Plastics Industry has made an admirable effort to advance this technology by standardizing test methods, establishing quality standards, and conducting annual seminars. However, despite their efforts, the technical information so necessary to the tool designer, tool engineer, or tool builder still only appears widely scattered throughout various technical journals, trade magazines, and vendor literature. It is, in many cases, not readily accessible to the majority of the people who could put the information to good use.

Fortunately, the publisher of this book realized the need for a single source of information on the present state of the art of plastic tooling. It was felt that American industry needed a book presenting the basic fundamentals of plastic tooling, physical property information on various plastic tooling materials, design criteria for plastic tools, cost advantages and disadvantages of plastic tools, and the most recently developed fabrication techniques. Above all, such a book had to be practical and down-to-earth.

With this in mind, this book was written, hopefully, to satisfy the needs of many people. This book is intended to serve the following purposes:

1. Provide industry management with a better understanding of the capabilities of plastic tooling, in order that they may make optimum use of this growing technology.

2. Provide tool engineers and tool designers with information on strength characteristics of plastic tooling materials, design criteria for plastic tools, and information on the most successful applications of plastic tools.

3. Provide industry in general with a reference book on plastic tooling. In addition to providing the basic fundamentals of plastic tooling, it also deals with some of the most advanced tool fabrication techniques.

4. Provide patternmakers and tool builders with a shop handbook containing the most recently developed plastic tooling materials and detailed fabrication techniques.

5. Provide a textbook that can be used by many of the vocational and trade schools that are now offering programs in plastics.

The author is very enthusiastic and optimistic about the future of plastic tooling. The reader will no doubt sense this sentiment as he goes through this book. Tooling itself is an exciting, challenging field that offers the individual an opportunity to exercise his creativity as well as utilize his technical knowledge or manual skills. To the author, the versatility of plastic tooling materials, leading to new concepts in tooling, offers a very rewarding career. It is hoped that this book not only will encourage newcomers to careers in plastic tooling, but will serve to build a greater awareness among management, technical, and production personnel as to the capabilities of plastic tooling. The optimum utilization of plastics in tooling is dependent on these people having a thorough knowledge of the advantages as well as the disadvantages of plastic tooling, and a good working knowledge of the proper way to design and fabricate plastic tools.

I would like to express my appreciation to McGraw-Hill for giving me the opportunity to write this book. I am also indebted to the members of the Plastics for Tooling Division of the Society of the Plastics Industry who have been very helpful in providing me with some of the photographs, technical data, and other information contained in this book.

William P. Benjamin

Plastic Tooling

CHAPTER ONE

Tooling Concepts and Materials

The field of tooling offers one of the most interesting and exciting challenges available to the young man launching out on a career in the modern industrial world. There are very few other areas in present-day manufacturing that offer the individual as much opportunity to exercise his creativity and ingenuity as well as his technical or manual skills. Tooling is so basic to all manufacturing operations that the opportunities in this field are virtually unlimited.

The use of plastics as tooling materials has provided many new opportunities for the creative plastic engineer and tool engineer to advance the state of the art and improve tooling costs. The very dynamic nature of the plastic industry promotes constant change and improvement. Through the continued development of new materials, new applications, and new tool fabrication techniques, the plastic tooling industry has steadily grown. It has progressed from a "black art" to a modern approach to tooling based on accepted chemical and engineering principles.

In order to sustain this growth, the industry must develop the necessary knowledge on the part of the management, engineers, and toolbuilders to enable them to make proper use of the materials and to avoid misapplications. Numerous young people, about to make decisions with regard to their life's work, have only a vague, generalized picture of our industrial world. In order that the tooling industry be capable of attracting able young men, there must be a means available of providing them with insight into the field of tooling. For this reason, this book will begin with a discussion of tooling itself and its relationship to modern industry. It will then proceed into the specialized area of tooling that this book is all about, plastic tooling.

Tooling is a very broad field; consequently it is very difficult to define. In the industrial sense, tooling must be considered as all the effort that goes into the manufacture of any product from the original engineering drawing to the point of actually going into production. Tooling includes the fabrication of all the models, patterns, jigs, dies, or assembly tools required to produce any manufactured item.

From this broad description it is apparent that a tool can be anything from a mold used to encapsulate miniature electronic components to a giant assembly jig used to locate and join sections of today's "jumbo jets."

Tooling is a prime consideration in the decision-making processes involved in the planning of the manufacture of any product. It is obvious that because the tooling costs are part of the manufacturer's investment, these costs must be recovered as part of the price of the product. Therefore, before the decision is made to produce a product, the manufacturer must make very detailed plans with regard to the identification of the required tooling and the estimating of the tooling cost. When the tooling costs have been determined, they will be combined by management with estimates on manufacturing costs, marketing costs, desired profit margins, and various other considerations. This will result in a determination of the price at which the product must be sold in order to provide the manufacturer with a satisfactory return on his investment. It cannot be overemphasized at this point how important it is that the forecasted costs be accurate. This is particularly true for the estimated tooling costs. In most industries, the tooling costs represent a substantial part of the investment. Consequently, an error or underestimate of the total tooling costs could mislead management into undertaking an unprofitable venture.

Imaginative, innovative tooling management can set a company apart from others in its industry. There are many companies today that are still in business and operating profitably because they have competent tooling personnel that consistently provide them with an edge over their competition.

FORMULATING A TOOLING PLAN

We have discussed that whenever the manufacture of any product is being considered, a detailed tooling plan must be developed. The objective of the tooling plan is to identify a family of tools that will be accurate and economical, make the part within the desired tolerances, last the required number of cycles, and be easy to maintain and repair. A great deal of technical knowledge as well as practical experience is required to develop a good tooling plan.

For example, consider the knowledge required by the design engineer in order to determine the design of the tool as well as the material from which the tool will be made. He must first be well informed on the material from which the part will be produced. If it is a metal product, he must know how the metal is best formed to the desired shape.

He must also know what problems are presented by the part design with regard to the elimination of wrinkles during the forming of the metal. If the product is to be made of plastic, he must know the temperatures and pressures at which the material is cured, as well as the shrinkage of the production material during processing. He must also know the quantity of parts that will be produced, for this consideration alone may very well dictate whether the tooling material is metal or plastic. For example, an automotive company with a requirement to form 1 million steel parts would in all likelihood select steel dies, while an aircraft manufacturer needing only 1,000 aluminum parts might very well select a less-expensive plastic tool.

In order to design tools properly, a knowledge of the production equipment is also required. Unless the tooling plan is being developed for a very simple product, the talents of several people with complementary backgrounds will be required to develop a comprehensive, accurate plan.

In addition to a knowledge of the materials from which the product will be made and the manufacturing processes, there are other considerations that must be made before the tooling plan is complete.

A considerable body of knowledge of the available tooling materials and tool fabrication techniques must be put to use in order to design the tooling properly. In the case of plastic tooling, the manufacturer is dealing with a rapidly advancing technology. He must therefore be abreast of the latest state-of-the-art advances to ensure that he incorporates only the best materials and tooling procedures into his tooling plan. The tool designer, for example, must have a knowledge of the various tooling materials available to choose from and select the best for his particular application. He must be familiar with the physical properties of many materials as well as the best method of putting this material into the desired form or configuration. A well-designed tool will be a less-expensive tool because it will reflect the designer's knowledge of the tooling material, the tool fabrication method, and the way in which the tool will be used.

If all this knowledge is properly combined, the resulting tooling plan will provide the manufacturer with information on the number of tools required, the anticipated flow time required to fabricate the tools, and an accurate estimate of what the tooling family will cost.

If the manufacturer becomes committed to produce this product, it will be up to the tool fabrication department to stay within the predicted tooling costs.

BASIC CONCEPTS OF TOOLING WITH PLASTIC

It is apparent from the previous discussion that tools may be fabricated from either metal or plastic. While both of these materials can be worked or formed to an identical shape, there are some great differences in the methods used to arrive at a desired shape with either metal or plastic. It is important to know the basic differences in the two tooling approaches. In making metal tools the material is either cast or extruded to a rough shape and machined or hand-finished to the desired configuration. Another method of making metal tools is to stretch sheet metal to the desired contour by the use of a forming tool. The stretched sheet becomes the tool. In most cases, the manufacture of metal tooling requires expensive equipment and considerable handwork.

The basic concept of making plastic tools is quite different. For the most part, the materials used in plastic tooling are resins in the liquid state that are capable of forming solid, stable shapes through the use of a suitable catalyst or hardener. This permits the use of plastic tooling materials to be formed to a net configuration. Normally, hand finishing is kept to a minimum.

The concept of using plastic materials to make tools or molds is not new. The basic concept of plastic tooling can be traced back to the early Egyptian dynasties. Archaeologists have discovered that over 5,000 years ago the Egyptians were using molds to reproduce shapes in plaster for ornamental and decorative objects. Although these techniques are now considerably refined, the same basic concept prevails. Stated simply, the basic concept of plastic tooling is that, *given a desired shape or configuration, plastic materials can be used to accurately reproduce the reverse shape and that the reverse shape can in turn be utilized to reproduce the original shape or configuration.* This concept is illustrated in a very simple form in Figure 1-1. The part illustrated in this figure is a section of decorative molding. The model is sculpted or carved by hand and a reverse mold made from the model. Duplicate parts are then cast into the mold. Many of the theaters constructed early in this century have decorative moldings of this type which were cast in plaster, cut to proper length, bonded into place, and painted.

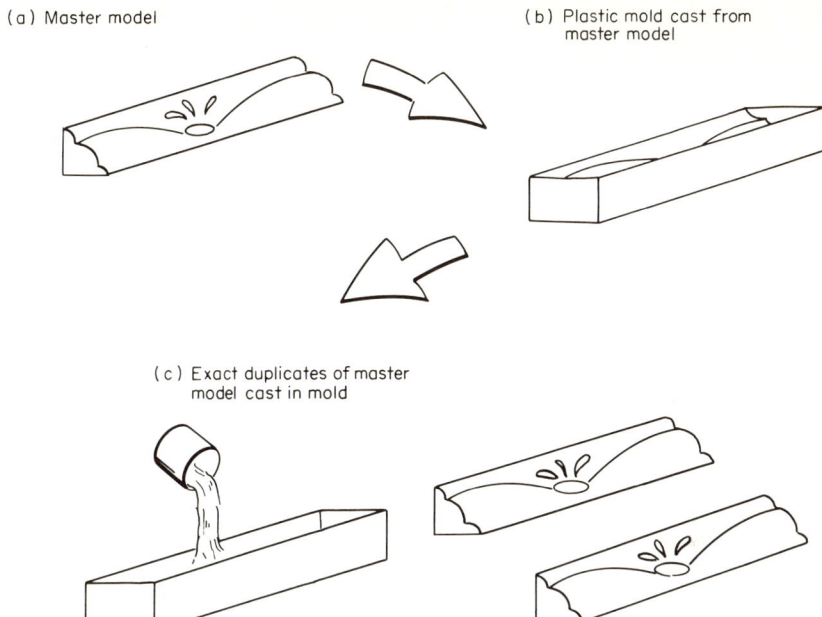

Fig. 1-1 Basic concept of plastic tooling.

It should be pointed out that, while this example serves well as an illustration of the basic plastic tooling concept, it is oversimplified. Plastic tooling materials do not reproduce shapes to the exact dimensions. As a general statement, it can be said that plaster products expand slightly upon curing. Conversely, most tooling resins shrink slightly. Since both the expansion of plaster and the shrinkage of tooling resins is uniform in all directions, the dimensions upon completion of cure are predictable. For example, the plaster used to make the plaster molding in Figure 1-1 expands 0.0018 inch per inch. While this is relatively unimportant for an ornamental item of this type, one quickly sees that the expansion of plaster must be a consideration on large parts with critical dimensions. If this material were being used to make a mold for a large aircraft tool with normal tooling tolerances of plus or minus 0.010 inch, the expansion would have to be compensated for in some way in order that the final production tool be accurate. Expansion and shrinkage factors of all the various plastic tooling materials will be discussed in detail in the appropriate sections of this book.

Sequence in Industrial Tooling

From the foregoing discussions, it is an obvious conclusion that tooling plays a very important part in the determination of the final cost of

6   Plastic Tooling

any manufactured product. In general, the fewer the number of parts that will be produced, the greater the impact of tooling costs on profits. For example, if a tool will only be used to produce a few hundred parts, the manufacturer cannot withstand tooling cost overruns that a manufacturer in another industry is able to amortize over several hundred thousand parts. For this reason, tooling plans must be very thorough and must carefully outline the tooling sequence to avoid duplication and wasted effort. A typical tooling sequence is shown in Figure 1-2. A similar sequence will be used in the development of every tooling plan. As in all cases, the point or origin for the tooling plan is the engineering drawing. The engineering drawing specifies the configuration of the part as well as the dimensions and tolerances. The engineering drawings are used to develop tool design drawings. In many large tooling programs, tool design drawings are made for all master tools.

However, for the other types of tools, tool design drawings are made for only a few typical tools of each type, and the tool fabrication shop is thus provided with the basic design criteria for the other tools. For example, if 150 thermoforming molds were required in the tooling plan, tool design drawings might be made for seven or eight configurations that were typical of all the shapes in the total package. The other tools would be designed by the tool fabrication shop, using the criteria established in the seven or eight tool design drawings.

In studying Figure 1-2, it should be noted that all tooling is developed from the master model. It is common tooling practice to coordinate all completed tooling to the master model within close tolerances (usu-

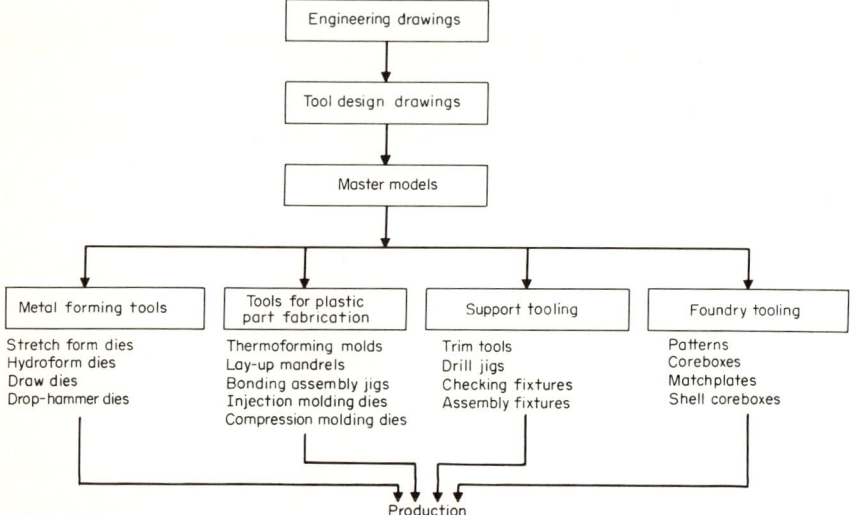

Fig. 1-2   Typical tooling sequence.

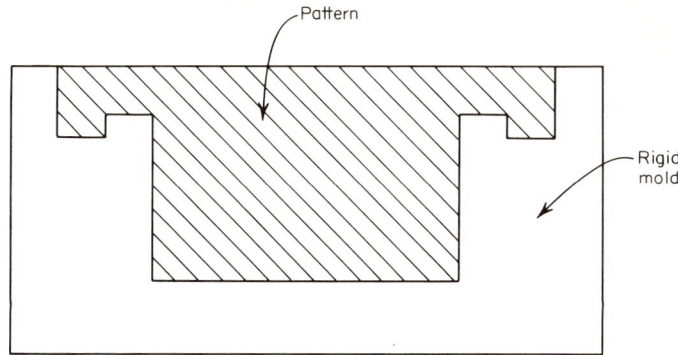

Fig. 1-3 Design with no draft. It would be virtually impossible to remove this pattern without incurring damage to either the pattern or the mold.

ally 0.010 inch). Following this approach, one can see that a production part made on a stretch form die (metal-forming tool category) will coordinate to an assembly fixture (support tooling category) because they are both made from accurate transfers taken from the same master model. Because all tooling is coordinated back to the master model, it is common industry practice that once a master model has been approved by the quality control organization for accuracy, it becomes the controlling reference for all subsequent tooling and, in effect, supersedes the engineering drawing.

The Concept of Draft

In order to design tools and molds properly, it is important to have a good understanding of the meaning of the tooling term *draft*. Draft is the term used to describe the taper given to the sides or vertical faces of a pattern to facilitate its withdrawal from a mold. Generally a taper of $\frac{1}{8}$ inch per foot, or approximately 2 degrees, is considered "good draft." Designers of plastic molded parts are encouraged to design all parts with a minimum of 2 degrees of draft whenever possible.

When a pattern or model has vertical walls, it is referred to as having "no draft." The pattern illustrated in Figure 1-3 has no draft. The removal of this pattern from the mold without damaging either the pattern or the mold would be extremely difficult, if not impossible. As an example, if the pattern were made of wood, even the slightest amount of wood grain on the vertical sides of the pattern would cause the pattern to lock itself inside the mold. In such a case, there are basically two alternative solutions to the problem:

8   Plastic Tooling

1. The part (consequently the pattern) could be redesigned to provide adequate draft. Figure 1-4 shows how the part could be redesigned to provide good draft. Such a redesign would make part removal relatively simple.

2. If the part could not be redesigned, the mold could be made using a flexible material. This would permit the flexing of the mold walls outward, enabling the part to be withdrawn from the mold.

Backdraft is the term used to describe a part or pattern with taper on the vertical sides that prevents removal of the object from the mold. Figure 1-5 illustrates a pattern having backdraft. This pattern would obviously be impossible to remove from a one-piece rigid mold. If we assume in this case that the design of the part cannot be changed, there are again two alternatives:

1. The mold can be designed as a rigid two-piece mold. This would enable the mold halves to be separated and the part withdrawn.

2. The mold can be made from a flexible plastic material. The walls of the mold would then be able to flex outward, permitting removal of the pattern.

In studying Figures 1-3 and 1-4, it can be seen that it would not be possible to use a two-piece mold to make either of these parts. The ridges in the base of the pattern would prevent the mold halves from being separated on a horizontal plane. This serves to point out that an understanding of draft is very important to the design of good tools and molds.

Since it is such an important tooling consideration, draft should be

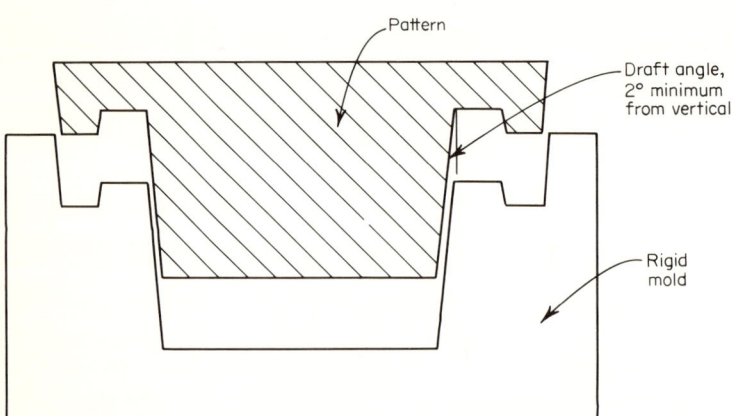

Fig. 1-4 Design with adequate draft. Pattern designed with adequate draft (2° minimum from vertical) can be easily removed from the rigid mold.

Tooling Concepts and Materials 9

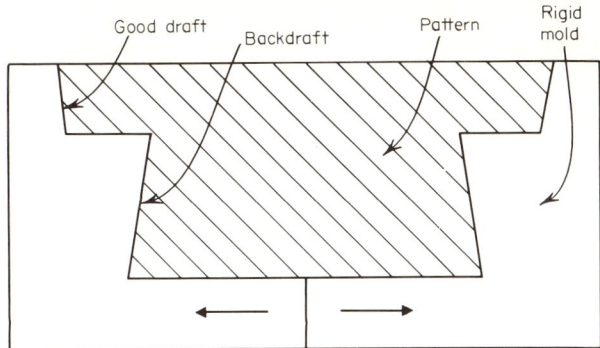

Fig. 1-5 Design with backdraft. The taper of this pattern makes it impossible to remove from a one-piece rigid mold. In this case a two-piece rigid mold has been designed. Part removal is achieved by moving the mold halves in the directions indicated by the arrows.

planned in the design of any production part. If draft considerations are overlooked, the result can be expensive redesign or the incurrence of unnecessarily high tooling costs. All too frequently, production parts, particularly decorative items, are designed from the aesthetic standpoint with very little consideration given to the tooling and manufacturing problems associated with the production of the part. When this occurs, tooling shop personnel may call it to the attention of the design organization. This often enables slight modifications to be made in the design, resulting in a much lower cost to manufacture the part.

Locating and Indexing

Because tooling with plastics involves making a series of transfers, methods of accurately locating and indexing various tools and transfers of tools becomes very important. Often the configuration of the part itself will permit adequate indexing. Frequently, however, the part contour is such that some other means must be devised to maintain proper coordination. Various techniques are employed, and they will be discussed in the appropriate sections of this text. For the present, we will discuss the most common method of locating and indexing a simple two-piece mold.

In constructing a two-piece mold, it is important that provisions be made for locating and indexing the mold halves together. If the two mold halves do not mate properly, the part will be distorted and unacceptable. Figure 1-6 illustrates this point. This condition is commonly referred to as a "mismatch." In Figure 1-6, cylindrical part B was made in a two-piece mold that did not match properly.

10   Plastic Tooling

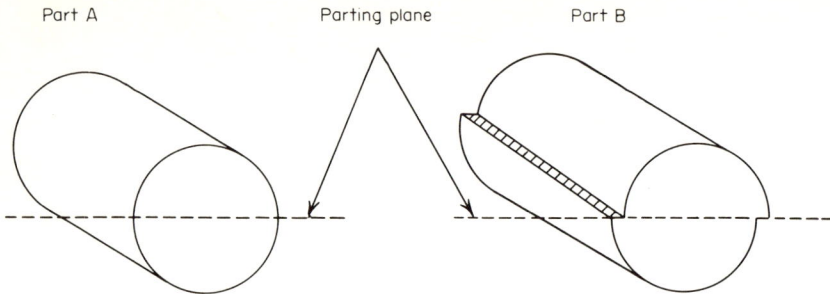

Fig. 1-6 Results of properly and improperly matched molds. Part A was molded in a two-piece mold that was properly indexed. Part B was made in an improperly matched two-piece mold. It is important that proper coordination be maintained throughout the tool fabrication sequence.

Provisions for locating and indexing should be considered prior to the actual fabrication. The necessity of indexing two mold segments after the fabrication has been completed can be an expensive chore.

The use of "match-buttons" is perhaps the simplest and most straightforward method of locating and indexing mold segments. The procedure, although simple, is a very accurate way of matching two mold halves, such as the molds required to make the part illustrated in Figure 1-6.

To make a two-piece mold for a cylindrical part such as the one illustrated in Figure 1-6, the first step is to mount the part model on a surface table in a fixed position. Modeling clay or plaster may be used for this purpose. In this case, the parting plane bisects the part. After determining how far beyond the part the mold will extend, the silhouette of the part at the parting plane is cut out of wood or thin-gauge metal. The parting plane is established by supporting the board in its proper relationship to the part model (see Figure 1-7). Modeling

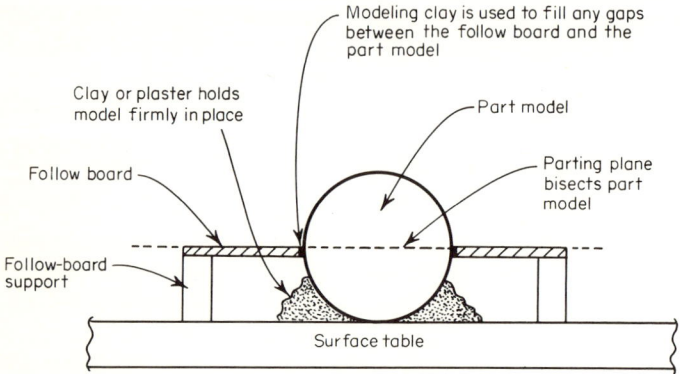

Fig. 1-7 Establishing the parting plane for a two-piece mold.

Tooling Concepts and Materials   11

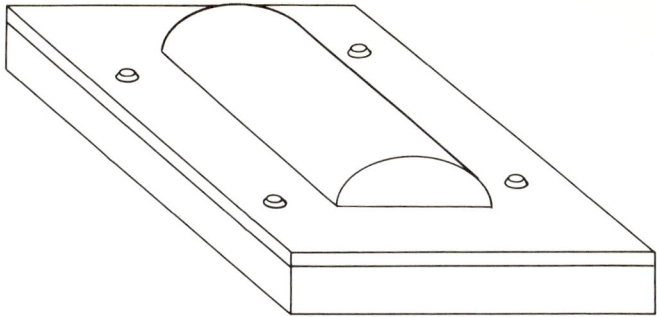

Fig. 1-8 Typical location of match-buttons.

clay is then used to fill in any gaps between the follow board and the part model. The modeling clay is worked with a modeling tool to ensure that it is a flat extension of the follow board and is perpendicular to the tangent of the part. This provides a sharply defined parting plane for the two mold halves.

Holes are drilled in the follow board at four locations. The holes should be $\frac{1}{8}$ inch greater in diameter than the stub of the match-button. A small amount of modeling clay is applied to the stub of the match-button, and the match-button is pressed firmly into the predrilled holes. Any cracks between the base of the match-button and the follow board are filled with modeling clay. This will prevent resin from running under the match-button and causing it to lock to the tool during subsequent operations. Figure 1-8 is a sketch showing the location of the match-buttons in relation to the follow board and part model. Figure 1-9 is a detail of the method of attaching the match-buttons to the follow board as well as a detail showing the use of clay to extend the parting plane to the tangent point of the part model.

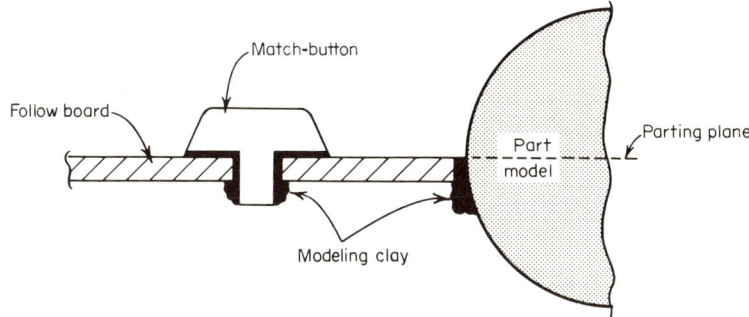

Fig. 1-9 Detail of the use of modeling clay to locate match-button and fill in gaps between the follow board and the part model. Note that the clay meets the part model perpendicular to its tangent.

Fig. 1-10 Locating pins are used to properly index this two-piece mold. (*Hysol Division, The Dexter Corp.*)

The model and follow board are then coated with an appropriate parting agent. One-half of the mold is then made by either casting or laminating. Upon completion of the resin cure, the pattern, follow board, and top mold half are carefully inverted. The follow board is then carefully removed, taking great care not to separate the part model from the plastic mold half already completed.

When the follow board is removed, the stubs of the match-buttons are protruding above the parting plane, which is now reflected in the plastic mold half. The match-buttons are removed from the mold with a pair of pliers, leaving four depressions showing in the plastic mold half. Parting agent is applied to all the exposed surfaces of the part model and the mold section already completed. The second mold half is then made in the same manner as the first section. Upon completion of cure of the plastic materials, the part model is removed. This provides a two-piece mold that is an accurate mirror image of the part model and is precisely coordinated. Figure 1-10 shows a plastic mold that was fabricated using the procedure described in the preceding section. In this case, locating pins were used and were left imbedded in the mold.

MATERIALS USED IN PLASTIC TOOLING

The materials used in plastic tooling fall under two general categories of plastic materials, the *thermosetting materials* and the *thermoplastic materials*. The preponderance of plastic tools are fabricated using thermosetting materials. However, since a large number of plastic tools are used to form thermoplastic materials into desired shapes, it is well at this point to have a thorough understanding of both categories of plastic materials.

It will not only provide a better understanding of some of the production processes used to manufacture plastic parts, but it will provide greater insight into why thermosetting materials are preferred as tooling media.

Since this book is not intended to be an engineering reference on the chemistry of plastics, the definitions and explanations of various plastic materials will be kept very simple. For our purposes, it is sufficient to define *plastics as organic materials that at some stage in their processing can be caused to flow and take up a desired shape upon the application of adequate heat and pressure and to retain this shape when the applied heat and pressure are withdrawn.*

Thermosetting plastics are by far the most commonly used in plastic tooling. Normally, these materials are resins in the liquid state that are capable of forming solid, stable shapes through the use of a suitable catalyst or hardener. When the two components are combined in their proper ratio and formed into a desired shape, they remain stable at all temperatures below their decomposition temperature. The structure that is formed when these molecules are chemically linked together is called a *crosslinked structure*.

Because of the manner in which they are linked together, they are normally very dimensionally stable. Figure 1-11 illustrates the crosslinked structure of thermosetting materials.

Typical examples of thermosetting materials used in plastic tooling are the epoxy resins, the polyesters, the silicones, and both the polyurethane elastomers and the foams.

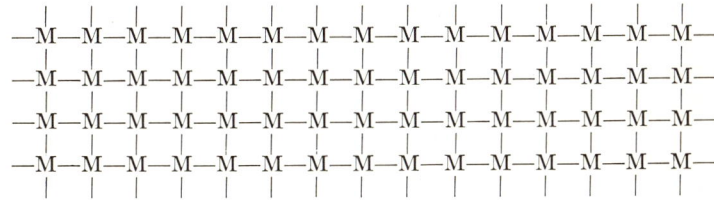

Fig. 1-11 Structure of thermosetting plastics.

The other category of plastic materials is called the thermoplastics. The thermoplastic materials are also composed of monomers linked together to form long chains. However, these monomers are linked together in a different structural pattern than the thermosetting materials and consequently possess different properties. Figure 1-12 illustrates the structure of the thermoplastic materials. It is important to note that, while these molecules are linked together to form long chains, these chains are not crosslinked to one another. Therefore, because of their basic structure, the thermoplastic materials are not as inherently stable as the thermosetting materials.

—M—M—M—M—M—M—M—M—M—M—M—M—M—M—M—M—M—
—M—M—M—M—M—M—M—M—M—M—M—M—M—M—M—M—M—
—M—M—M—M—M—M—M—M—M—M—M—M—M—M—M—M—M—
—M—M—M—M—M—M—M—M—M—M—M—M—M—M—M—M—M—

Fig. 1-12 Structure of thermoplastic materials.

When a thermoplastic material is heated up and pressure applied, the chains are able to slide past one another. In this manner, the material can be manipulated or formed into another shape. This process, usually referred to as *thermoforming*, can be repeated several times as long as the material is not heated beyond its decomposition temperature. This characteristic has been used to great advantage by industry to produce a variety of plastic consumer items such as bottles, luggage, containers, pipes, and even items of furniture.

For tooling purposes, the thermosetting materials offer the advantages of strength, dimensional stability, rigidity, and the ability to operate over a larger temperature range than the thermoplastics. These materials are all commercially available from tooling resin formulators, usually in a two-component liquid state.

The industry group known as the Plastics for Tooling Division of the Society of the Plastics Industry has developed around the requirements of the tooling shop. The member companies are specialists in compounding a wide range of formulations for specific plastic tooling applications. Moreover, their compounds have been developed over a period of time on the basis of long experience in tooling and familiarity with the specific problems of the toolbuilder.

Physical property data, useful to the tool designer as well as to the tooling shop supervisor, are readily obtainable from the member companies. To the toolbuilder, the field representatives of member companies provide technical assistance as well as contact with a broad spectrum of industry engaged in plastic tooling. Much valuable information about new tooling concepts, materials, and fabrication techniques is disseminated in this manner.

Perhaps one of the greatest advantages of the tooling resin formulators is reliability. They are able to offer the manufacturer of plastic tools a high degree of quality and uniformity from batch to batch. The toolbuilder is thus assured that he can rely on the materials to provide him with consistently good quality tools.

Through the outstanding efforts of the Plastics for Tooling Division of the Society of the Plastics Industry, test methods have been developed which provide meaningful physical property data on a wide range of tooling resin formulations. Largely through their efforts, plastic tooling has emerged from a black art to a sophisticated industry with established basic material standards and proven success in a wide range of tooling applications. Plastic tooling has emerged into a position of wide acceptance and recognition as a reliable, economical tooling media.

Classification of Plastic Tooling Materials

Plastic tooling resin compounds may be classified either by their chemical classification or by their function. The nature of the products make them difficult to discuss thoroughly using a single method of classification. Even though there is a certain degree of overlapping in using both methods of classification, it is felt that the subject can be covered more completely in this manner. A discussion of plastic tooling materials using either a chemical classification or a functional classification alone would be incomplete.

Functional Classification of Plastic Tooling Materials

Casting Compounds: Casting of plastic tooling compounds represents the quickest and easiest method of making plastic tools. The use of casting compounds permits simply mixing the two components in their proper ratio and pouring of the mixture slowly into a cavity. This method provides the greatest labor savings of all plastic tooling methods. Casting compounds are usually of low viscosity (10,000 centipoises or less) in order to facilitate pouring without entrapment of large amounts of air. They are usually filled systems; i.e., they incorporate the use of fillers such as metallic powders or clays.

Casting compounds are usually formulated from slow-reacting thermosetting resins. This minimizes the exothermic heat generated in the casting, enabling large masses to be cast and still retain dimensional accuracy. Casting compounds usually require a minimum of 16 hours cure at room temperature before they can be demolded.

Gel Coats or Surface Coats: Gel coats or surface coats are specifically formulated to be applied to the surface of a model in a thin layer, usually no greater than $1/16$ inch. When properly backed up by either a laminate or a casting, the gel coat becomes the surface of the tool.

Gel coats and surface coats are usually characterized by their high degree of thixotropy and high viscosity when in the liquid state. *Thixo-*

tropy is the ability of a material to adhere to vertical surfaces without sagging or running off.

A wide variety of fillers are incorporated into a gel coat system to provide specific properties. For example, a metallic filler such as silicon carbide may be incorporated into a gel coat system to provide abrasion-resistant characteristics. Unless they possess wear-resistant characteristics, tooling gel coats are usually white in color. This makes it easier to see scribed lines and/or defects on the surface of a tool.

Gel coats are recommended for all laminated tools on which tooling lines must be subsequently scribed.

Laminating Systems: Laminating compounds are specifically formulated to impregnate fiber glass cloth during the process of making a fiber glass laminated tool. Consequently, these materials are normally low in viscosity (in the 3,000- to 5,000-centipoise range), have some degree of thixotropy, and have the ability to "wet" or penetrate fiber glass cloth or other fabrics. Because laminating is a time-consuming operation, laminating compounds normally have a working life of a minimum of 30 minutes. The use of laminating compounds enables large tools to be made with very low material costs. Further, laminated tools are much lighter weight than either metal tools or cast plastic tools. While the labor costs involved in making a laminated tool are higher than labor costs for casting, the savings in materials on a large laminated tool may offset the additional labor.

Paste Compounds: Tooling plastics are formulated as both semiflow and thixotropic pastes for a variety of applications. These paste compounds are normally used for such purposes as splining master models, repairing damaged tools, potting bushings, and bonding reinforcements to tools. Their working time and curing time varies considerably, depending on the type of resin being used and the application for which it is being used. For example, a paste repair compound may have a working time of only 10 to 12 minutes and cure hard enough to sand within 30 minutes. On the other hand, a paste splining compound may have a working life of 45 minutes and require an overnight cure.

Chemical Classification of Plastic Tooling Materials

Polyesters: Polyester resin compounds are used in tools and molds in applications where dimensional accuracy is not a critical factor. The two main advantages of polyesters are that they can be cured rapidly and they are substantially lower in cost than the other thermosetting materials used in tooling. The major disadvantage of polyesters is their high shrinkage. Where tooling tolerances are not critical, polyester–fiber glass laminates are utilized to take advantage of the lower material costs. However, where greater accuracy and interlaminar strength are required, the epoxy resins have become the standard.

Epoxies: Of all the thermosetting plastics used for tooling, the epoxies have proven to be the most versatile. The epoxy resins are available in the widest variety of compounds formulated for specific applications of any of the other tooling materials chemical categories. The advantages of the epoxies as tooling materials are their low shrinkage, high flexural and compressive strength, dimensional stability, and good resistance to corrosion, weathering, and ordinary chemicals. Because epoxies are excellent adhesives, epoxy tools can be easily repaired with the same material from which they were made.

Silicones: Silicones are predominantly used in tooling as a liquid casting system for making flexible molds. Silicone compounds may be poured and cured at room temperature. Most often, silicones are used as casting systems. However, it is possible to make laminates with silicone compounds by using a suitable primer on the fiber glass cloth. Flexible molds made of silicone elastomers may be used at temperatures up to 600°F. The cost of silicone compounds is higher than other flexible moldmaking materials. However, the cost is often offset by the ability of the silicones to release from other plastic materials without the use of parting agents.

TABLE 1-1 Typical Physical Properties of Thermosetting Tooling Plastics

Material	Shrinkage, inches/inch	Compressive strength, psi	Flexural strength, psi	Tensile strength, psi	Bond strength, psi	Typical applications
Polyester laminate	0.10	15,000	28,000	18,500	800	Lay-up molds
Epoxy laminate	0.0003	20,000	35,000	25,000	1,750	Trim tools, drill jigs
casting	0.002	12,500	8,500	6,000	1,800	Forming tools, rigid molds
Silicone	0.002	......	......	750	200*	Flexible molds
Polyurethane elastomers (Shore D 60)	0.05	......	......	3,000	4,000	Flexible molds, forming pads
foams (12-lb density)	0.00	480	410	......	......	Tool reinforcement

* Shear strength.

This is a distinct advantage over other flexible moldmaking materials since the others all require the use of parting agents. On parts that require finishing or painting after they have been cast, a manufacturer can often achieve economies by using silicone molds, thus eliminating the need for expensive cleaning of parting agents from parts prior to finishing.

Polyurethanes: The polyurethanes perform a dual role as tooling materials. They are commercially available as both elastomeric grades and foamable compounds. The polyurethanes have only been used as tooling materials in recent years. However, their advantages are becoming increasingly apparent as resin technology has improved to make these materials easier to handle. In addition to low shrinkage, they possess a high degree of toughness and durability. Polyurethane elastomers have found wide usage as pads for metal-forming operations, outlasting other elastomeric materials used for this application by a wide margin. The polyurethane foams have been widely used to provide rigid, lightweight reinforcement to thinly fabricated plastic tools. The recent introduction of self-skinning polyurethane foams offers some unique possibilities for these products as tooling materials. Both polyurethane elastomers and polyurethane foams are commercially available as two-component liquid systems capable of being poured and cured at room temperature.

Parting Agents Because most thermosetting materials used in plastic tool fabrication are also excellent adhesives, a parting agent or mold release must be applied to the model before application of the tooling plastic. It cannot be overemphasized that the application of a suitable release agent to a model is one of the most critical steps in the fabrication of a plastic tool. Improper selection or improper application of the parting agent will result in the tool's bonding itself to the surface of the model. As a consequence, a large expenditure of labor will be required to restore the model and/or the tool to usable condition. There have been occasions when both the tool and the model have been lost altogether because either the wrong parting agent was used or the parting agent was not applied properly.

Preparation of the Model Surface: It should be kept in mind that plastic tooling materials will reproduce every detail of the model surface including even the most minute surface detail such as wood grain and fingerprints. It is important to recognize that the finish on the surface of the tool can only be as good as the original model. If the model surface has defects, the plastic tooling compound will reproduce the defects just as accurately as it will reproduce the desirable details such as scribe lines. For this reason, great care should be exercised to ensure that the model surface is perfect before application of the parting agent.

A few minutes invested in preparing the model surface properly will save a considerable amount of time and effort at a later point in time to rework the tool in order to obtain the desired surface finish. Another point to consider is that reworking the tool to anything but a minor degree will frequently put the tool out of tolerance. It makes very little sense to be careless in preparation of the model surface and then have to expend many times the effort reworking the surface of the tool. In the fabrication of any plastic tool, the prime objective should be that when the tool is removed from the model it should have the desired surface quality.

Selection of the Proper Parting Agent: The selection of the proper parting agent is largely determined by the surface from which the tool is going to be taken. Plastic tools are fabricated from a variety of coordination media such as plaster, wood, metal, other plastics, or combinations of these materials.

Each model material presents a different problem in the selection of parting agents and in the techniques for applying them. For this reason, the techniques for sealing and releasing from each model material are discussed individually in this section.

In general, porous materials such as plaster and wood must be sealed prior to the application of a parting agent. Nonporous surfaces, such as metal and plastics, need not be sealed prior to the application of the parting agent. Several new release agents have recently been introduced on the market. These materials reportedly perform the dual role of sealer and release agent in one application. Before using any of these materials on production tools in lieu of the method recommended in this section, a small test should be conducted to ensure that the desired results are obtained.

The selection of a particular manufacturer's parting agent should be accomplished with the assistance of the company providing the tooling materials which will be used. Each member company of the Plastics for Tooling Division of the Society of the Plastics Industry will be able to recommend specific brands of parting agents that work well with the resin compounds which they manufacture. For this reason, this book will not attempt to specify parting agents by brand name but will instead refer to these materials in generic terms.

The release of plastic tools from various surfaces will be discussed in general terms. General considerations that must be made in each case will be pointed out. Release from various materials will be discussed in order of decreasing difficulty; i.e., the most difficult material to release from, plaster, will be discussed first. This will be followed by a discussion of the release of plastic tools from wood, metal, and other plastic materials, in that order.

Release from Plaster Models: A substantial number of plastic tools are direct transfers from plaster models. Although plaster is a generic term used to refer to both plasters and gypsum cements, the term plaster will be used here to simplify the discussion of parting agents. A more thorough discussion of the various types of plasters is given in Chapter 2.

The plaster model poses two challenges to good release of plastic tools: (1) it contains moisture, and (2) it is porous. Moisture is probably the greatest problem to overcome because moisture can interfere with the cure of the resin compound. For example, polyurethane elastomers are particularly sensitive to moisture and if exposed to even the slightest amount of moisture will produce a tool with a badly pitted surface.

All plaster models contain moisture. When plaster is mixed with water, an amount of water in excess of what is required to cause the chemical reaction is added to the plaster in order to make a pourable slurry. After the chemical reaction has taken place and the plaster reaches a solid state, there is a certain amount of free water in the plaster casting.

Thermosetting materials rely on exothermic heat generated from the chemical reaction of the two components to cause complete curing of the compound. There can be a considerable amount of heat generated during the cure of plastic tools, particularly on large tools. If the surface of the model reaches a high enough temperature, the free water in the model will turn to steam. The steam will pass through the parting agent and settle between the mold surface and the resin. This condition will result in numerous defects on the surface of the tool, usually in the form of pinholes and voids. For this reason, plaster models should not be used for the fabrication of high-temperature plastic tools that will require curing in the oven at elevated temperatures. Plastic-faced-plaster models should be used for making high-temperature plastic tools. The fabrication and use of plastic-faced-plaster models will be discussed in detail in Chapter 6, High-temperature Plastic Tools.

With the foregoing in mind, it is obvious that the first consideration in preparing a plaster model is to ensure that the plaster model is thoroughly dry. The following general rule of thumb may be used to determine whether a plaster model is dry enough to be used to make a plastic tool: A plaster model or transfer medium should be allowed to dry at room temperature for a minimum of 10 days before being used to make a plastic tool. If schedule requirements do not allow a waiting period of this duration, the plaster model should be dried in an air-circulating oven at a temperature of 125°F for a period of 12 hours for every inch of thickness of the plaster model. For example, a plaster transfer medium with a 2-inch wall thickness should be sufficiently dry after 24 hours in an air-circulating oven set at 125°F.

After the model surface is thoroughly dried, two coats of lacquer should be applied to the surface of the plaster model. A clear automotive lacquer thinned with approximately 30 percent by volume of lacquer thinner is normally used for this purpose. The first coat should be brushed or sprayed on and allowed to dry for approximately 20 minutes. The second coat is then applied and allowed to dry until it is odor-free. After the second coat of lacquer has sufficiently dried, two coats of a high-quality paste wax should be applied over the lacquer. The wax should be buffed between coatings. This will impart a high gloss to the surface of the model.

The next step in preparing the surface of a plaster model is the application of a film-forming plastic by either brushing or spraying. A polyvinyl chloride formulation is recommended over polyvinyl alcohol for this application because polyvinyl alcohol is soluble in water, which could create problems if the plaster is not thoroughly dry. If the film-forming plastic is sprayed, it should be sufficiently dry in approximately 45 minutes at room temperature. If the parting agent is applied by brush, it will take a minimum of 2 hours to dry. After the film-forming plastic is dry, another coating of paste wax is applied. The excess wax is wiped off but not buffed. Buffing of the final wax coating can result in peeling or wrinkling of the film-forming substrate. If this occurs, it will be necessary to remove the entire polyvinyl chloride coating and reapply both the film-forming plastic and the final coat of wax.

Release from Wood Models: Wood patterns are also porous and contain moisture. Therefore, the surface of a wood pattern should be pre-

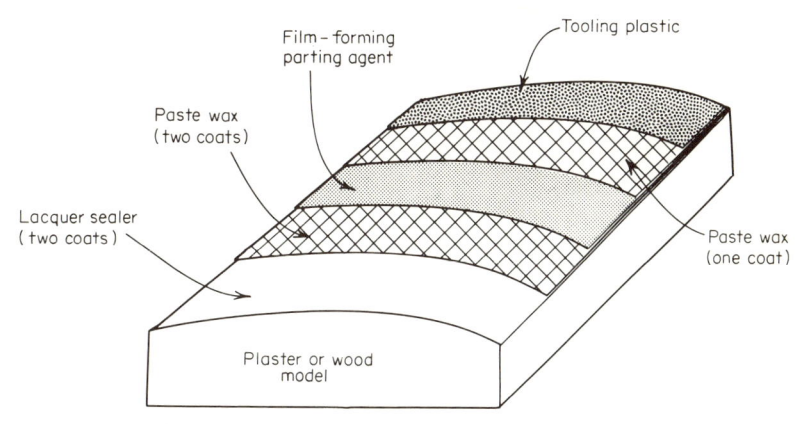

Fig. 1-13 Surface preparation of plaster or wood models.

pared in a manner very similar to the preparation of a plaster model. On wood patterns with very little draft, great care should be exercised to ensure that all wood grain has been sanded out. If this is not done and wood grain remains on the vertical walls of the model, it will cause the plastic to bind or "hang up" and make removal from the model very difficult. On patterns where the removal of all wood grain presents a problem, a coating of lacquer base sanding sealer is often required.

After the surface of the wood pattern has been sanded, and if necessary sealed with sanding sealer, two coats of either lacquer or shellac are applied. Judgment must be exercised as to the amount of thinner required, since different types of wood have different degrees of porosity. The first coat should be thinned sufficiently to enable it to penetrate into the wood. The second coat should be allowed to dry until it is odor-free. Two coats of high-quality paste wax are then applied to the model surface. The first layer of wax should be buffed prior to the application of the second layer.

The second coat of wax should be a light coat and should also be buffed. To provide additional assurance that a good release will be obtained, it is recommended that a film-forming parting agent such as polyvinyl chloride be applied either by brushing or by spraying. When the film-forming parting agent has dried, an additional coat of paste wax is applied. The wood pattern is then ready for use in making a plastic tool.

Release from Metal Surfaces: In comparison to plaster and wood surfaces, it is relatively easy to obtain good release from metal surfaces. A metal surface does not require sealing prior to the application of a parting agent. A resinous film-forming mold release, such as a silicone grease, is recommended. This type of material is usually applied to a clean metal mold or model surface and then baked into the metal in an oven at approximately 250°F for 1 to 2 hours. Normally, the mold release is applied and baked into the metal at least three times in succession prior to use to fabricate a plastic tool. The treatment of a metal mold or model in this manner will provide a surface capable of several releases before the parting agent has to be reapplied. This method is the same method used to release production parts from metal molds at temperatures up to 500°F.

Release from Other Plastics: Normally, the release of plastic tooling materials from other plastics is easily accomplished. Like metal surfaces, plastics do not require sealing prior to the application of a parting agent. There is a wide variety of parting agents, ranging from paste waxes to clear films, that work well when used in accordance with the manufacturer's instructions. In selecting the most suitable parting agent for release from plastics, the main thing that must be considered is the temperature at which the tool will be cured. Sad experience has shown that parting agents that release extremely well at cure temperatures under 150°F can prove to be excellent adhesives at cure temperatures up to 400°F. It is extremely important to keep this point in mind when selecting parting agents for fabrication of high-temperature plastic tools.

For room-temperature curing epoxy compounds, two coats of high-quality paste wax, buffed after each coat, will normally be sufficient to provide good release. However, most tooling shops prefer to have additional assurance that the tool will release from the model. In such cases, an application of either a polyvinyl chloride or a polyvinyl alcohol is commonly used. When the film-forming material has dried, an additional coating of paste wax is applied. The excess wax is carefully removed. The surface is not given a final buffing. The plastic model surface is then ready for use.

For tools that will be cured at elevated temperatures, an inorganic paste wax is recommended. It is suggested that the manufacturer of the high-temperature resin system being used be consulted for his recommendation on release agents. The manufacturer will be able to recommend specific release agents that are known to work well with his particular formulation.

ADVANTAGES AND DISADVANTAGES OF PLASTIC TOOLS

The tremendous growth in the use of plastics for tooling in recent years is testimony to the many advantages of plastic tools. Although plastics have been used to build tools for approximately 30 years, there is still a large segment of American management that is unfamiliar with the advantages of plastic tooling. Various misapplications of plastics for tooling have also created a reluctance on the part of some managers to utilize plastic tools. For this reason, many American executives tend to fall back on the metal tooling, or "hard tooling," that they used earlier in their careers. This human tendency to stand by the familiar, *tried and true*, older methods can only be overcome by developing familiarity and confidence in plastic tooling in modern industry. It is hoped that this book will be useful in putting the picture of the present state of the art of plastic tooling in its proper perspective for the benefit of all of those who can utilize plastic tools to their advantage.

In almost every segment of American manufacturing, one can find metal tools being used where plastic tools could have been utilized at lower fabrication cost and with less expensive maintenance. To cite some specific examples of this, let us consider first the experience of one automotive manufacturer. A set of 12 fixtures, designed in steel with plastic surfaces, were needed for use as masters in making a group of welding fixtures. These, in turn, were to be used for checking the production sheet metal as it came from the stamping plant and to set the welding units on the stamping presses. The estimated cost in steel was $68,000 with a delivery time of 22 weeks. In order to shorten the schedule, the fixtures were fabricated in plastic at a cost of $33,000 and a flow time of 7 weeks. In another instance, an aircraft manufacturer encountered schedule problems on the fabrication of 14 large metal tools to be used for curing fiber glass–honeycomb parts. In order to meet schedule requirements, the decision was made to fabricate the tools out of high-temperature plastic. The tools were made in less than 8 weeks at approximately 40 percent of the predicted cost of the metal tools. Although the plastic tools were intended to be used only as interim tooling, they were used successfully for over 3 years. The high-temperature plastic tools performed well enough so that the originally scheduled metal tools were never fabricated.

Instances similar to those cited above are occurring almost daily throughout American industry. New materials, processes, and applications are constantly being developed. The Plastics for Tooling Division of the Society of the Plastics Industry has been instrumental in this growth. The successes of plastic tooling have succeeded in bringing managers to a point where they are asking themselves objectively, "Where is the payoff? Where can I save money by using plastic tools?"

It should not be overlooked, however, that plastic tooling does have several limitations. In order to achieve the optimum benefits from the use of plastic tools, it is important that the disadvantages as well as the advantages be thoroughly understood. It can be just as expensive to choose a plastic tool for an improper application as it can be not to use a plastic tool for an ideal application. At the present time, the avoidance of misapplications for plastic tooling is one of the greatest challenges faced by tool engineers and plastic engineers.

Advantages of Plastic Tooling

Through the use of plastic in tooling, lower total tooling cost is possible. One of the greatest advantages of plastic tools is that they can be cast or laminated to finished dimensions. This eliminates the need for the expensive machining or handworking to contour that is necessary on other forms of tooling. The more complex the surface, the greater the advantage of plastic tools.

Normally, flow time on plastic tools is much shorter than the flow time on metal tools. Frequently plastic tools are completely fabricated in the same shop, providing shorter flow time and reduction in problems of coordination of the efforts of several different shops to fabricate parts of a tool. Flow time on plastic tools can be measured in days or weeks; whereas, the same tool in metal would require weeks or months to fabricate.

In general, plastic tools are lighter in weight than metal tools. This is extremely apparent in large tools. This advantage has recently been put to good use by the aircraft industry to make lightweight, epoxy laminated stretch form blocks reinforced with urethane foam. The use of these tools has greatly reduced the transportation and handling problems associated with metal tools of the large sizes required to form aircraft skins.

Disadvantages of Plastic Tools

There are several disadvantages of plastic tools that should also be pointed out. For example, the surface hardness of most epoxy resin systems is about two-thirds that of aluminum. Consequently, plastic tools are more prone to damage by rough handling or scratching with sharp objects. Also, the strength of plastic is generally lower than the strength of metals. The flexural, tensile, and compressive strengths of plastic tooling materials are less than half the strengths of most metals. For this reason, careful attention must be given to the design of plastic tools in order that they can adequately perform their function.

Because plastic materials are organic, there are definite limitations on the temperature at which they may be used. Although some high-temperature plastic tooling materials have performed satisfactorily at pro-

TABLE 1-2 Comparison of Metals and Plastics for Tooling

Item of consideration	Comparison result
Capital investment	Less for plastic
Skilled supervision	Generally equal
Labor cost	Less for plastic
Material cost	Generally equal
Lead time	Less for plastic
Equipment for tooling	Less for plastic
Large tool cost	Very favorable for plastic
Tool weight	Approximately 25% less for plastic
Repair and design changes	Very favorable for plastic
Short runs and prototypes	Very favorable for plastic
Long runs	Metal tools generally better
Ease of duplication	Favorable for plastic
Corrosion resistance	Very favorable for plastic
High-temperature strength above 500°F	Metal tools generally better
Thermal conductivity	Unfavorable for plastic

longed oven and autoclave temperatures up to 400°F, present plastic tooling materials are not normally recommended for use above 500°F, except for very short periods of time. The silicones are an exception to this general rule, since they may be used at temperatures up to 600°F.

Another disadvantage of plastic tooling is that it is prone to errors made by shop workers during tool fabrication. The quality of plastic tooling materials is adversely affected by improper mixing and curing of plastic tooling materials. The improper selection of a resin system for a particular application can result in high exothermic heat, causing excessive shrinkage and/or distortion of the tool. The failure to maintain the proper resin-to-glass-cloth ratio in the construction of a laminated tool can also result in excessive shrinkage or warpage. These problems can be overcome by proper training of shop workers and careful attention to detail during the tool fabrication processes. However, they do represent caution areas that, if neglected, can result in tool failures and excessively high tooling costs.

In summary, it can be said that when properly utilized plastic tooling offers the following advantages over conventional metal tooling:

1. Lower total tooling costs
2. Shorter tool fabrication flow time
3. Lighter-weight tools
4. Tools that can be easily modified or repaired

The success of any plastic tooling program is largely dependent upon the ability of the plastic engineers and tool engineers to make the proper material selection, to employ the correct fabrication procedures, and to use plastic tooling in the right applications. If this is done, the field of plastic tooling will continue the steady growth that it has experienced in recent years.

REFERENCES

Baldanza, Nicholas T.: *A Review of Plastics for Tooling,* Plastics Technical Evaluation Center, Picatinny Arsenal, Dover, N.J.

The Techniques of Using Epoxy Plastic Tooling Materials, Ren Plastics, Inc., Lansing, Mich., April 1964.

CHAPTER TWO

Models and Modelmaking

The prime objective of tooling is to enable a manufacturer to make identical parts of products. Depending on the complexity of a manufactured item, a single tool may be required or, more frequently, several tools may be required. If several tools are required, it is essential that they coordinate very accurately with one another. If proper coordination is not maintained, individual parts made on different tools will not fit properly when placed together in an assembly.

From the preceding, it is apparent that in order to ensure that all parts of a given product fit together properly, a dimensional standard or coordination medium is required. The two-dimensional engineering drawing will not serve this purpose, and so it becomes necessary to translate the two-dimensional engineering drawing into a three-dimensional representation of the part or product to be manufactured. In the tooling industry, this three-dimensional object is referred to as the *master model*. The master model is constructed to extremely close tolerances and, once completed, serves as the dimensional standard for all subsequent tooling.

Before discussing models and modelmaking, it is appropriate to clearly define some of the commonly used terms. Four terms in particular are used in an overlapping and often incorrect manner that causes unnecessary confusion for the reader: *master model, prototype, model, and mock-up*. By establishing at this point exactly what is meant by each of these terms and by referring to them in the properly defined sense in this text, it is felt that a good deal of confusion can be avoided.

A *master model is a full-scale, three-dimensional object which establishes the complete outside or inside of a part or assembly as defined by the engineering drawing*. It contains all the information given on the engineering drawing such as reference data and loft lines. Usually, it also has coordination data such as trim lines and tooling holes. The master model is the starting point for making a family of tools for manufacturing production parts. The master model provides a dimensional standard for use by quality control and inspection personnel to check the accuracy of production parts. The master model is the only place where the exact contours of the design are established for reference. Once the master model has been approved for accuracy, it usually supersedes the engineering drawing as the dimensional standard. Master models are usually made from plaster, plastic, wood, or sometimes clay.

The term *model* is frequently confused with the term master model. The main difference between a model and a master model is that the model does not necessarily have to be full-scale. A model is used for the purpose of providing a three-dimensional representation of the part or the product for further design study or for a visual review to determine the aesthetic appeal of the product. Models are usually made from plaster, plastic, wood, or clay.

A *prototype* is a full-sized, handmade, three-dimensional representation of the final product or part. It is usually constructed from the same materials that will be used to make the production item. Prototypes are functional models and are capable of doing everything that the production part will do. Prototypes are normally used for testing and evaluation prior to commitment to production.

The term *mock-up*, when properly used, means the same thing as the term master model. Unfortunately, the term is used very loosely to refer to models and prototypes as well. In order to avoid confusion, the term mock-up will not be used in this text.

THE USE OF PLASTER FOR MASTER MODEL CONSTRUCTION

Plaster is one of the most commonly used materials in master model construction. The term *plaster* is a generic term that is used to refer to a variety of products that are derived from the mineral gypsum. Because there are a variety of plaster products, it is important to understand the various products available in order to be able to select the type of plaster specifically designed for a particular need. Although plastic is finding increasing usage as master model material, the great majority of master models are still fabricated using plaster. For this reason, it is important that tooling personnel have a good understanding of what plaster is, what types are available, and what specific application each type was developed for.

Plaster is made from the mineral gypsum. Gypsum is calcium sulfate, and its chemical formula is $CaSO_4 \cdot 2H_2O$. Some 200 years ago it was discovered that when gypsum rock was heated to temperatures in excess of 800°F, it turned into a powdery mix. Further, it was found that this powdery mix could subsequently be mixed with water to form a pourable slurry, and that this mixture would quickly harden into a solid rocklike mass resembling its original state. For this reason, gypsum is referred to as "the mineral with a memory."

Continued research effort has resulted in the development of this simple chemical reaction into a huge industry. There is presently a wide range of plaster products to choose from. These products are easily divided into two general categories: the molding grade plasters, and the gypsum cements. It can be noted from the physical data presented in Figure 2-1 that the gypsum cements possess higher strength and exhibit less expansion during setting than molding grade plasters. Because of their low setting expansion, gypsum cements are preferable

TABLE 2-1 Physical Data on Plasters and Gypsum Cements

Material	Pouring consistency (parts water to 100 parts by weight dry plaster)	Setting time, minutes	Setting expansion, inches/inch	Compressive strength, psi(dry)	Uses
Industrial molding plaster (atmospheric calcined)	64–66	25–30	0.0018	2,000	Temporary patterns and waste molds
Gypsum cement (pressure calcined)	46–49	45–55	0.0005	3,800	Diesinking patterns and master models
Expansion plaster (special purpose)	44–50	25–35	0.010–0.020	2,100	Foundry patterns. Gives uniform expansion in all directions

to ordinary molding grade plaster for tooling purposes. This is particularly true in the case of master model construction in the aircraft and aerospace industries where extremely close tolerances are required on extremely large master models. The use of gypsum cement to fabricate master models, molds, and patterns has become a standard throughout the tooling industry.

Gypsum cement products have also been formulated to give controlled uniform expansion of a pattern in all directions. This expansion is used very effectively in some industries for foundry applications where patterns are required to compensate for the shrinkage of various metals such as kirksite and aluminum.

Advantages of Gypsum Cements

When mixed and used properly, gypsum cements offer the following advantages:

1. *Economy*—Gypsum cements are the lowest-priced tooling material commercially available. In addition to savings on material costs, the use of gypsum cements enables the user to achieve savings in time and labor of up to 50 percent over conventional wood patternmaking methods.

2. *Accuracy and dimensional stability*—Because of their extremely low expansion, gypsum cements can be used to construct extremely accurate master models. It is common practice in the aircraft industry to achieve tolerances of 0.005 inch on large master models. Since gypsum cement models are unaffected by normal variations in temperature and humidity, they do not shrink or warp. It is not uncommon for large gypsum cement master models to be utilized for up to 10 years and still retain their original dimensional accuracy.

3. *Versatility*—Gypsum cements are particularly adaptable for use in forming master models with complex curves or contours. If engineering changes are released after the model has been completed, the area to be changed can be chipped away and made to conform to the new configuration.

Handling and Mixing of Gypsum Cements

In order to achieve optimum results with gypsum cements, they must be used properly. In this regard, several factors such as storage, handling, and mixing must be taken into consideration. If the following recommendations are observed, a high level of consistent results will be obtained.

Gypsum cement possesses the capability of absorbing moisture slowly out of the atmosphere. For this reason, plaster should be stored in a warm, dry place at all times. Dampness not only causes lumps; it also causes accelerated or nonuniform set in any plaster or gypsum cement. Gypsum cement should be stored in pallets at least 4 inches off concrete floors and at least 18 inches from masonry walls. Gypsum cement should only be ordered in quantities that can be used within a 6-month period of time. A system should be established for using the oldest gypsum cement first. A simple "first in, first out" system in the storage area will accomplish this objective. Gypsum cement that has become lumpy due to improper storage should never be used.

The plaster shop, as well as the equipment in the shop, should be kept as clean as possible. Because of the nature of plaster work, it is easy to allow the floor of the shop to become covered with plaster dust and drippings. Poor housekeeping of that sort usually leads to problems such as lumpy plaster, pinholes in plaster castings, and accelerated set. The use of polyethylene mixing containers is one way to ensure that small chunks of plaster from previous mixes do not remain in the mixing container. Polyethylene has a built-in release system from plaster. Plaster can be mixed in these containers and can then be removed from the container by simply flexing the polyethylene container after the plaster has become hard.

Always use water that is fit to drink. Using water that is free from sediment and dissolved chemicals will ensure that impurities will not affect the setting time. The water should be at room temperature and not allowed to vary more than plus or minus 10°F. The temperature of the water has an effect on the setting time and expansion. For example, the use of water that is lukewarm will greatly accelerate the setting of the plaster. Conversely, the use of cold water will not only retard the set, it will also increase the expansion.

Experience has indicated that in mixing gypsum cements, the most consistently successful results are obtained when the water and plaster are both weighed. Shop workers should not be allowed to make rough volumetric estimates or "eyeball" the quantities of plaster and water, since uniform results cannot be obtained in this manner.

The optimum amount of water required to mix 100 parts by weight of plaster to a standard degree of fluidity is referred to as the material's "normal consistency." When weighing gypsum cement and water, the correct proportions required to make a slurry at the normal consistency should always be used. The normal consistency is expressed as a whole number and not as a percentage. For example, a gypsum cement with a normal consistency of 46 will require 46 pounds of water to be combined with 100 pounds of the gypsum cement to produce a slurry of a standard degree of fluidity, or normal consistency.

It is interesting to note that a variation in the consistency of a gypsum cement has a significant effect on the strength of the gypsum cement after it has set. The strength of a gypsum cement is the result of the development of numerous needlelike crystals during setting. These crystals interlace tightly among each other to give the gypsum cement its strength. As more water is added to the gypsum cement mixture, the final resulting crystals are pushed further apart by the free water. Consequently, an increase in the amount of water produces a decrease in the compressive strength of the gypsum cement. This serves to emphasize that the material should be mixed to its normal consistency and that both the water and the plaster should be weighed.

After the gypsum cement and water have been weighed in the correct proportions to give the normal consistency, the gypsum cement is strewn or sifted evenly and slowly into the water. It is important to note that the gypsum cement is slowly scattered into the water. Water should *never* be poured into a mixing pail containing dry plaster. After the entire weighed quantity of plaster has been strewn into the water, it should be allowed to sit undisturbed for 3 to 4 minutes.

After soaking, the gypsum cement and water are mixed until the slurry has undergone an increase in viscosity, or "creamed." Batches under 25 pounds are usually mixed by hand using a spatula. Quantities ranging from 25 to 50 pounds can best be mixed by using a $\frac{1}{4}$-inch drill motor with a speed of approximately 1760 rpm, with a 5-inch-diameter rubber disc mounted on a shaft. Mixes over 50 pounds will require a $\frac{1}{2}$-horsepower mixer. Best results are obtained when the propeller shaft is set at an angle of approximately 15 degrees from vertical and a little off-center of the bucket. The rubber disc should clear the bottom of the mixing container by approximately $1\frac{1}{2}$ to $2\frac{1}{2}$ inches. Mixing normally takes 2 to 5 minutes, depending on the size of the slurry being mixed. At this point, the gypsum cement is ready for use.

There are basically three methods of working with gypsum cements to make a model or a mold: (1) *pouring*, (2) *splashing*, and (3) *screeding*. Normally, the method used to construct a particular model is determined by the size and shape of the model to be constructed or reproduced. Each of these methods is discussed in detail in this chapter.

Pouring Gypsum Cement The pouring method is used for reproducing an existing shape, and it is the simplest method of forming a shape with gypsum cement. The use of this method is usually confined to small- or medium-sized shapes. Basically, all that is involved is applying a release agent to a model or pattern, pouring a fluid gypsum cement slurry over the model or pattern, and removing the gypsum cement after it has set or become hard. Due to the nature of this method, it is obviously impossible to make an original model from an engineering drawing using the pouring method. The pouring method is used, therefore, solely for making a mirror image of an existing shape. Although the basic method is simple, there are some techniques essential to the achievement of good results that are not initially apparent and are therefore worth discussing in detail.

The process of pouring a gypsum cement casting begins with the construction of a frame around the model. Wood is the most common material used for constructing the frame, although metal and plexiglass have also been used. The frame and the model are sealed as required, depending on the material from which the frame is constructed. Then the model and inside surfaces of the frame are coated with an appropriate release agent. The gypsum cement and water are weighed in the proportions that will yield the normal consistency of the material. The gypsum cement is slowly strewn into the water and mixed as outlined earlier in this chapter.

The resulting gypsum cement slurry is then poured slowly into one of the four corners so that it will flow evenly across the model. This technique is of great value in eliminating small voids or pinholes caused by entrapped air. Pouring a large quantity of the slurry directly onto the model is likely to create numerous air voids or pinholes on the working surface of the gypsum cement casting. Another technique that helps eliminate entrapped air on the surface of the gypsum cement casting is vibrating or jiggling the workbench while the slurry is being poured. This technique is also helpful when fine detail in a pattern or model is being reproduced.

It is important to know the precise time to remove the gypsum cement casting from the model or pattern. If the casting is removed too soon, it will crack because it has not had sufficient time to develop strength. However, if the casting is removed too late, the gypsum cement will have expanded, and the casting may bind or "hang up" on the model. This usually results in either having to break up the casting with a hammer and chisel, repeating the pouring process after the model has been cleaned; or in trying to force the casting from the model. In either case, there is considerable risk of incurring damage to the model.

The best time to remove a gypsum cement casting is between 45 and 55 minutes after it has been poured. The chemical reaction that causes the gypsum cement slurry to become hard is an exothermic reaction; that is, the heat generated during the process of the chemical reaction results in the material's setting. The setting time of most gypsum cements ranges from 45 to 55 minutes. At that point, the casting has reached its maximum heat and will begin to cool down. The gypsum cement casting will begin to expand at this point. Therefore, it is essential that the casting be removed at the time the casting begins to cool down, or slightly prior to that time. The use of this simple rule of thumb will enable the casting to be removed after it has developed sufficient strength to prevent it from being damaged, but before it has expanded enough to cause it to bind.

Removal of the gypsum cement casting from the model can be accomplished by either of two methods. The first method is simply to drive small wood wedges between the model and the casting along the parting plane. Care must be exercised to spread the wedges out around the entire periphery of the casting in order to avoid causing the gypsum cement casting to crack. Another method, which is preferred by most tooling shops, involves the use of compressed air. In this method, a tube is affixed to the surface of the model prior to the pouring of the gypsum cement. Usually, three or four tubes are located on the model, outside the part trim line. When the casting has been poured, these tubes provide a pathway for air to the model surface. When it is time to remove the gypsum cement casting, air pressure is applied to the tubes. This is usually a very effective means of breaking the seal between the model and the casting.

Splashing Gypsum Cement The splashing technique is widely used in making transfers from large objects such as aircraft or automobile models. Gypsum cement casts made by splashing usually have controlled thickness and are generally lighter and easier to handle than the same contour duplicated by pouring. In many respects, splashing is very similar to pouring, except that it is not necessary to confine the gypsum cement within a framework as it is in the pouring method.

The success of the splashing technique depends on the successful utilization of the *period of plasticity* of the gypsum cement. The period of plasticity is a phase of the gradual thickening stage of the gypsum cement, during which the slurry becomes more viscous and begins to have body. At this point it is no longer free-flowing, as it is when the gypsum cement and water are first mixed at normal consistency. Using the gypsum cement when it has reached the period of plasticity enables the material to be applied to gradual contours and stay in position. In this manner, large contoured splashes with uniform wall thicknesses can be fabricated.

In the splashing method, the area to be reproduced is masked off with masking tape. Heavy kraft paper is applied to the surface of the model outside of the area to be reproduced to prevent damage to the model by spillage of gypsum cement. The exposed surface of the model is then sealed and prepared with a suitable parting agent (see Figure 2-1).

The gypsum cement and water are then carefully weighed and mixed at normal consistency. Immediately after mixing, the gypsum cement

Fig. 2-1 Preparation of model surface prior to splash casting. (*U.S. Gypsum Co.*)

is fluid and free-flowing; however, a few minutes later, the gypsum cement begins to thicken. It has now reached the period of plasticity and is ready for use in the splashing technique.

At this point, the gypsum cement is literally splashed onto the surface of the model (see Figure 2-2). It should be spread over the entire surface of the area to be reproduced to a thickness of approximately ½ inch. During the early stages of the period of plasticity, the gypsum cement must be handled delicately and not be built up too thick; otherwise it will slump and lose shape. As the period of plasticity progresses, the slurry becomes thicker and thicker and the "splash" can be built up to a greater thickness, as desired. At this point, the gypsum cement can be easily formed with a splining rod or spatula. Normally the surface is built up to approximately ½ inch. It is usually smoothed out as much as possible.

After the first mix has been applied to a thickness of ½ inch over the entire area to be reproduced, a second batch of gypsum cement is mixed at normal consistency. At this point, reinforcement is added to the gypsum cement splash. The most common material used to reinforce gypsum cement splashes is manila fiber. Manila fiber is the product of a tropical plant called *abaca,* and consists of a long, soft, pliable strand that is considered one of the best materials for making large ropes. This material usually comes in either 80- or 100-pound bales, and is usually manila fiber that is unsuitable for the making of rope. As

Fig. 2-2 Gypsum cement being splashed onto model surface. (*U.S. Gypsum Co.*)

received, the fiber is matted in balings and must be picked apart by hand to loosen the individual strands. The unraveling should be done prior to the mixing of the second batch of gypsum cement.

The technique for reinforcing the splash with manila fiber is to make a small bat, approximately 8 inches in diameter, out of the fibers. The bat is then soaked in the gypsum cement to thoroughly saturate it. The saturated bat is then applied to the model on top of the original ½-inch layer of gypsum cement. In this manner, after setting, the manila fiber saturated with gypsum cement becomes an integral part of the splash. This procedure is used to apply bats saturated with gypsum cement over the entire surface of the splash to a thickness of approximately 1½ inches.

Although manila fiber is the most common form of reinforcement, other materials such as wire mesh, metal rods, expanded metal, and honeycomb are also used. These reinforcing materials are generally placed as near the neutral axis of the splash as possible; they should be nonferrous. Nonferrous materials are recommended because the water in the gypsum cement causes iron or steel reinforcements to rust. The expansion resulting from the formation of rust frequently causes the splash to warp, rendering it useless. Rigid reinforcements should not be applied until after the setting expansion of the plaster has taken place. If reinforcements are applied prior to that time, stresses are often developed which result in the distortion of the splash.

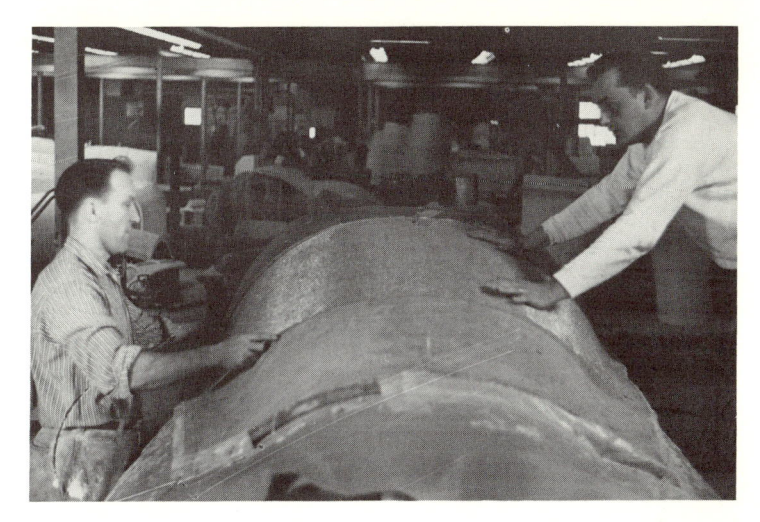

Fig. 2-3 Placing wire mesh over first layer of gypsum cement splash casting. (*U.S. Gypsum Co.*)

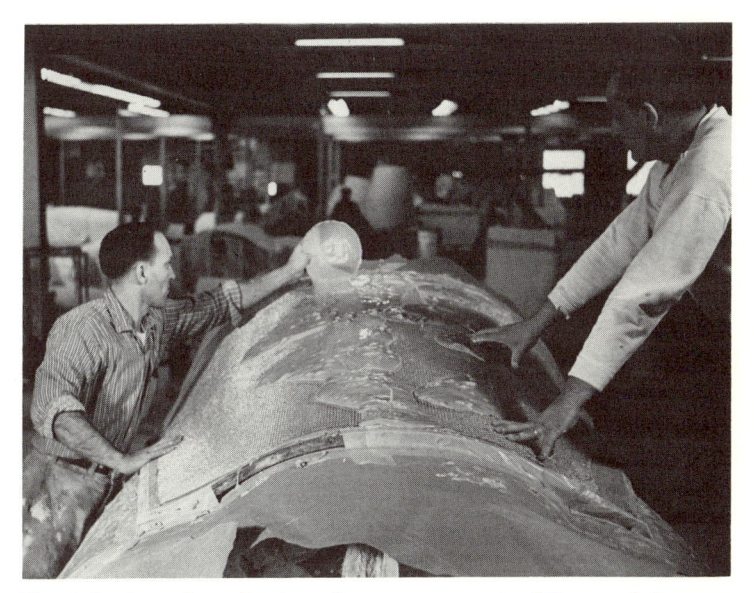

Fig. 2-4 Second application of gypsum cement. Wire mesh becomes an integral part of the splash casting. (*U.S. Gypsum Co.*)

38 Plastic Tooling

Under no circumstances should wood reinforcements be used if they are to be buried in the plaster. The reason for this, of course, is that the wood will swell when it becomes wet. The expansion of the wood will either crack or warp the gypsum cement splash. However, wood, when properly sealed, can be and often is used on the outside of splashes where it can be kept dry.

After the splash has been allowed to set up at room temperature for approximately 2 hours, the substructure or supporting frame is added to the splash. Normally the structural support is made up of metal rods, pipes, or tubing that has been either bolted or welded together. This framework is placed on the backside of the splash, while the splash is still in position on the model and is tied into the splash with manila fiber bats impregnated with gypsum cement (see Figures 2-5 and 2-6).

With regard to reinforcing splashes, a few words of caution are appropriate at this point. Frequently, steel pipes or tubing are bent and welded together to form the structural support for the splash. In all such cases, before they are tied into the splash, these reinforcements should be normalized to relieve any strains or stresses that may have developed during fabrication of the framework. Also, if wood reinforcements are used, great care must be taken. It is recommended that only kiln-dried wood be used, and that all wood surfaces be given at least three coats of lacquer before being fastened to the splash. This

Fig. 2-5 Positioning metal framework onto backside of the splash casting. (*U.S. Gypsum Co.*)

Fig. 2-6 Framework being "tied in" to splash casting using manila fiber saturated with gypsum cement. (*U.S. Gypsum Co.*)

is very important because, as we discussed earlier, the free water in the gypsum cement can penetrate unsealed wood, causing it to warp. In the opinion of the author, wood reinforcements should only be used as a last resort when no other materials are available.

Screeding with Gypsum Cements Screeding is the working of gypsum cement during its period of plasticity. This involves the use of a metal template to shape the gypsum cement while it is in a plastic condition. Some screeding methods involve the template's being moved in relation to the object being formed; other techniques involve moving the object being formed in relation to a stationary template. Screeding is the most commonly used method of translating a two-dimensional drawing or blueprint into a three-dimensional object.

There are four basic variations of the screeding method: (1) the loft template method, (2) the straight run molding method, (3) the circular turning method, and (4) the rod or cylindrical turning method. Of these four variations, the loft template method is most frequently used to make master models in the aircraft, aerospace, and automotive industries.

The Loft Template Method

FORMATION OF IRREGULAR SHAPES: Briefly described, the loft template method involves setting up a series of templates on a rigid base, placing gypsum cement between the templates, and using the templates as a

40   Plastic Tooling

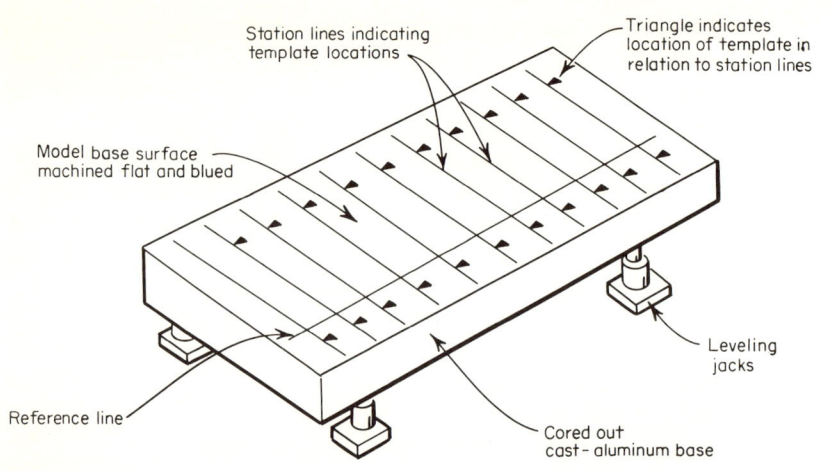

Fig. 2-7 Master model base indicating station lines for template setup.

baseline for screeding off the excess gypsum. While this method requires a higher degree of skill on the part of the worker, it is the most widely used because of its versatility. There is virtually no irregular or complex shape that cannot be formed using the loft template method.

THE BASE: The model base must be properly designed so that it will remain rigid under the weight of the completed gypsum cement model. A variety of materials is used for model bases; but, for the most part, model bases are either steel or aluminum. If the model base is a casting, the underside of the base is usually cored out to decrease the weight of the base while still maintaining the required strength and rigidity. The upper surface of the base is machined flat to extremely close tolerances. After machining, the top surface of the model base is blued, and the station lines and template locations are laid out and scribed onto the surface of the base. Great care is exercised in laying out the necessary lines since the accuracy of the location of the templates will determine the accuracy of the completed master model.

THE TEMPLATES: Each template, sometimes referred to as a *header*, defines the contour of the master model in a specific plane. The templates are made by transferring layout lines from the engineering drawing to metal template stock. Most commonly, templates are made from heat-treated aluminum. Steel is sometimes used where the additional weight is not an important factor. However, the cutting and filing is easier on aluminum stock than it is on steel, a factor which makes aluminum a preferred template material. The thickness of the metal template stock will vary from 0.050 to 0.125 inch, depending on the size and shape of the model, as well as the individual preference of the tool designer. Experience has proved that wood or plywood should never be used for making templates because the moisture in the gypsum cement will cause the veneer of the plywood to swell and warp out of shape.

Each time a change in contour occurs, a station line is established for the master model. By making a template for each station line and locating it in its proper relationship to the other templates, a skeleton of the part or model is developed. The configuration of each template is established by transferring layout lines from the blueprint to the template stock. The templates are then cut and hand-finished to the exact configuration, normally to within 0.005 inch of the loft lines. During the hand-finishing operation, it is important that the edges of the template determining the surface of the model be free from file marks, nicks, or scratches. Flaws of this type will cause imperfections on the surface of the completed master model. Holes are also normally designed into the templates to provide ventilation and decrease the weight. The ventilation holes provide a path for air circulation, enabling the

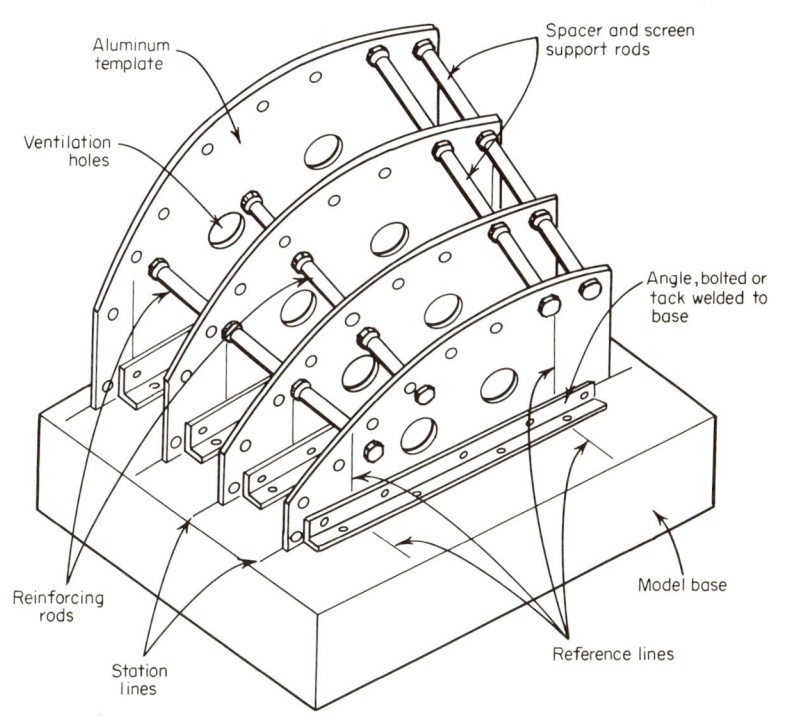

Fig. 2-8 Method of attaching templates to the base and installing spacer and screen support rods.

gypsum cement to dry from the inside as well as from the face of the model.

The templates are then mounted to the model base at the location corresponding to the proper station line which has been scribed on the model base. A series of templates mounted in this manner in proper relation to a common base is called a *template setup*. Again, accuracy in mounting the templates to the model base is essential since the ultimate accuracy of the completed master model can be no better than the accuracy of the templates. Generally, aluminum angle is used to mount the templates to the base, as shown in Figure 2-8. The angle is usually installed in the precise location of the template and bolted or tack-welded into position. The template is then bolted to the aluminum angle.

Because the gypsum cement is slightly alkaline, electrolysis occurs between the aluminum templates and the adjacent plaster. This causes degradation of the aluminum templates, as well as erosion of the plaster on either side of the template. It is advisable at this point to coat the templates with an epoxy coating to ensure that such rusting or corrosion does not occur. Such a precaution taken at this point will save many man-hours at a later time in reworking and maintaining the master models.

After all the templates have been precisely located and securely fastened to the model base, the model is further reinforced with threaded steel rods. Actually, there are two sets of threaded steel rods. One set provides reinforcement for the model, and the other set of rods provides a base for the metal lath or screen upon which the gypsum

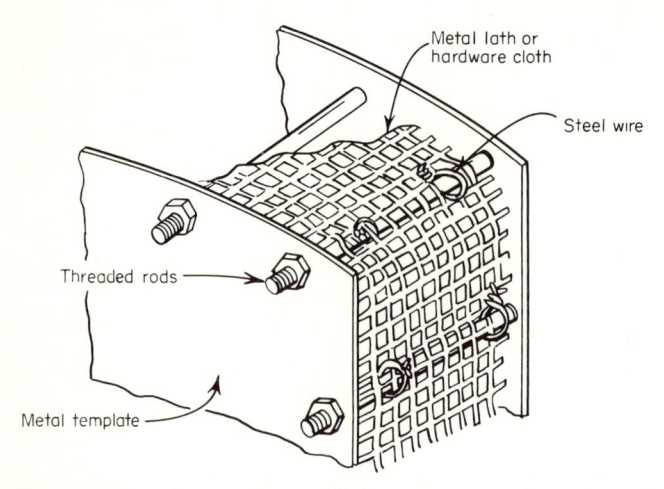

Fig. 2-9 Attachment of metal lath to support rods with steel wire.

Fig. 2-10 Initial application of gypsum cement onto metal lath. (*U.S. Gypsum Co.*)

cement will be placed. The second set of rods are normally 0.50-inch-diameter threaded steel rods, and are passed through predrilled holes located 1 to 1½ inch from the periphery of the model. After the rods have all been installed, the template setup is closely inspected for accuracy before proceeding further.

The next step is to provide a base upon which the gypsum cement will be placed. Usually metal lath, hardware cloth, or expanded metal is used for this purpose. The metal lath is cut to widths that will allow it to fit between the templates. The metal lath is then positioned between the templates and held in place by hog rings or wire passing through the mesh and around the metal rods (see Figure 2-9).

APPLYING THE GYPSUM CEMENT: Before the screeding of the final surface of the model takes place, it is necessary to provide a base of gypsum cement to work on. To accomplish this, gypsum cement is mixed with water to the proper ratio to give a normal consistency. Manila fiber bats are then dipped in the gypsum cement slurry and placed onto the metal lath. This procedure is used to build up the gypsum cement and manila fiber to a level approximately ¼ inch below the templates. At this point, another mix of gypsum cement is applied to the entire surface with a sawtooth scraper, maintaining the height of the gypsum cement at approximately ⅛ inch below the templates. The striated surface produced in this manner will provide a good mechanical bond, as

Fig. 2-11 Using sawtooth scraper to provide striated plaster surface. (*U.S. Gypsum Co.*)

well as a chemical bond, when the final mix of gypsum cement is applied (see Figure 2-11).

Because the material applied from this point on will be the surface of the completed model, it is important that all steps in the operation be done properly. The gypsum cement is mixed to its normal consistency and is allowed to reach its period of plasticity before being used. When it has reached its period of plasticity, the cement is applied to the striated surface by hand or with a spatula and is built up to a height slightly greater than the templates. A metal bar, thin enough to be flexible, is then used to screed or spline the plaster to the proper configuration (see Figure 2-12). This process is repeated until the entire surface of the model is completed. After the gypsum cement has hardened, the necessary reference and trim lines are scribed onto the model (see Figure 2-13). The model is then given two coats of lacquer to seal the surface.

At first glance, the loft template method of making master models seems a relatively straightforward, simple matter. However, the success of this method requires a considerable degree of skill on the part of the model builder. Even with the templates to provide the basic profile, it requires craftsmanlike skill to arrive at the desired configuration. For example, if the model builder does not pass the spline along at least three templates at the same time, flat spots on the model surface will result. Figure 2-14 illustrates the result of improperly screeding a gypsum cement model. In order to achieve the true, smooth-flowing con-

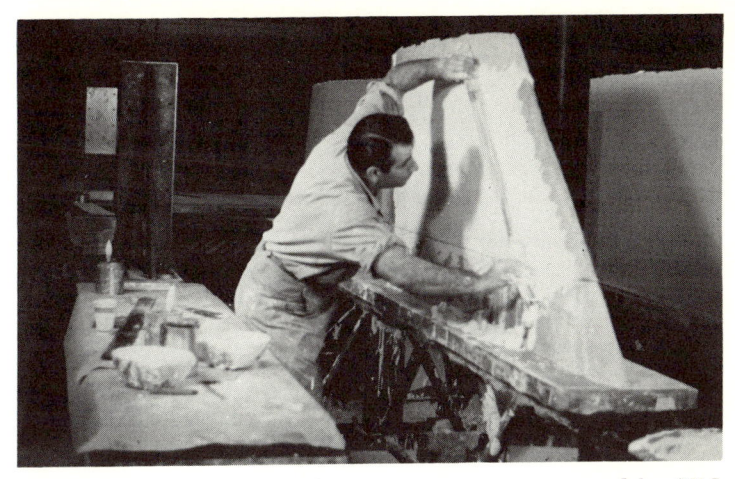

Fig. 2-12 Finish splining of gypsum cement master model. (*U.S. Gypsum Co.*)

tour, it is essential that at least three template stations be touched by the screeding bar at the same time.

ALTERING OR REPAIRING SCREEDED MODELS: In the event that engineering changes occur or that the gypsum cement model is damaged, it can easily be changed or repaired. In the case of engineering changes, the gypsum cement is chiseled away, and the existing templates in the

Fig. 2-13 Putting reference lines on completed master model. (*U.S. Gypsum Co.*)

46   Plastic Tooling

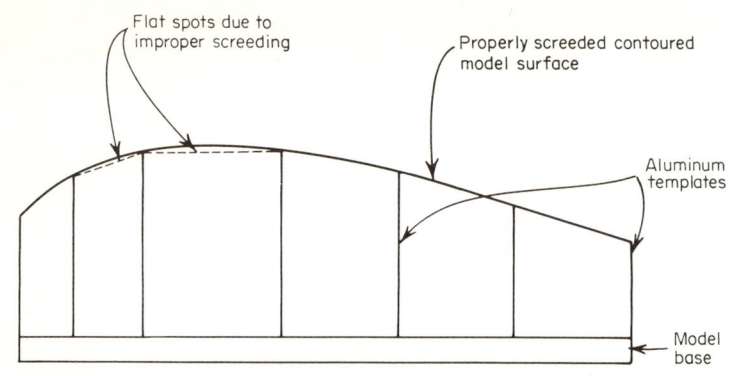

Fig. 2-14 When screeding, it is important that a minimum of three templates be spanned with a thin, flexible straight edge. This will assure the development of the true contour. The broken lines in the sketch indicate the error in contour that occurs when only two template stations are used.

area requiring change are cut away. New templates are then prepared to the new design and located in proper relationship to the rest of the model. The area is then screeded in with gypsum cement, using the same procedures described earlier in this section.

Repairs can be made by first thoroughly cleaning away the parting

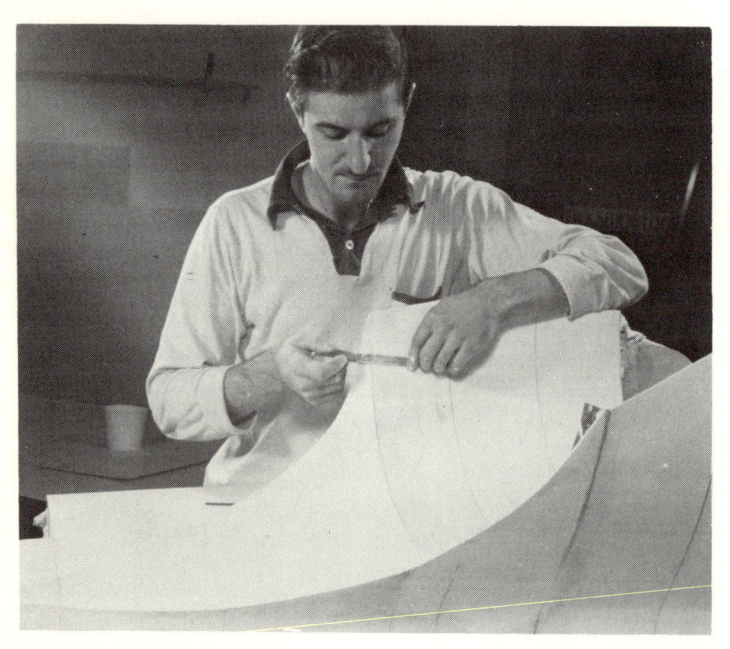

Fig. 2-15 Repairing gypsum cement model. (*U.S. Gypsum Co.*)

agent and lacquer sealer that may be on the surface of the model. The gypsum cement in the area to be repaired is then moistened with water. If this is not done, the hardened gypsum cement model will absorb water from the gypsum cement slurry that is being used to make the repair, making the slurry difficult to screed properly. The gypsum cement is then screeded to the proper configuration in the area requiring repair (see Figure 2-15).

The Straight Run Molding Method: The straight run method of screeding gypsum cement is used to produce models or patterns having parallel edges to form a straight molding. These straight moldings can then be cut up into sections to form letters or patterns for picture frames. There are no restrictions on the complexity of the contours that can be made by this method. Also, the straight run method of screeding gypsum cement has the lowest-skill requirement of any of the other methods covered in this chapter.

The first step in making a pattern by the straight run method is to construct a template. First, aluminum template stock, varying from 0.050 to 0.125 inch thick, is sprayed with Dychem or bluing. The contour of the part is then transferred from the engineering drawing to the template stock. The template is then cut with a band saw and hand-finished to the desired configuration. It is important at this point that the template be carefully finished so that it is free from file marks or other irregularities. If the template has any irregularities whatsoever,

Fig. 2-16 Splined gypsum cement master model. (*U.S. Gypsum Co.*)

48   Plastic Tooling

they will be reflected as either ridges or depressions along the entire length of the model.

A "sled" is then fabricated from 1-inch wood stock. It is advisable to seal the wood with two or three coats of lacquer thinned with 30 percent lacquer thinner. This will prevent the wood from swelling and creating drag later on in the screeding process. The aluminum template is then positioned and fastened to the sled, normally by the use of screws. Figure 2-17 illustrates the method of construction of the sled as well as the method of attaching the template to the sled. The sled is now ready for use in making a model or pattern by the straight run method.

It is recommended that a surface table be used for the model fabrication. A normal workbench may be used, provided that the edge of the bench is perfectly smooth and free from irregularities. Ridges or high spots on the top surface of the bench will make the subsequent steps in this operation more difficult. The use of a surface table is highly recommended since it eliminates subsequent problems. Once the work area has been selected, a suitable release agent is applied to the surface of the bench. There are many suitable release agents, although normal automotive grease or outboard motor oil is adequate for this purpose.

The first batch of gypsum cement should be mixed slightly below normal consistency; that is, less water should be used to make the first batch. Once the gypsum cement has been mixed, it should be allowed to thicken or cream and enter into its period of plasticity before it is applied to the bench or surface table. Using a spatula, the gypsum

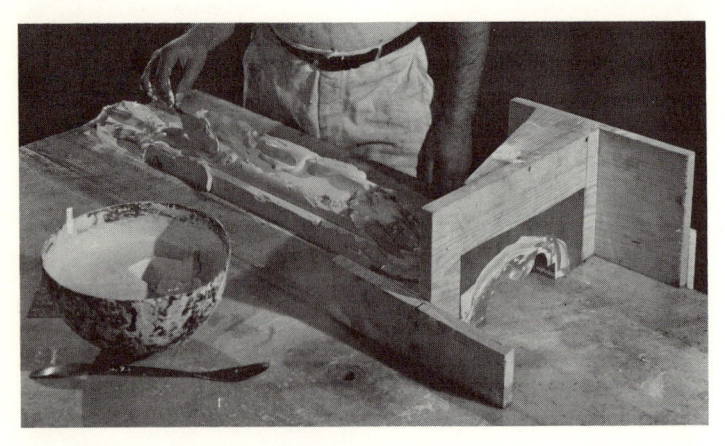

Fig. 2-17 Straight-run screeding of gypsum cement. The second mix of gypsum cement is being applied into the voids left in the original run. (*U.S. Gypsum Co.*)

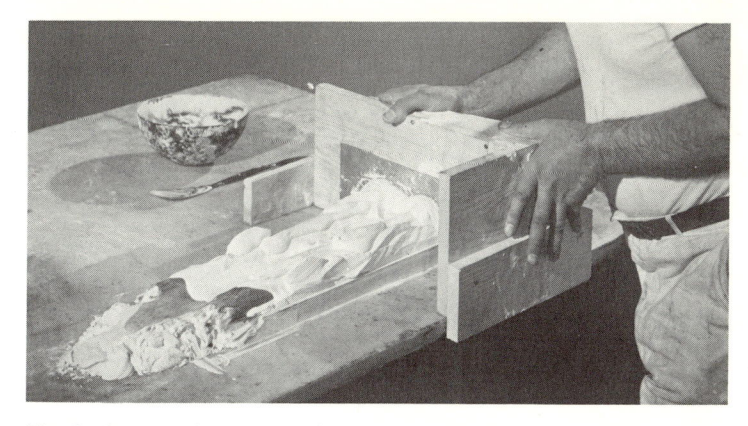

Fig. 2-18 Straight-run screeding of gypsum cement. The template is now pushed through the gypsum cement to form the model. Note how the cement, which is in a very plastic state, "rolls" as the template screeds it. The function of the guide board of the sled is clearly demonstrated in this photograph. (*U.S. Gypsum Co.*)

cement is spread in a line along the top of the table in a shape roughly resembling the outline of the template (see Figure 2-17). It is important not to build up too great a mass at one time. The buildup of too great a mass may result in the generation of excessive heat during the setting process. This can result in enough warpage or expansion of the cast to cause the template to stick on subsequent operations. It is preferable to build up the gypsum cement to the desired thickness or mass by stages.

The next step is to index the runners of the sled to the edge of the surface table and to push the template firmly through the gypsum cement while it is in its period of plasticity (see Figure 2-18). It is essential that the sled must touch the bench in all locations. This can be accomplished by pushing the sled slowly, while exerting an even, downward force on the sled to keep it from rising. The sled should be pushed through the gypsum cement mass in one direction only. After the sled has been pushed through the mass once, it should be removed, and the template should be thoroughly rinsed with water. The sled may then be returned to its starting position and pushed through the mass again.

Normally, by the time two passes have been made, the gypsum cement will have progressed far enough through its period of plasticity so that it will no longer screed smoothly. At this point, a mistake frequently is made by trying to extend the working life of the gypsum cement by the addition of more water. This is not a good practice since the material will become chalky and have very poor strength characteristics.

50   Plastic Tooling

Fig. 2-19 Straight-run screeding of gypsum cement. The completed pattern will be sawed to the proper length before being removed from the workbench. (*U.S. Gypsum Co.*)

Once the gypsum cement has progressed to a point where it no longer screeds smoothly, the shop worker should stop using it. Most of the mass of gypsum required for the model will have been used by this time. It is advisable to allow the mass to cure and not to continue working it until the gypsum cement has cooled back down to room temperature.

The second batch of gypsum cement should be mixed to normal consistency. This mix is allowed to cream slightly and then is applied to the low spots and voids with a spatula. The sled is indexed properly at the starting point and pushed through the mass of gypsum cement. This procedure is repeated as often as necessary to obtain the desired configuration and surface smoothness. Sometimes a third, fourth, or

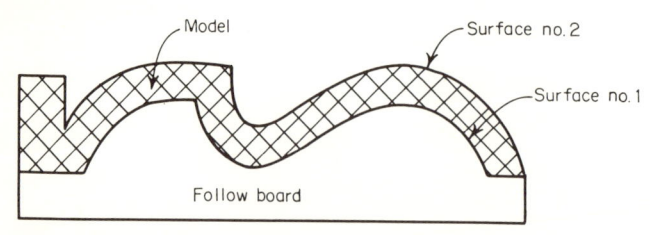

Fig. 2-20 Typical model, having two parallel contoured surfaces, produced by the straight-run molding method of screeding. This type of model requires two templates to produce. Surface no. 1 is generated first and serves as a follow board. The template is then changed, and surface no. 2 is formed to complete the model.

even fifth batch of gypsum cement will be required to build up all the high areas of a model. Once the model is completed, it is allowed to dry and then is sealed with three coats of clear lacquer.

The straight run method may also be used to fabricate a model or pattern with two contoured sides, such as illustrated in Figure 2-20. Since a great number of metal castings fall into this category, this method is frequently used to make prototype foundry patterns or master models for production foundry patterns. Fabricating a model with two contoured sides requires the use of a follow board.

If, for example, a model of the configuration shown in Figure 2-20 were required, the procedure would be as follows:

1. Separate templates would be prepared to the configuration of surface no. 1 and surface no. 2.

2. Using the straight run method, surface no. 1 is created.

3. Surface no. 1 is then allowed to dry. It is sealed with three coats of lacquer and coated with an appropriate parting agent.

4. The template for surface no. 2 is attached to the same sled, and surface no. 2 is screeded with gypsum cement.

5. Surface no. 2 is allowed to dry and is then sealed with three coats of clear lacquer. The model is then cut to the proper length and removed from the follow board.

The straight run method is also used to construct contoured models or patterns having square, rectangular, or oblique shapes. In doing

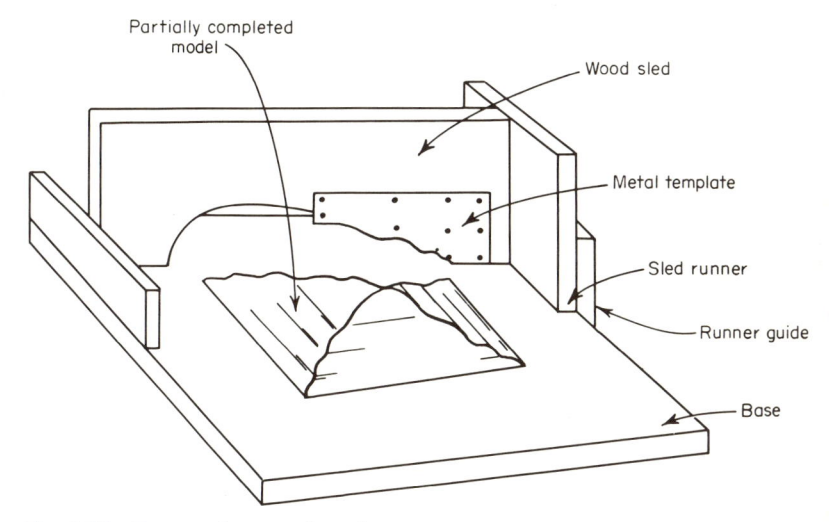

Fig. 2-21 Basic technique of producing square shapes by straight-run molding method of screeding.

52 Plastic Tooling

this, a base conforming to the shape of the desired model, only larger, is used (see Figure 2-21). This base is used as the surface that the sled rides on instead of the edge of the surface table or bench. The sled is then pushed along each side of the base, creating the desired shape. Patterns made by this method need no mitering, since the template produces the miter.

The Circular Turning Method: The principle of using a template and a sled to form contoured shapes with gypsum cements can be modified slightly to produce circular shapes having low profile. In making circular shapes, the template is rotated around a center post to produce a symmetrical pattern. This concept is illustrated in Figure 2-22. This method can be used to produce models or patterns of virtually any diameter. The accuracy of the finished work depends on the accuracy of the template and sled, as well as the skill of the workman. However, it is common to make models accurate to within 0.005 inch using this method. Examples of models of production parts made in this manner are washing machine liners, bases for floor lamps, and automobile tires.

As in the straight run molding method, a template is made from aluminum template stock. However, for circular turning, a template is made of the drawing only to the centerline of the part. The template is usually cut away beyond the centerline. The template is drilled and then nailed or screwed to the work sled. A hole is drilled in the work sled in the location corresponding to the centerline of the part which has been scribed on the template. In some cases, an oversized hole is drilled in the sled and a bushing potted in. The use of a bushing ensures that the sled will rotate smoothly around the center post serving as the pivot point.

A hole is drilled in the center of the slab on which the model will

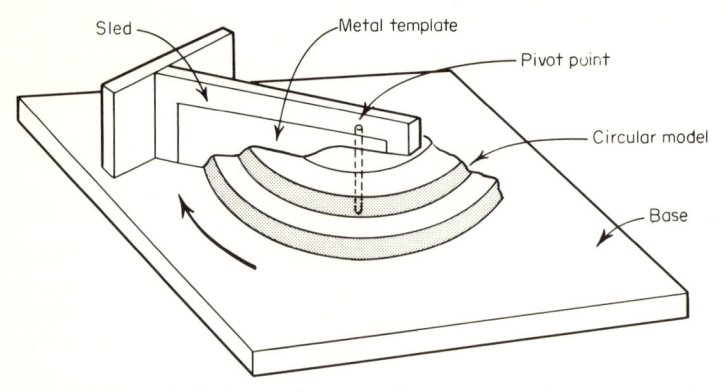

Fig. 2-22 Method of screeding a model or pattern having a circular shape. The template is rotated around a pivot point to produce a symmetrical pattern.

be made. The center post, around which the template will rotate, is placed in this hole and fastened so that it is absolutely rigid at the top. It is recommended that the center post have a running thread, with a double nut arrangement to enable height adjustment.

The procedure for mixing and handling the gypsum cement for the circular method is basically the same as the procedure used in the straight run molding method. The initial mix of gypsum cement should be below normal consistency. When it has started into its period of plasticity, it is applied to the slab with a suitably sized spatula. The template is then rotated several times to form the rough configuration of the part. In doing this, the sled should be held firmly and rotated with an even pressure. Unless this is done, the mass of the gypsum cement can cause the sled to rise on the pivot point and to produce high spots in the model surface. As in the straight run molding method, the sled should be removed frequently and cleaned thoroughly.

The second mix, as well as subsequent mixes of gypsum cement, should be at normal consistency. The mix is applied to the model with a spatula, filling voids and low spots. While the gypsum cement is being applied to the model, the sled is rotated. Gypsum cement is continually directed to the low spots with the spatula while the sled is being rotated. In this manner, the details of the model are built up. The process is repeated until the desired shape is achieved. Whenever a slurry of gypsum cement loses its plasticity, it should be discarded and a new batch mixed. When the model is completed, excess material is removed by rotating and lifting the sled simultaneously. In this manner, the template will pick up the excess gypsum cement. If the template was made properly and is free of nicks, gouges, or file marks, no hand-finishing of the model will be required. The completed model is allowed to dry and is then sealed with two coats of clear lacquer.

Circular models or patterns having two parallel contoured surfaces can be made by this method. In doing this, two templates are required. The procedure is the same as outlined in the section on straight run molding for models having two contoured sides.

The Rod or Cylindrical Turning Method: The box or rod-turning method is the best way to make models of cylindrical shapes. By this method, the gypsum cement is formed onto a rod which is rotated horizontally in journals in a box. As it is rotated, the excess gypsum cement is screeded by a stationary template attached to the box. It should be noticed that in this method the work is rotated, rather than the template.

The box itself is constructed from 1-inch wood and is sealed with three coats of lacquer. This prevents the wood from absorbing water from the gypsum cement and subsequently warping. The journals in

54   Plastic Tooling

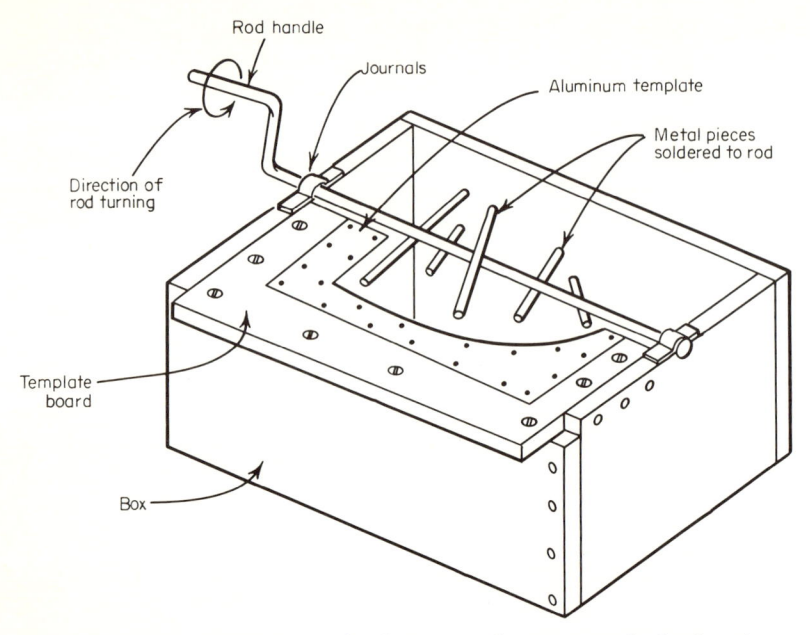

Fig. 2-23 Basic arrangement for box or rod-turning method of making gypsum cement models.

the box must fit the size of the rod that is being used. A handle, such as a lathe-dog, is clamped to the rod and is used for turning the rod during the fabrication of the model (see Figure 2-23).

The template is fabricated from thin aluminum template stock in the manner described earlier in this chapter. However, the true center of the template must be cut away to allow for the radius of the rod. Therefore, an arbitrary line must be established on the template in order to locate it on the template board in its true position. The template is then drilled and screwed to the template board in its proper position. The template board is then fastened securely to the box, which supports the template at the centerline height.

If the rod is going to be removed from the model after it is completed, twine is wrapped around the rod to provide a mechanical bond between the rod and the initial mix of gypsum cement. However, if the rod is going to be left inside the pattern, pieces of metal can be soldered to the rod in various locations to provide a base for the cement to adhere to the rod and to help support the cement when it is applied. The pieces of metal soldered to the rod should be at least $\frac{1}{4}$ inch less than the radius of the model at that location. The use of metal fastened to the rod in this manner is highly recommended whenever possible.

Models and Modelmaking   55

When the template is fastened into position and the rod located in its journals, the buildup of the model can begin. A small batch of gypsum cement is mixed at below normal consistency (see Figure 2-24) and allowed to reach its period of plasticity. At this point, the mix is applied slowly to the rod along the entire length of the pattern. The rod is rotated slowly and, as the gypsum cement creams, more mix is added. Care should be taken not to apply too much gypsum cement at one time, since its own weight will cause it to sag away from the rod if applied in too great a quantity. The worker should be aware that all that is desired at this point is for the first mix to provide a good bond to the rod and create a firm foundation for the subsequent mixes of gypsum cement.

All subsequent mixes should be prepared at normal consistency and applied in small quantities to the model along the entire length of the rod. The rod should be continually turned while the gypsum cement is being applied. It is important that the rod be turned in one direction only, that direction being toward the template. Occasionally, it is preferred that two templates are used to make a model of this type. One template is made to the engineering drawing; while a second template is made approximately $\frac{1}{8}$ inch undersized, with a sawtooth surface. The striated surface produced on the model by this template will provide a good mechanical bond, as well as a chemical bond, for the final applications of gypsum cement (see Figure 2-24).

When the gypsum cement mix has passed beyond its period of plastic-

Fig. 2-24 Gypsum cement at below normal consistency is applied to form a body to which the finish coat may be applied. Note that a striated template is being used to provide a mechanical bond for subsequent mixes. (*U.S. Gypsum Co.*)

56 Plastic Tooling

Fig. 2-25 The gypsum cement for the finish coat is applied at normal consistency. Note that striated template has been replaced with smooth template with desired configuration of completed pattern. (*U.S. Gypsum Co.*)

ity it should be removed and discarded. No attempt should be made to salvage a batch of material by adding water. At this stage, tiny crystals are forming and will only cause defects in the model surface. It is important that the template be kept free of waste or excess material. If it is not kept clean, it will not produce a satisfactory model surface.

If a sawtooth template is used, it should be removed when the desired thickness is built up. The template that has been cut to the engineering drawing is then substituted and the process is repeated (see Figure 2-25). At this point, during the application of the final mixes, it is important to be aware of glazed surfaces.

Glazed surfaces are formed when gypsum cement is allowed to set undisturbed for too long a period of time. If this occurs, the glazed surface should be roughened with coarse sandpaper before subsequent mixes are applied. If the glaze is not removed in this manner, subsequent applications of gypsum cement will not bond well to the substrate and are likely to peel off. Figure 2-26 illustrates the worker roughing up the model surface before applying the final mix of gypsum cement.

Mixes of gypsum cement at normal consistency are applied until the desired surface is achieved. After the model has cured, it is removed from the box by lifting out with the rod. After the model has dried for approximately two days at room temperature, two coats of clear lacquer are applied, and the model is ready for use. This method has

Fig. 2-26 A workman removes the glazed surface with coarse sandpaper prior to the application of a finish coat of gypsum cement. (*U.S. Gypsum Co.*)

Fig. 2-27 Completed gypsum cement missile nose master model made by rod-turning method. (*U.S. Gypsum Co.*)

been widely used to make radome, aircraft cowling, and missile nosecone master models.

PLASTIC MASTER MODELS

As discussed earlier in this chapter, splined master models are the first step in the fabrication of a family of tools required to produce a complete aircraft or missile configuration. For many years, the standard for master models had been to construct them from splined gypsum cement. Gypsum cement had the advantages of low cost of materials, easy working characteristics, low expansion, and dimensional stability.

Although the use of gypsum cement is an excellent way to construct master models, there are some basic disadvantages of gypsum cement models that should be noted at this point. These disadvantages have become more apparent in recent years with the increased size of aircraft and missiles. The main drawback pointed up by the increased size of master models is that gypsum cement models are extremely heavy. While this does not present much of a problem to tooling shops engaged in the fabrication of relatively small models and patterns, it does present a considerable problem to tooling shops making master models of the size required for some of our modern, large, commercial aircraft and space vehicles. Models for these products are retained for several years and are constantly used for reference purposes. Some of these models constructed with gypsum cement are so massive that they are impossible to move. Consequently, a large gypsum cement master model has come to be regarded as a necessarily permanent object located in the tooling shop, significantly reducing the floor space available for other operations.

In addition to their sheer weight, there are other problems associated with gypsum cement models. These problems, which tend to magnify in proportion to the increased size of the models, are as follows:

1. Even if a gypsum cement model is small enough to be moved, it cannot be stored outdoors because it is prone to damage from water.

2. Gypsum cement is susceptible to damage. The splashes taken from the gypsum cement master model occasionally cause fragments to break away from the surface of the model. This is attributable to either poor application of parting agent, excessive exotherm, or poor bond between the finish coat of the model and the gypsum cement substrate. Sometimes important information is lost because it is not always possible to restore this information exactly where it belongs.

3. Large master models are difficult to maintain dimensionally stable. This is attributed to the different coefficients of thermal expansion of the various materials used in gypsum cement models.

For these reasons, among others, the aircraft industry has turned to plastic for master model construction in a number of instances. For the most part, paste-type epoxy resins are used for constructing splined plastic master models. From the standpoint of materials' cost alone, splined plastic master models are considerably more expensive than gypsum cement models. Also, epoxy splining resins do not handle as well as gypsum cement. Epoxy splining resins have a tendency to drag on the steel spline; consequently, they require more man-hours to achieve the final configuration. In addition, because epoxy splining materials shrink upon curing, changes in the template arrangement are required. For example, templates for a plastic master model should not be spaced more than 6 inches apart or small cracks between the plastic and the template will result.

However, despite some of these problems, the aircraft and aerospace industries are turning more toward plastic master models. It is apparent that the tremendous increase in size of aircraft and missiles has brought the industry to a point where the tried-and-true, successful methods of the past cannot solve the problems created by the constantly advancing technology of today. It is generally agreed that plastic splined master models have the following advantages over gypsum cement models:

1. Plastic master models are considerably lighter than gypsum cement models.
2. A plastic surface has high-strength characteristics without necessitating large mass.
3. A plastic surface is tough and durable. The surface of plastic master models is normally not damaged when splashes are taken from it.
4. Scribed lines and other tooling information can be permanently added to plastic model surfaces.

Splined epoxy master models do not represent the only approach to the use of plastics for master model fabrication. Considerable work has been done to develop the use of lightweight epoxy syntactic foams for use in master models. This technique involves applying a lightweight epoxy syntactic foam over a rough honeycomb core and numerical controlled machining it to the desired configuration. This approach, however, is restricted to master models whose configuration is mathematically defined and available on numerical controlled tape.

Splined Plastic Master Models

The basic concept for fabricating splined plastic master models is very similar to that of gypsum cement models. The splined plastic model consists of a series of templates mounted on a rigid base, tied together with rods and screen, and splined with plastic material between the templates to create a smooth, contoured surface. However, because the epoxy splining resins have different physical characteristics than the gypsum cements, there are significant differences in the fabrication technique as well as the master model design. In order that these differences may not be overlooked, we will discuss the construction of splined plastic master models in detail.

The Skeleton of the Splined Plastic Model The skeleton of the plastic master model or template setup consists of a base, a series of templates mounted to the base, and rods passing through the templates (see Figure 2-28). The rods are covered by screen or mesh, upon which the plastic material is placed. The base of the model can be constructed of a variety of materials. Machined aluminum sheet stock that has been stress-relieved is a commonly used material on small models, as is stress-relieved welded steel construction, 3-inch-thick honeycomb panels, and cored-out cast aluminum structures.

The material selected for the base will largely be determined by the size of the model, as well as the individual preference of the tool designer. For example, some tool designers prefer a plastic-faced honeycomb base because they feel it reduces movement in the completed master model. This movement is caused by differential thermal coefficients of expansion between dissimilar materials over a range of temperature variations. Other tool designers prefer to stick with the materials they know best, usually metal. Again, the size of the model can have a significant bearing on the choice of material used for the model base. Any base structure is satisfactory, provided that it is flat, stable, and self-supporting; i.e., it must not flex if the model is moved from one location to another.

The templates are normally made from 0.050-inch aluminum or steel

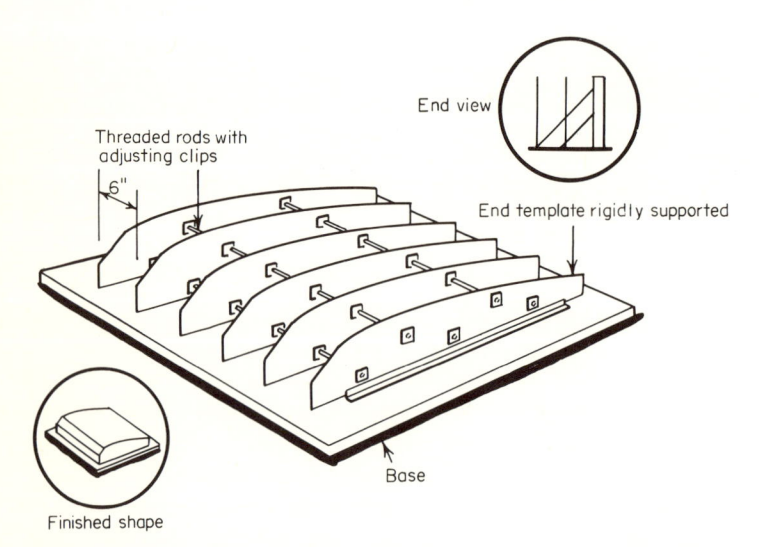

Fig. 2-28 Template setup for splined epoxy master model. (*Ren Plastics, Inc.*)

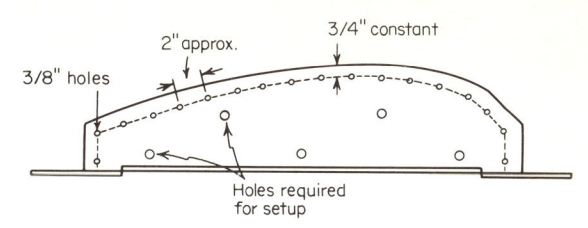

Fig. 2-29 Detail of template hole pattern for splined epoxy master model. (*Ren Plastics, Inc.*)

template stock. Aluminum is the preferred material because it is easier to cut and file to the desired shape. The metal stock is sprayed with Dychem or bluing, and the loft lines are scribed on the metal stock. The templates are machined or cut to the proper contour and filed to within 0.005 inch of the true configuration.

The templates contain two sets of holes. The larger holes seen in Figure 2-29 are for threaded $\frac{1}{4}$- or $\frac{5}{16}$-inch rods with adjusting clips. These rods are for the purpose of strengthening and stiffening the template setup. The smaller holes are for the rods used to support the plastic material, and are not used in setting up the templates. The templates are mounted in a common plane, usually perpendicular to the base, and located on reference lines established on the base.

After the template setup is completed and inspected for accuracy, the plastic supporting rods are slid into $\frac{3}{8}$-inch holes, which are spaced 2 inches apart and $\frac{3}{4}$ inch from the model surface as determined by the templates. The rods can extend from one end of the model to the other if the holes are in line. If the holes are not in line, the rods should extend through a minimum of three template spaces. The templates are washed with clean solvent. The rods are then bonded to the templates with a paste epoxy adhesive, which is allowed to cure overnight at room temperature. In mounting these rods, great care must be taken not to cause the template edges to move out of their exact position.

Next, the wire screen is attached to the rods. Normally, hardware cloth with a $\frac{1}{4}$-inch mesh is used for this purpose. The screen is cut to the proper width, placed on top of the plastic support rods, and attached to the rods with "hog rings" or ties. At this time, the templates and the hardware cloth should both be washed with a clean solvent such as methylene chloride. The sides of the templates above the screen should be sanded lightly with 80- or 120-grit sandpaper to ensure a clean, fresh surface for the epoxy material to bond to. Great care should be taken in this operation to avoid sanding or otherwise affecting the control surfaces of the templates.

Application of the Plastic Materials Two different types of epoxy resin compounds are used in the construction of a splined plastic master model. One type provides a lightweight base coat; the other type provides a hard, smooth, finished model surface. The base material is an epoxy resin compound, usually a thixotropic paste, that is heavily filled with microballoons. The material, because of its light weight, is commonly referred to as a syntactic foam, although it is not a true foam. Typical physical properties of low-density epoxy tooling compounds are given in Table 2-2. The splining resin that provides the finished surface of the model is also an epoxy tooling compound. It is normally a creamy, thixotropic paste and is usually white in color.

Great care should be exercised in mixing these materials to ensure that they are thoroughly blended. Because they are thixotropic pastes, it is difficult to mix the two components thoroughly by hand. Normally, only batches of 500 grams or less are mixed by hand. Low-density materials should not be mixed in a container by hand. Experience has shown that thorough mixing by this method is not possible and usually results in soft spots throughout the material after it has cured. It is strongly recommended that mixes that are mixed by hand be placed on a large flat surface and blended with the use of a putty knife. Batches larger than 500 grams should be mixed with a suitably sized mixer on a drill press at a speed of approximately 250 rpm.

Application of the Base Coat: The use of a scrim cloth is recommended for applying the low-density base coat to the hardware screen. In this method, the scrim cloth is cut to the proper width to allow it to fit between two templates. The scrim cloth is then laid out on a clean flat table. The low-density epoxy tooling compound which has already been mixed is then applied to the scrim cloth to a thickness of approximately ¼ inch. The scrim cloth is then placed onto the hardware screen with the low-density material facing downward. The scrim cloth is then pressed lightly into the screen, either by hand or by the use of

TABLE 2-2 Typical Physical Properties of Low-density Epoxy Tooling Compounds

Shrinkage, inches/inch	0.002
Specific gravity	0.65
Compressive strength, psi	4,000
Bond strength, psi	1,500
Deflection temperature, °F	140
Pot life, minutes	50
Gel time (¾-inch thickness), hours	4
Coefficient of thermal expansion, inches/inch/°F $\times 10^{-5}$	3.0–4.0
Shore D hardness	60

a roller. This will cause the major portion of the low-density compound to pass through the hardware screen to a depth of $\frac{1}{8}$ to $\frac{1}{4}$ inch. When it has cured, the low-density tooling compound will be firmly locked in place.

The use of the scrim cloth in the application of the initial layer of the low-density tooling compound has three main advantages over applying it directly to the hardware screen with a spatula. These advantages are:

1. Loss of material due to excessive penetration through the hardware cloth is greatly reduced. The scrim cloth acts as a barrier and does not permit penetration of the low-density base material beyond the $\frac{1}{4}$-inch thickness. If the scrim cloth is not used, the application of subsequent layers of low-density compound will cause the material to penetrate through the screen much like hamburger coming out of a hamburger grinder. A great deal of material is wasted by direct application.

2. The use of the scrim cloth will result in a lighter-weight model, since less material will be used.

3. Labor costs are reduced when scrim cloth is used. If the low-density compound is applied directly to the hardware cloth, the shop worker must exercise great care not to force an excessive amount of material through the screen. The application rate is considerably slower because of the extreme care required.

Using scrim cloth, low-density material is applied to the hardware cloth over the entire model. Immediately following the application of the scrim cloth, additional low-density epoxy compound is mixed and applied over the scrim cloth. The material should be built up to a level that is almost even with the template control surfaces. A splining tool, such as the one illustrated in Figure 2-30, is then used to screed the low-density compound to a height of approximately $\frac{1}{8}$ inch below the template surfaces. The low-density compound is applied to the entire surface of the model in this manner. It should then be allowed to cure for a minimum of 12 hours before the application of the finish splining compound.

Application of Finish Splining Compound: The finish splining compound is the material that provides the completed surface of the splined plastic master model. In the early years of plastic tooling, a great deal of difficulty was encountered in attempting to spline with plastic. Consequently, a great deal of research and development effort has been expended by the tooling resin formulators to achieve an epoxy splining compound that would provide handling characteristics comparable to those of gypsum cements. New epoxy splining compounds have been

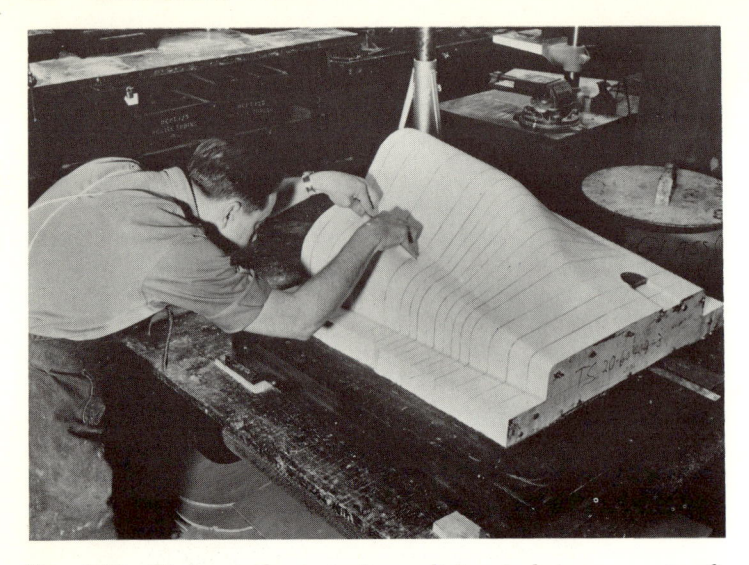

Fig. 2-30 Workman demonstrating splining technique on aircraft splined epoxy master model. (*Ren Plastics, Inc.*)

gradually improved to a point where they provide a minimum drag, a minimum of entrapped air bubbles, and an easy and smooth application in "feather" or very thin coats. When properly fabricated, splined plastic master models provide a smooth, durable, and accurate surface.

Typical physical properties of epoxy splining compounds are provided in Table 2-3. When mixed, epoxy splining compounds are creamy, thixotropic paste compounds. They are formulated to be used in thicknesses up to ⅛ inch. Experience has shown that, if used in thicknesses exceeding ⅛ inch, excessive shrinkage will result. Therefore, it is important that these materials not be used in thicknesses greater than ⅛ inch in order to achieve optimum model accuracy.

TABLE 2-3 Typical Physical Properties of Epoxy Splining Compounds

Shrinkage, inches/inch	0.005
Shore D hardness	85
Compressive strength, psi	10,000
Bond strength, psi	2,000
Deflection temperature, °F	150
Coefficient of thermal expansion	2.9
Gel time, minutes	75
Specific gravity	1.4
Pot life, minutes	35–45

Because epoxy splining compounds are high in viscosity, it is recommended that any batches weighing over 250 grams be mixed by mechanical means. The speed of the mechanical mixer should not exceed 250 rpm. Mixing speeds of over 250 rpm will cause the entrapment of small air bubbles in the mixture. Since this material provides the model surface, it is important that entrapped air be minimized.

As soon as the splining compound has been thoroughly mixed, it should be "buttered on" the low-density base compound with a spatula. At this point, it is advisable to only add splining material to every other space and not to fill in adjacent spaces. Since splining compounds require several hours to cure, this technique allows the material in one space to be worked without disturbing semicured material in a finished section.

The splining compound is applied to a height slightly exceeding the

Fig. 2-31 Splined epoxy master model of forward fuselage—Jet Commander. Worker at left is using transit to align straight edge held by worker in center of photo. This is used to scribe the centerline on the master model. Worker at right is using a scale to check for deviation in station templates. (*Ren Plastics, Inc.*)

template surfaces. The excess is then removed with a standard splining tool. The shop worker should not expect to achieve a perfect finished surface on the first application of the splining compound. On the first application, it is sufficient to apply material to the entire model up to the template edges. It is important that no splining compound be allowed to project above the template surfaces. If this happens, the projecting material will have to be sanded or ground to the proper level. Once the operation is complete, the splining compound should be allowed to cure for a minimum of 12 hours before any subsequent operations.

After the splining compound has cured for 12 hours, subsequent applications are made to achieve the model surface. The final work on the surface may take several applications of splining compound, depending on the skill of the shop worker and the accuracy required on the surface. At this stage, applications will be only a few thousandths of an inch thick. It is therefore recommended that only small batches, approximately 200 grams, be mixed in order to avoid wastage of material. If large batches are used, they are liable to cure or "kick off" in the container while the toolbuilder is carefully splining the final surface.

The splining tool, which is normally made of spring steel, should be kept clean by wiping frequently with acetone or denatured alcohol.

Fig. 2-32 Splined epoxy master model of automobile fender. (*Rezolin, Inc.*)

The finish splining operation should be done in a manner that enables at least three adjacent templates to be touched by the splining tool at the same time. In order to accomplish this, it may be necessary for the toolbuilder to bend or flex the splining tool. The splining tool should be held at approximately a 45° angle to the model surface. Experience has shown that a splining tool with a rounded edge provides superior results to a splining tool with two sharp edges. If these steps are followed carefully, the result will be a master model with an accurate, smooth, and durable surface.

REFERENCES

Box or Rod-turning Cylindrical or Kindred Shapes, IGL-120, U.S. Gypsum Company, Chicago, Ill.

Industrial Tooling with Hydrocal Gypsum Cements, IGL-121, U.S. Gypsum Company, Chicago, Ill.

Industrial Tooling with Hydrocal Gypsum Cements—Circular Shapes, IGL-111, U.S. Gypsum Company, Chicago, Ill.

A Review of Plastics for Tooling, Plastics Technical Evaluation Center, Picatinny Arsenal, Dover, N.J., March 1964.

Run-Work-Straight Moulding, IGL-109, U.S. Gypsum Company, Chicago, Ill.

The Techniques of Using Epoxy Plastic Tooling Materials, Ren Plastics, Inc., Lansing, Mich., April 1964.

CHAPTER THREE

Laminated Plastic Tools

GENERAL DISCUSSION

Laminated plastic tools are perhaps the most commonly selected form of plastic tool. A laminated plastic tool consists of glass cloth impregnated with resin, usually epoxy. During the fabrication of the tool, alternate layers of glass cloth and liquid resin are applied to the surface of the model being reproduced. The liquid resin penetrates or impregnates the glass cloth. When the laminate is completed and the resin allowed to cure, the end result is a laminated tool which is a mirror image of the surface from which it was molded.

This chapter concerns itself with laminated tools made with epoxy resin compounds, cured at room temperature, and used in production applications at temperatures below 140°F. The fabrication sequences of the two most frequently used methods, i.e., hand lay-up and spray laminating, are discussed in detail. While other types of resin, such as polyester, are used in some industries for tools which do not require close dimensional accuracy, the great majority of laminated plastic tools are made with epoxy resin compounds. Therefore, this chapter will deal only with laminated plastic tools made with epoxy resin compounds. The procedures and design considerations for other resin systems are similar enough that they can be adapted, if desired, to the information contained in this chapter.

Laminated epoxy–fiber glass tools are used wherever accuracy, strength, and weight are prime considerations. Epoxy laminated tools experience less shrinkage during cure than any other type of plastic tool. This feature is particularly important on extremely large tools. For example, if the shrinkage of an epoxy laminated tool is 0.0003 inches/inch, a laminated tool 20 feet long would only be 0.072 inch smaller than the model from which it was made. On the other hand, a cast tool, the same size, experiencing shrinkage during cure of 0.002 inches/inch, would be 0.48 inch undersize. For this reason, laminates are selected whenever possible on large tools.

Laminated tools are also preferred in many instances because they are lighter in weight. By using the laminating technique, extremely large tools can be fabricated that are only a fraction of the weight of a cast tool. Table 3-1 gives some typical physical properties of room-temperature-cured epoxy laminates that will be helpful to the tool designer.

When properly designed, epoxy laminated tools provide the greatest accuracy and best dimensional stability of any form of plastic tooling, regardless of size. For this reason, laminated tools are most frequently the choice throughout industry for master gauges, checking fixtures, diesinking patterns, assembly models, and inspection fixtures.

The one disadvantage of laminated tools is that they are time-consuming to fabricate, both in man-hours expended and in flow time required. These disadvantages must be weighed by the tool designer against the advantages of laminated tools and compared with the advantages and disadvantages of other types of plastic tooling approaches. The selection becomes difficult because there are no hard-and-fast rules for making such determinations. Each tool must be considered individually on the basis of its size. General ground rules that can be helpful in

TABLE 3-1 Typical Physical Properties of Room-temperature-cured Epoxy Laminates*

Flexural strength, psi	34,000
Flexural modulus, psi $\times 10^5$	2.3
Tensile strength, psi	25,000
Hardness, Shore D	90
Shrinkage, inches/inch	0.0003
Deflection temperature, °F	150
Thermal expansion, inches/inch/°F $\times 10^{-5}$	0.7

* Epoxy laminating resin, no. 1500 glass cloth, Volan A finish, hand lay-up, cured at 72°F ± 5°F for 7 days.

TABLE 3-2 Desirability Factors for Various Types of Plastic Tools

	Laminate	Metal core surface cast	Mass cast	Paste
Dimensional stability	1	3	4	2
Shrinkage, during cure	1	3	4	2
Least weight	1	4	3	2
Labor cost	4	3	1	2
Material cost/lb	4	3	1	2
Strength	1	2	3	4
Toughness	1	2	4	3

NOTE: The above table is intended to be used only as a guide. Specific conditions in any particular application may alter these factors.
SOURCE: Ren Plastics, Inc.

determining which plastic tooling approach is to be used for a given tool are illustrated in Table 3-2. The ratings shown, established from the standpoint of desirability, are as follows: (1) most desirable, (2) satisfactory, (3) fair, and (4) least desirable.

Fiber Glass Fabrics—Why They Are Used

Fiber glass fabrics are relatively new engineering materials whose usage has contributed significantly to the growth of the plastic industry. Fiber glass fabrics have many unique and outstanding characteristics which have provided design flexibility, decreased fabrication costs, and produced tools and products with superior strength-to-weight ratios over any other engineering material. Because they are highly engineered, desired physical properties can be predetermined by careful selection of weave, finish, etc. Fiber glass fabrics have five main characteristics that make them desirable for combination with epoxy resins to make laminated tools.

Outstanding Dimensional Stability The fiber glass yarns used in the manufacture of glass fabrics will not stretch or shrink—maximum elongation at break is 3 percent. Even at elevated temperatures, fiber glass fabrics maintain their dimensional stability.

Superior Strength Fiber glass fabrics have one of the highest-known strength-to-weight ratios. Fiber glass fabrics are treated with many special finishes to increase their compatibility with the numerous resins with which they are used. With a properly prepared surface, the glass and resin can be joined chemically to create a laminate with strengths far superior to the components. With proper selection of fabric, unidirectional or bidirectional strengths can be designed into a laminated structure.

Excellent Corrosion Resistance Glass fabrics are made from superfine filaments of pure glass. Consequently, glass fabrics will not rot, mildew, or deteriorate. Glass fabrics will resist all organic solvents and most acids and alkalies.

Good Thermal Properties Fiber glass fabrics have a low coefficient of thermal expansion and a relatively high thermal conductivity. Glass fabrics dissipate heat more rapidly than asbestos or organic fibers.

Low Cost Fiber glass fabrics themselves are not expensive. In addition, they often permit the use of faster, more efficient manufacturing techniques than other materials would allow.

Basic Considerations of Fiber Glass Fabrics

Fiber glass fabrics are highly engineered products. Therefore, many factors must be considered when selecting a fiber glass fabric for a particular application. For example, strength requirements for a particular application must be matched to the right combination of glass fabric weight, thickness, and construction. It is therefore important to know the basics of how fiber glass fabrics are made and to understand the descriptive terminology associated with fiber glass fabrics.

The Yarn Fiber glass is glass in fiber form. All forms of glass fibers begin with the same manufacturing process. The various ingredients are mixed in a batch to make a specific formulation. The mixture is then heated to convert the mix into molten glass. From the molten glass, continuous filaments are attenuated (drawn or pulled rapidly) through precise multihole bushings. The filaments are coated with a protective lubricant or binder to protect them from damage during processing and weaving. A strand is produced by combining individual continuous filaments.

The Weave Weaving consists of interlacing a series of fiber glass yarns at right angles. All standard fabric weaves can be produced with fiber glass yarns. The most widely used industrial weaves are illus-

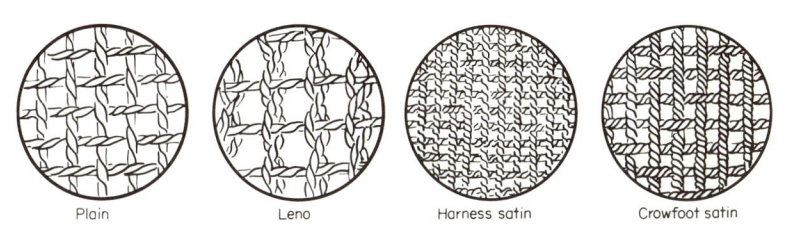

Fig. 3-1 Fiber glass cloth weaves commonly used in plastic tooling. (*J. P. Stevens & Co., Inc.*)

TABLE 3-3 Technical Data on Standard Fiber Glass Fabrics Used in Tooling

Style no.	Weight, oz/sq yd	Thickness, in.	Thread count/in. Warp	Thread count/in. Fill	Avg. breaking strength, lb/in. of width Warp	Avg. breaking strength, lb/in. of width Fill	Yarn Warp	Yarn Fill	Weave
120	3.16	0.0040	60	58	125	120	450-½	450-½	Crowfoot satin
181	8.90	0.0085	57	54	340	330	225-⅓	225-⅓	8 harness satin
1500	9.66	0.014	16	14	450	410	150-⅔	150-⅔	Plain
1544	19.20	0.022	28	14	745	830	150-⅔	150-⅔	Plain
1800	9.10	0.0125	16	14	500	350	18-⅙	18-⅙	Plain
2532	6.85	0.010	16	14	300	230	25-⅙	25-⅙	Plain
7500	9.66	0.014	16	14	450	410	150-⅔	150-⅔	Plain
7544	19.20	0.022	28	14	745	830	75-⅔	75-⅔	Plain
7587	20.00	0.030	40	21	750	450	75-⅔	75-⅔	Mock leno

SOURCE: J. P. Stevens & Co., Inc.

trated in Figure 3-1. The plain weave is used for most tooling applications. It has good bidirectional strength characteristics and is the most stable weave available. It also has good handling characteristics, and because of its open nature, air entrapment during laminating is minimized.

To summarize the foregoing discussion, it can be safely concluded that fiber glass fabrics with a Volan A finish and a plain weave are the most commonly used for tooling applications. Style no. 1500 is by far the most universally used for epoxy laminated tools. Sixteen layers of no. 1500 fiber glass fabric and epoxy laminated tools. Sixteen duce a laminate with a cured thickness between 0.24 to 0.30 inch depending on the resin system used. Table 3-3 provides technical data on various styles of fiber glass fabrics used for plastic tooling applications.

FABRICATION OF ROOM-TEMPERATURE EPOXY LAMINATED TOOLS

Hand Lay-up Method

The hand lay-up method is the most commonly used method of fabricating room-temperature epoxy laminated tools. This method consists of applying alternate layers of resin and fiber glass cloth onto the model until the desired thickness is reached. Normally, resin formulators will recommend that the laminate not be built up to exceed a thickness of 0.30 inch, since the exotherm generated by the curing plastic will cause excessive shrinkage or warpage of the tool. As a rule of thumb, a 16-layer laminate of 0.013-inch glass fabric will produce a laminate with a cured thickness between 0.24 to 0.30 inch. Thicknesses of laminates made by hand lay-up will vary considerably, depending on (1) the resin system being used, (2) the skill level of the shop worker, and (3) the method used. Even though there are variables, extremely good quality laminated tools can be fabricated by the hand lay-up method if a few basic rules are followed and if materials are accurately measured and properly blended.

The basic procedure for hand lay-up is as follows:

1. Inspect the surface of the model for accuracy and/or surface defects. Keep in mind that the laminate you are going to make will be a mirror image of the surface that you are inspecting. Every surface imperfection will be reproduced. To avoid the necessity of handworking the laminated tool after it has cured, the surface should be free of defects. All defects or surface imperfections should be repaired before proceeding on to the next step.

2. Prepare the model surface with the appropriate sealers and parting agents as described in Chapter 1.

3. The surface-coat resin and hardener should be carefully weighed and mixed thoroughly. Mixing for 2 to 3 minutes with a drill motor or 4 to 5 minutes by hand is sufficient. The surface coat may be applied by brush, squeegee, or sprayer. The surface coat should be allowed to cure until it has become "tack-free." The surface coat is considered tack-free when your finger will leave a fingerprint in the material, but the material will not stick to your finger. At this point, the next operation may be started.

Note: The next step should take place within 3 hours. If for some reason (such as change of shift) the surface coat resin is allowed to harden beyond the tacky stage, the surface should be sanded before the next operation. This will ensure a good bond between the surface coat and the laminate. If this precaution is not observed, the surface coat is likely to chip or separate from the cured laminate.

4. Sharp corners and projections should be filled with a mixture of milled glass fibers and catalyzed laminating resin. This will simplify subsequent laminating steps. This mixture, usually referred to as a "glass paste" or "putty mix," is prepared as follows: (*a*) A predetermined amount of laminating resin and hardener are mixed in their proper ratio. (*b*) Milled glass fibers, preweighed to 20 to 25 percent of the total weight of the laminating resin and hardener, are slowly added to the catalyzed laminating resin. The mixture should be stirred as the glass

fibers are being added to ensure that the fibers are thoroughly wetted by the resin. The resulting glass paste is then applied to projections and sharp radii with a small putty knife or spatula. It is best to make the glass paste as thick as possible because the exposure to laminating resin in the next step will cause the putty mix to sag and lose its shape if it is mixed too thin initially. The glass paste can be allowed to cure for 30 to 35 minutes, during which time the fiber glass cloth to be used in the subsequent laminating operation can be cut to the required shapes and dimensions.

5. Small strips of glass cloth or glass tape are then applied over areas where the glass paste had previously been applied. This is accomplished by mixing a small amount of laminating resin and hardener in the correct ratio, and then applying it sparingly over the areas previously filled with glass paste. The glass tape is then carefully applied and stippled with the hairs of the brush. This precaution will provide the areas filled with glass paste with some support and will help prevent the glass paste from moving out of position during subsequent steps of the laminating process. Proceed immediately to the next step.

6. When mixing laminating resin and hardener, never mix more material than it is possible to use in 30 minutes. A thin coat of laminating resin is applied to the model by either brush or squeegee. Fiber glass cloth, which has previously been cut up into 18-inch squares (approximately), is then applied to the wet resin. The use of small squares of cloth will help prevent bridging during the laminating of the first few layers. This technique is particularly helpful on tools with complex shapes. Once the cloth is in position, it is squeegeed or stippled with a brush to ensure that it is tight against the model and contains no voids. When squeegeeing the resin and cloth, start at the middle and work the air out to the edge. If excess resin appears, add another layer of cloth without adding more resin. Keep resin to a minimum.

7. Laminating resin is again applied, and the operation described in step no. 6 is repeated. It is important to note that resin is first applied, and then worked up through the cloth which is applied over the resin. This ensures thorough wetting of the fiber glass cloth and creates a much better tool.

8. Step no. 7 is repeated until the desired tool thickness is reached. Normally 16 layers of no. 1500 tooling cloth will provide a tool of adequate thickness (0.24 to 0.30 inch). If a tool thickness greater than 0.30 inch is desired, it is recommended that it be fabricated in two stages. The first stage consists of 16 layers. These 16 layers should be allowed to cure and to cool down to room temperature. If the surface is glossy, it should be sanded before the second stage is applied. If this precaution is not observed, excessive heat generated by the exo-

thermic reaction of the curing plastic can cause shrinkage or warpage of the laminated tool.

9. After the tool has been built up to the desired thickness, it is allowed to cure a minimum of 16 hours at room temperature prior to the application of the reinforcement. After the reinforcement is applied, the tool should be allowed to cure on the model at room temperature for a minimum of 24 hours before it is removed from the model. The reinforcement or framework should always be applied before the tool is removed from the model. This provides a curing period of 40 to 48 hours for the tool face and ensures that it has reached its full strength before it is deprived of the model's support.

Spray-laminating Method

Spray laminating offers an excellent opportunity to reduce the labor costs involved in fabricating laminated tools. Commercially available equipment allows the resin and hardener to be mixed in the correct ratio, sprayed from a gun toward the model surface, and combined with chopped fiber glass. It has been estimated that labor costs on a spray-laminated tool are approximately 40 percent of the labor costs of a hand-laminated tool.

The following are proven advantages of the spray-laminating method:

1. Weighing and mixing by hand of the resin and hardener components are eliminated.
2. Measuring and cutting of fiber glass cloth are eliminated.
3. Chopped fiber glass strands are lower in cost than woven glass fabric used in hand lay-up.
4. Rapid buildup of the desired laminate thickness is possible.
5. Greatly reduced labor costs.

Spray-laminating equipment consists of two basic components: a pumping unit and a spray gun coupled to a glass roving chopper. The entire unit is mounted on a base with wheels, making it possible to move from one work area to another.

There are special requirements for an epoxy resin spray-laminating system. A spray-laminating system must have outstanding wetting properties, low tack, a minimum of runoff or sag when applied to a vertical surface, the ability to mix easily in the mixing chamber of the spray gun, and the ability to cure without excessive shrinkage. The epoxy resin formulators have been equal to the task, and spray-laminating materials with typical physical properties shown in Table 3-4 are readily available.

Basic Spray-laminating Procedure The sequence in the fabrication of a spray-laminated epoxy tool is as follows:

1. A suitable parting agent is applied to the model or pattern. The selection of proper parting agent and application techniques is described in detail in Chapter 1 of this text.

2. The glass roving chopper is adjusted so that its output will equal the weight of the mixed resin and hardener.

3. The glass roving chopper is adjusted to make the chopped strands coming out of the chopper intersect the resin-hardener stream approximately 1 to 2 inches in front of the gun nozzle.

4. The gun is held approximately 3 to 4 feet away from the model or pattern, and resin and chopped glass are sprayed onto the pattern in horizontal sweeps. Each pass is overlapped slightly.

5. The next layer is sprayed onto the pattern in vertical sweeps. This is done to ensure that uniform laminate thickness be obtained.

6. The glass fibers are compressed by rolling them into the laminate using a commercially available "disc-harrow" roller. Spray laminates should be rolled when the laminate is 1.16-inch thick, and in $\frac{1}{8}$-inch increments thereafter.

7. The laminate should be allowed to cure a minimum of 16 hours at room temperature before it is removed from the model.

It must be emphasized at this point that the quality of the laminate depends to a great extent on controlling the resin-to-glass ratio, and on thoroughly rolling out the laminate during the fabrication sequence. If this is not done, the laminate will be resin-rich and will lack strength. In addition, a resin-rich laminate will shrink excessively, putting the tool out of tool tolerances.

In instances where a dense, well-compacted spray laminate is desired, the use of a vacuum bag is very effective. After the laminate has been sprayed and compacted with the roller, the laminate is enclosed in a bag made out of polyethylene film. A vacuum line is inserted in the bag and the air is evacuated. In this manner, atmospheric pressure is exerted evenly on all surfaces of the laminate.

Three purposes are accomplished by the use of a vacuum bag. First, it serves to produce a more dense laminate than is possible with only

TABLE 3-4 Typical Properties* of Epoxy–Chopped Glass Spray Laminates

Flexural strength, psi	32,000
Flexural modulus, psi $\times 10^5$	1.1–1.5
Hardness, Shore D	85
Shrinkage, inches/inch	0.0008
Deflection temperature, °F	140

* Cured at 72°F ± 5°F for 7 days.

rolling the glass fibers. Second, the laminate is made to conform more closely to the exact configuration of the model or pattern. Third, the use of a vacuum bag also helps to eliminate the characteristic tendency of sprayed chopped-fiber glass laminates to have pinholes on the surface between the laminate and the model.

The spray-laminating method is not entirely without disadvantages. One chronic problem is the effect that the resin and hardener have on the gaskets in the spray equipment. Several large tooling shops have expressed the feeling that the problems encountered in keeping the equipment operational and clean tend to offset the advantages of spray laminating. However, it must be conceded that the performance of any piece of equipment is directly proportional to the care and consideration given to it by the operator. For example, if the operator does not flush the unit thoroughly after use, it must be expected that the resin and hardener combined in the mixing chamber will set up inside the gun. If spray-laminating equipment is to be used effectively to reduce the cost of laminated tools, it must be recognized by the using shop that the equipment must be properly operated and maintained.

The fact that spray-laminating equipment requires a skilled and reliable operator is considered to be another major drawback by several tooling shops. Spray equipment in the hands of an inexperienced or careless operator will produce a lot of scrap tools. This is considered to be a particularly serious drawback by aerospace firms, who are constantly shifting and transferring personnel from tooling to production shops.

Some additional disadvantages of spray laminating are:

1. In many states, hygiene requirements necessitate the use of spray booths in conjunction with the operation of spray-laminating equipment. If large tools are to be built by the spray-laminating methods, the cost of a spray booth can be a major consideration. When evaluated from that standpoint, management may find that the savings achieved by spray laminating are more than offset by the cost of a spray booth. Unfortunately, there is no generalization that can assist management in making a decision of this type. The decision must be made with the particular situation in mind. This involves a consideration of the number of tools to be built, the size of the tools, the savings estimated per tool, and the cost of a spray booth or other suitable ventilation or air-exhausting equipment.

2. As a general rule, spray laminates have 15 to 20 percent less strength than laminates made by hand lay-up with woven glass fabrics. Depending on the type of tool being considered, this may or may not be of significant consideration.

The foregoing discussion was aimed at pointing out that significant labor savings are possible through the use of spray-laminating equipment. It was also intended to point out that spray-laminating equipment, like any equipment, has to be used properly and has to be maintained properly on a regular basis. If these factors are recognized and if management considers the cost of the equipment required, associated facilities, skill and reliability of shop workers, and size and number of tools to be fabricated, the decision as to whether or not to use spray-laminating equipment should be relatively straightforward. Many shops have considered the matter. Some have purchased spray-laminating equipment and are using it to good advantage. Other shops have evaluated all the considerations and have elected to stay with the hand lay-up method.

REINFORCING LAMINATED TOOLS

A laminated tool is usually reinforced by the addition of a plastic framework which is attached to the laminated tool face. Usually the framework is made of the same resin system used to fabricate the tool face, or of similar materials. The use of similar materials prevents factors such as temperature changes, moisture, age, and weight from affecting the dimensional stability of the tool. Because the choice of the framework has a great effect on the dimensional stability of the tool, it is important that the reinforcement method and materials be selected carefully.

Basically, there are four methods of reinforcing laminated tools: (1) solid laminated sheet eggcrate reinforcement, (2) plastic tubing, (3) fiber-glass-faced honeycomb sandwich panels, and (4) lightweight aggregate coated with epoxy laminating resin. All four methods have proven effective in that they provide adequate strength, dimensional stability, and maintain the lightweight characteristic of the tool. There are several variations of the four basic methods, such as the use of urethane foam combined with solid laminated eggcrate reinforcement, but for the most part the four basic methods discussed in this chapter provide the foundation for reinforcing laminated tools.

It will become apparent to the reader, as he progresses through this chapter, that it is nearly impossible to establish rigid design criteria for laminated tools, or which reinforcement method to use on a particular tool. Variables such as the physical properties of the resin system used, size of the tool, configuration of the tool, skill of the laminator, and the intended use of the tool, all enter into this decision. It is necessary that the tool fabricator consider each tool individually and select the method for reinforcing the tool accordingly. In order to assist the reader, this chapter contains many sketches and photographs which illustrate good designs of laminated tools for various applications. These have all been carefully selected to give the reader insight into the design and reinforcement of laminated tools.

Solid Laminated Sheet Eggcrate Reinforcement

The use of a solid laminated sheet bonded to the back of a laminated tool in an eggcrate pattern (see Figure 3-2) is perhaps the most common method of reinforcing laminated tools.

Normally the eggcrate reinforcements are spaced approximately 18 inches apart. This can vary depending on the size of the tool, its intended use, and its configuration. For example, if the tool configuration is such that it has strength built into the tool face, the reinforcements may be spaced 24 to 30 inches apart. However, 18 inches is a good general rule of thumb suitable for most tooling applications. The following is a typical sequence for applying solid laminated sheet reinforcement to the back of a laminated tool:

1. Reinforcement locations are determined by measuring the tool, determining the number of reinforcements required, and laying out the reinforcement pattern on the exposed surface of the tool.

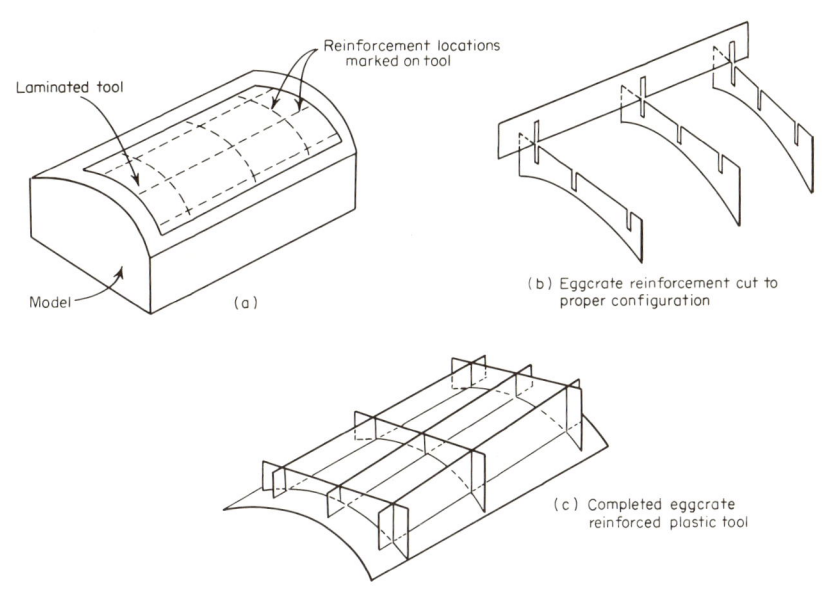

Fig. 3-2 Sequence of application of eggcrate reinforcement to laminated tool.

80   Plastic Tooling

2. An area 2½ inches wide on each side of the lines representing the header locations is sanded lightly to remove the gloss and to provide a good surface to which to bond the reinforcements.

3. Using heavy kraft paper or cardboard, templates conforming to the tool configuration at the reinforcement locations are made. The templates should be identified so that they can be placed in the proper position later.

4. The templates are then used as patterns for tracing the reinforcement configuration on ¼-inch solid laminates. These laminated sheets are normally laid up on a surface table and allowed to cure for 48 hours prior to this operation. The solid laminated sheets should be made from the same materials as the tool face.

5. The laminated sheet stock is then cut to the proper configuration and fitted onto the exposed surface of the tool. The reinforcement should fit the tool well enough so that there are no spaces in excess of ⅛ inch between the reinforcement and the tool.

6. A bead of glass paste is then applied over the lines on the tool representing the reinforcement locations. The reinforcement structure is then placed onto the tool and pressed into the bead. The structure is allowed to cure at room temperature until it is firm. Occasionally, tooling shops prefer to use a fast-setting adhesive for this step. However, in doing this, there is the risk of shrinkage marks showing on the tool face, caused by the heat and shrinkage of the fast-setting adhesive. If tooling schedules will permit, it is best to use a glass paste mix and wait until it has cured enough to proceed to the next step.

7. The glass paste mix is then used to make a fillet between the tool and the reinforcement. A fillet of approximately ⅜-inch radius will make subsequent operations easier. The glass paste should be allowed to cure at room temperature until firm.

8. Two or three layers of glass tape are then laminated as shown in Figure 3-3 to reinforce the bond between the reinforcement and the tool.

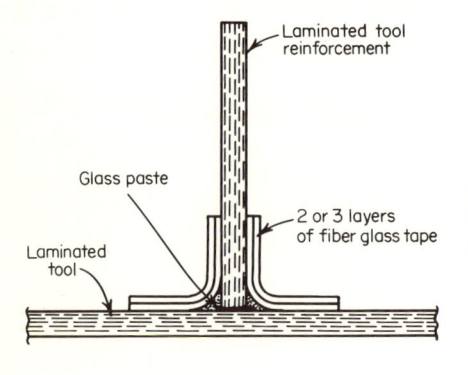

Fig. 3-3 Detail of method of bonding eggcrate reinforcement to laminated tool.

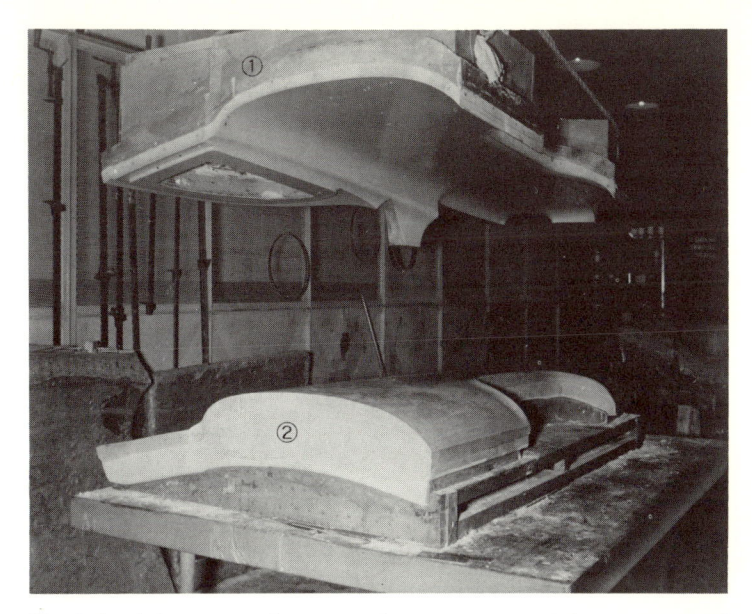

Fig. 3-4 (1) Laminated spotting fixture for automobile quarter panel taken from (2) laminated duplicate model. Both tools are constructed of room-temperature epoxy laminating compound and fiber glass cloth and are reinforced with an eggcrate structure consisting of $\frac{1}{4}$-inch laminate of same materials as the tool face. (*Hysol Division, The Dexter Corp.*)

The tool and reinforcement should be allowed to remain on the model at room temperature for 16 to 24 hours prior to removal from the model. The base of the tool should be leveled before removal.

Epoxy Tubing Reinforcement

There are many instances where it is advantageous to use epoxy tubing for tool reinforcement. Epoxy tubing has proved to be dimensionally stable as well as lightweight. It is commercially available in a wide range of sizes. Physical specifications of the most commonly used sizes are given in Table 3-5.

One of the advantages epoxy tubing has over sheet stock as a reinforcing material is that it can be easily applied in a short period of time by relatively unskilled labor. When using laminated sheet stock as a reinforcing material, a great deal of time and effort are consumed in making accurate templates from which to cut the laminated sheet and in cutting the sheet to the desired configuration. If the sheet does not conform to the back of the tool as well as required, expensive hand-

82 Plastic Tooling

TABLE 3-5 Sizes and Physical Specifications of Epoxy Tubing Used in Tool Reinforcement

Type of tubing	Round		Square	
Size of tubing	1 in. O.D.	1¾ in. O.D.	1¾ in. sq	2¼ in. sq
Flexure, 20-in. span: Deflection in center of 20-in. span, for each 10-lb load............	0.0357	0.0068	0.0028	0.0017
Uniform deflection to max. load of, lb.......	80	160	560	650
Compression parallel to axis: Crushing load, lb........	3,600	7,400	15,600	12,900
Deflection in inches/inch of height for each 1,000-lb load..........	0.003	0.001	0.0007	0.0005
Proportional limit.......	2,700	5,700	10,300	10,800
Compression perpendicular to axis on 1-in. length: Crushing load, lb........	150	90	890	510
Deflection for each 10 lb of load................	0.005	0.018	0.0005	0.0009
Uniform deflection to maximum load of, lb..	80	45	570	240
Wall thickness, in.........	0.058	0.069	0.122	0.112
Weight per foot, oz........	2.3	4.0	8.9	10.3

SOURCE: Ren Plastics, Inc., Lansing, Mich.

work is necessary. Epoxy tubing, on the other hand, can be spiral cut (as shown in Figure 3-5) and easily made to conform to any configuration.

The spiral-cut tubing is bonded into position on the backside of the tool with a fast-setting epoxy adhesive. After the adhesive has cured, a fillet is made with glass paste. The final step in fastening the tubing to the tool is to apply two or three layers of fiber glass tape and laminating resin as shown in Figure 3-6. This serves to securely tie the tubing into the tool face, making it an integral part of the tool and creating a rigid, dimensionally stable structure.

Another advantage of epoxy tubing is its lightweight characteristic. On tools with high relief, those reinforced with epoxy tubing are much lighter in weight than the identical tool reinforced with laminated sheet. Normally, in cases such as this, there is a substantial savings in materials when epoxy tubing is used.

Angle of saw table determines spacing of cuts

Tilt saw table approximately 25° and secure blocking material in back of saw blade with sufficient distance so as not to allow saw blade to cut more than 1/16" more than round tube wall thickness.

Saw table — Blade

Square tubing

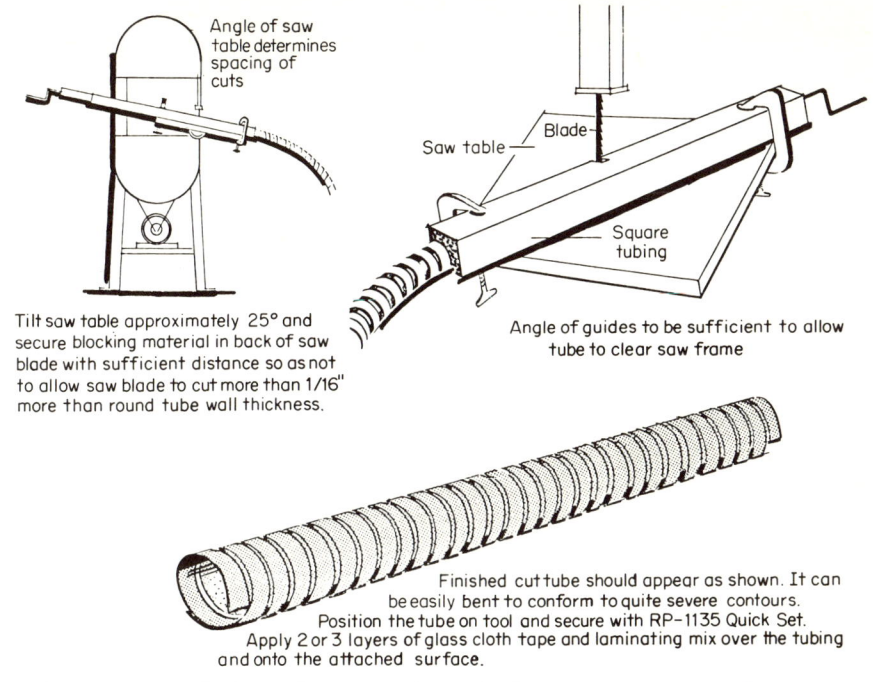

Angle of guides to be sufficient to allow tube to clear saw frame

Finished cut tube should appear as shown. It can be easily bent to conform to quite severe contours. Position the tube on tool and secure with RP-1135 Quick Set. Apply 2 or 3 layers of glass cloth tape and laminating mix over the tubing and onto the attached surface.

Fig. 3-5 Method of spiral cutting of round plastic tubing. (*Ren Plastics, Inc.*)

Tool face

2 or 3 layers fiber glass tape

Glass paste

Epoxy tubing

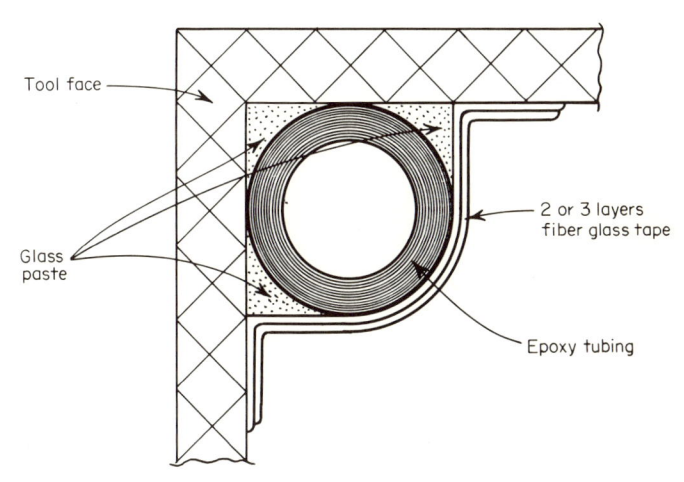

Fig. 3-6 Reinforcing the flanges of a tool with spiral-cut round tubing.

84   Plastic Tooling

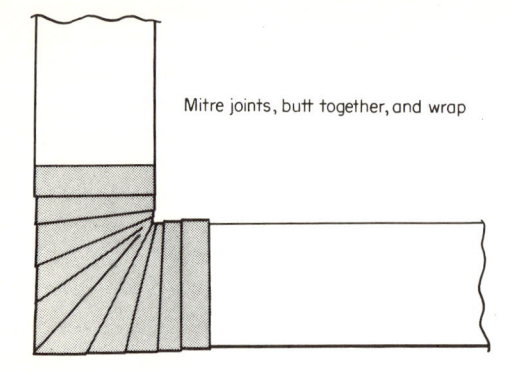

Mitre joints, butt together, and wrap

Fig. 3-7 Typical tubing joint wrapped with glass tape. Laminating resin is applied with a brush as tape is wound around joint. (*Ren Plastics, Inc.*)

Fiber-glass-faced Honeycomb Reinforcement

Frequently, fiber-glass-faced honeycomb sandwich panels are used to reinforce laminated tools. These panels are commercially available and are normally constructed of ⅜-inch cell—0.003 inch expanded aluminum honeycomb core faced on both sides with two plies of type 1500 fiber glass cloth which has been impregnated with epoxy laminating resin. The panels are usually sold in 4- by 8-ft sections in ½-, 1-, and 2-inch core thicknesses. Table 3-6 provides typical physical and mechanical properties of panels of this type.

Fig. 3-8 Model duplication and matched mold for aircraft part. Tools are constructed of room-temperature epoxy laminating compound and style no. 1500 fiber glass fabric, reinforced with laminated epoxy tubing. Note that the frame structure of square tubing is used for the base plane of these fixtures. (*Ren Plastics, Inc.*)

The main advantage of fiber-glass-faced honeycomb sandwich panels is their high strength-to-weight ratio. On large laminated tools, where tool weight is an important consideration, this type of reinforcement is advantageous.

Fiber-glass-faced honeycomb sandwich panels can be easily cut on a band saw, fitted, and attached to the back of a laminated tool in much the same manner used to apply solid laminated sheet reinforcements. Normally, no special tools are required. Good adhesion can be obtained without sanding the skins or other means of surface preparation prior to bonding.

Fiber-glass-faced honeycomb sandwich panels are used extensively in the construction of master models built by the numerical control machining method. Used as the supporting structure under the extruded low-density tooling compounds, they have proved to be highly dimensionally stable while providing strength and lightweight characteristics.

Lightweight Aggregate Reinforcement

Frequently, a lightweight aggregate coated with laminating resin is used to reinforce epoxy laminated stretch press dies, large foundry patterns, and Keller duplicating models. It has similar applications wherever tool rigidity, rather than weight, is critical. A cubic foot of this type

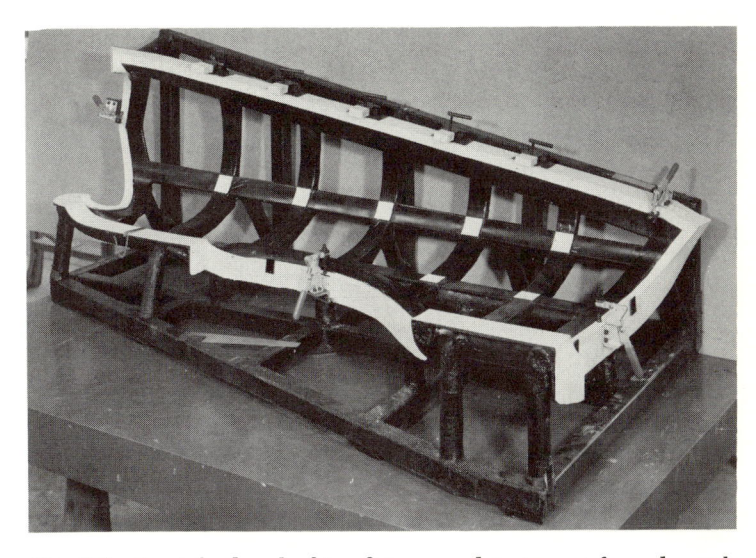

Fig. 3-9 Front fender checking fixture, used to inspect formed metal parts. Tool constructed of room-temperature epoxy–fiber glass laminate reinforced with laminated epoxy tubing. When set up on a surface plate, reference plane of base allows for easy inspection of fixture. (*Ren Plastics, Inc.*)

TABLE 3-6 Typical Properties of Fiber-glass-faced Honeycomb Tooling Panels

	Description of testing procedures	Typical test values 2-in. Core	1-in. Core	½-in. Core
Compressive test flatwise.......	Maximum load Proportional limit Modulus of elasticity	333 psi 285 psi 120,000 psi	388 psi 349 psi 90,000 psi	330 psi 300 psi 57,000 psi
Compressive test edgewise......	Maximum load*	3,900 lb	3,870 lb	3,590 lb
Compressive test edgewise......	Maximum load†	3,460 lb	3,510 lb	3,570 lb
Flexural test edgewise......	Breaking load* Uniform deflection to a maximum load of Deflection in center of 8-in. span, inches for each 10-lb load	813 lb 442 lb 0.001 in.	580 lb 230 lb 0.001 in.	740 lb 290 lb 0.001 in.
Flexural test edgewise......	Breaking load† Uniform deflection to a maximum load of Deflection in center of 8-in. span, inches for each 10-lb load	780 lb 404 lb 0.001 in.	640 lb 250 lb 0.001 in.	800 lb 290 lb 0.001 in.
Flexural test flatwise.......	Breaking load* Uniform deflection to a maximum load of Deflection in center of 20-in. span, inches for each 10-lb load	396 lb 271 lb 0.004 in.	310 lb 122 lb 0.015 in.	206 lb 50 lb 0.054 in.
Flexural test flatwise.......	Breaking load† Uniform deflection to a maximum load of Deflection in center of 20-in. span, inches for each 10-lb load	389 lb 263 lb 0.004 in.	334 lb 132 lb 0.015 in.	214 lb 61 lb 0.056 in.
Peel strength....	ASTM D-1781-T, in.-lb peel torque*	11	11	11
Peel strength....	ASTM D-1781-T, in.-lb peel torque†	11	11	11
Weight............................		1.67 psf	1.35 psf	1.20 psf
Panel thickness..................		2.075 in.	1.075 in.	0.570 in.

* Length is parallel to width dimension of aluminum honeycomb core.
† Length is perpendicular to width dimension of aluminum honeycomb core.
SOURCE: Ren Plastics, Inc., Lansing, Mich.

of reinforcement will usually weigh approximately 52 pounds. When a laminated tool is reinforced with a lightweight aggregate, experience has shown that the laminate thickness can be greatly reduced and still be sufficiently strong for its intended use. If properly applied, the aggregate can be used to fill a cavity of any size or thickness without fear of warpage due to excessive exothermic heat.

The most commonly used lightweight aggregate is a volcanic-type rock, sold commercially by tooling resin formulators under the name "Corefill." Because it is volcanic in origin and contains many interior gas cavities, the material is relatively lightweight when compared to sand or gravel. It is usually sold in pebble size with diameters ranging from ½ to 1½ inches.

Lightweight aggregate is relatively simple to use. When the laminated tool has been built up to its desired thickness, the aggregate is coated with laminating resin and used to fill the cavity behind the laminate. Figure 3-10 shows the cross section of a typical tool reinforced with Corefill.

The procedure for using lightweight aggregate to reinforce a laminated tool is as follows:

1. Immediately after the last ply of laminate has been applied, a batch of laminating resin and hardener are weighed in the correct ratio and mixed thoroughly. The container used should be 8 to 10 times the volume of the resin and hardener.

2. The lightweight aggregate is slowly added to the resin mixture. The aggregate is constantly stirred so that the laminating resin mixture coats all the surfaces of the aggregate. Aggregate should be added until the weight of the aggregate is approximately 5 times the weight of the laminating resin and hardener. A mixture of this ratio will produce an aggregate core with a compressive strength of approximately 4,000 psi.

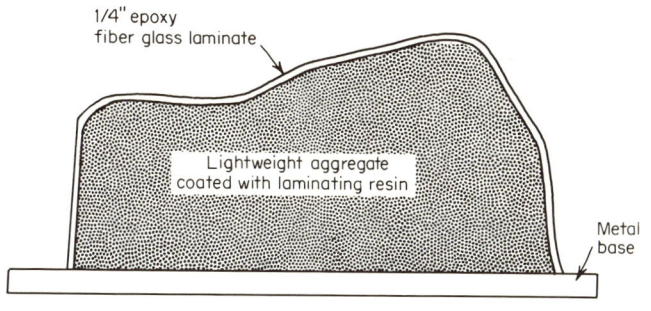

Fig. 3-10 Cross section of typical laminated tool reinforced with lightweight aggregate.

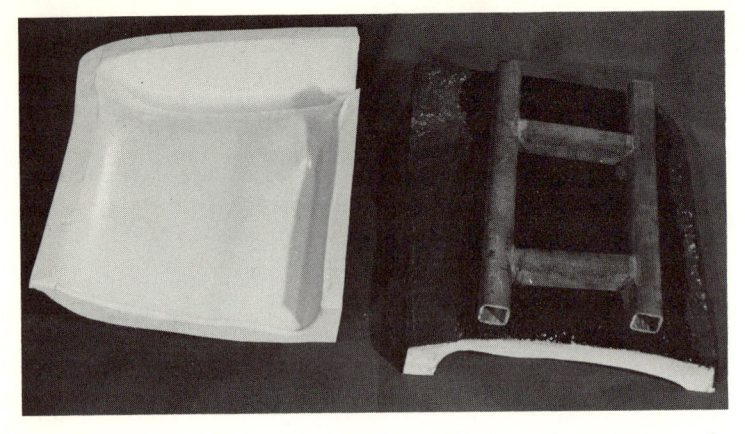

Fig. 3-11 Laminated model reinforced with lightweight aggregate and epoxy–fiber glass tubing. (*Hysol Division, The Dexter Corp.*)

3. After the aggregate and laminating resin have been mixed until all aggregate surfaces are coated, it is poured into the laminate cavity and tamped into place. Usually the butt end of a two by four works well for this purpose. The aggregate should be spread out as a uniform layer and tamped down to ensure that no large, open spaces exist.

4. The process is repeated until the laminate cavity is filled to the desired height. The working time for the mixture will range from 25 to 35 minutes, depending on the resin system used, after the resin and hardener are combined. Consequently, it is advisable to limit the batch to a size that can easily be handled within that time period.

5. The tool is then allowed to cure for 24 hours at room temperature before it is removed from the model.

A variety of other materials are used as fillers for aggregate reinforcement of laminated tools. Among these are walnut shells, sand, gravel, polystyrene beads, and a lightweight aggregate called Air-light.*

TYPES OF LAMINATED TOOLS

Epoxy laminated tools are used in virtually every phase of the manufacturing process. Epoxy laminated tools have virtually replaced machined metal tooling for a number of applications such as assembly and drill fixtures, spotting fixtures, inspection fixtures, short-run dies, and foundry patterns. Manufacturers who have used epoxy laminates for these purposes report substantial cost savings due to the particular suitability

* Trade name of Hysol Division of The Dexter Corp.

of plastics to large-size, complex configurated tools requiring close dimensional tolerances.

Epoxy laminated tools have also been found satisfactory for applications such as molds for casting plastic prototype parts and short-run dies for forming thin-gauge metal.

In the remainder of this chapter, we will discuss several of these specific applications for epoxy laminated tools and how these tools are fabricated. The sketches and photographs provide the basis for typical designs of these tools.

Assembly Fixtures

An assembly fixture is a tool which correctly positions two or more components of an assembly in proper relationship to one another while the components are being joined together to form a finished part. Frequently, assembly tools may be combination tools. For example, it may be a single-tool combination drill jig and assembly fixture used for holding the parts in accurate alignment while they are drilled and then assembled (see Figure 3-17).

Normally, the laminated assembly tool is made directly from a coordination medium containing bushings in order to obtain the exact contours and hole patterns. A *bushing* is a hardened steel sleeve with an accurate bore. It provides accurate, wear-resistant holes for receiv-

Fig. 3-12 Laminated spotting fixture for an automobile door panel. Tool is constructed of epoxy gel coat and room-temperature epoxy laminating compound and fiber glass cloth. Tool is reinforced with ¼-inch laminated epoxy eggcrate structure. (*Hysol Division, The Dexter Corp.*)

90   Plastic Tooling

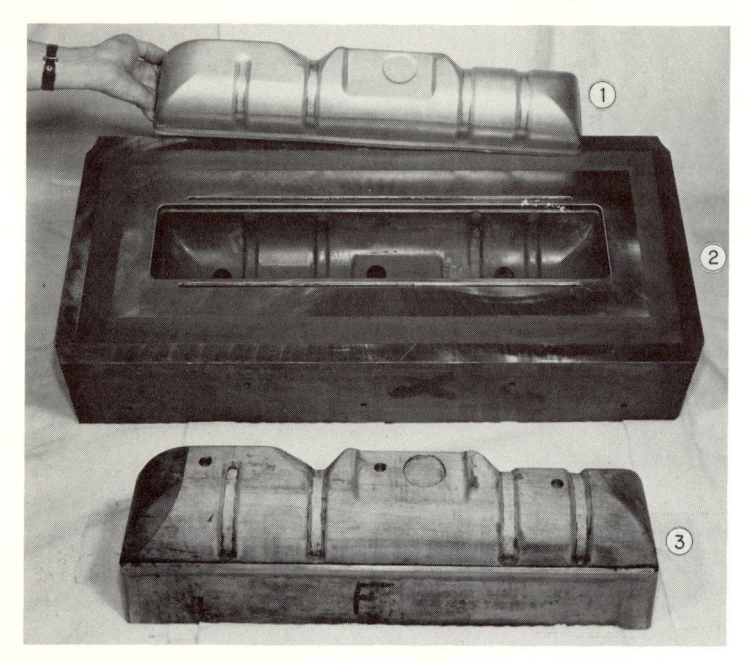

Fig. 3-13 From bottom to top: (1) Wood pattern of automobile radiator top used to fabricate (2) epoxy laminated metal-forming die in steel frame. (3) A prototype part made in plastic die. (*Hysol Division, The Dexter Corp.*)

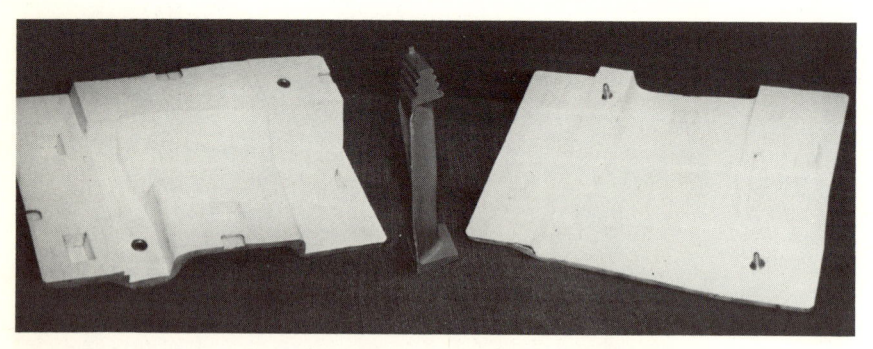

Fig. 3-14 Two-piece laminated mold for casting jet engine blade model. Tool is constructed of room-temperature epoxy laminating compound and fiber glass fabric. Note metal inserts for mold alignment. (*Hysol Division, The Dexter Corp.*)

Fig. 3-15 All-plastic drop-hammer dies, used in production forming of sheet metal aircraft components by Rohr Aircraft Corporation. Tools are fabricated with abrasion-resistant epoxy gel coat and epoxy laminating compound–fiber glass cloth. (*Furane Plastics, Inc.*)

Fig. 3-16 Metal-forming dies constructed of ⅜-inch-thick epoxy laminate reinforced with lightweight aggregate and laminating resin. (*Rezolin, Inc.*)

ing locating pins or for using as guides for drilling and reaming. The outside surface of bushings is usually notched, serrated, or knurled to prevent them from turning. Bushings may be installed during the laminating operation or potted in place after completion of the laminate.

Assembly tools have basically two types of holes cut in them: *lightening holes* and *access holes*. Lightening holes are holes which are cut in the tool to facilitate handling and decrease weight. They are located so that they do not interfere with the function of the tool. Access holes are put into tools for a variety of reasons, the main reason being to provide a means of inspecting the fit between the part and the tool at a particular location.

Drill Jigs

A *drill jig* is a tool which holds a production part or assembly in position for purposes of drilling holes in the part. A drill jig is usually an epoxy laminated tool into which drill bushings have been mounted in a specific hole pattern which has been coordinated to the master model.

A drill jig is frequently a two-piece tool (see Figure 3-18). The production part or assembly is clamped between the two tool sections during the drilling operation. Drill jigs are frequently designed as com-

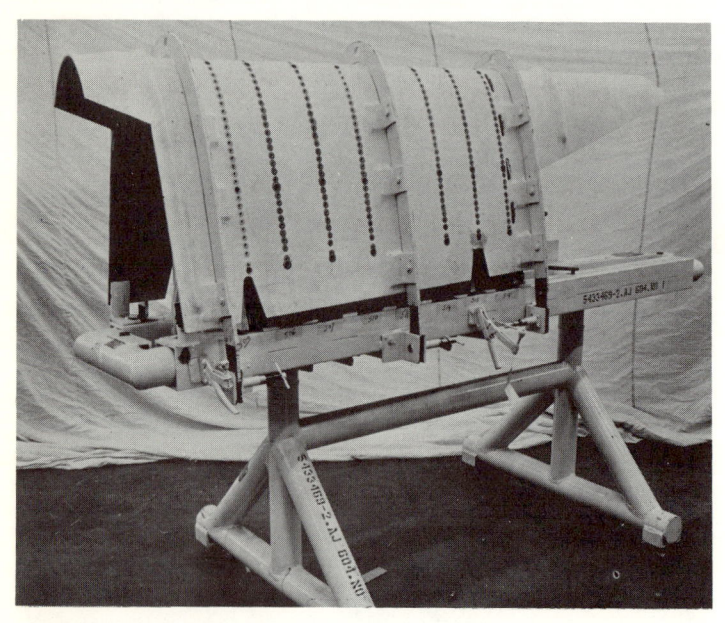

Fig. 3-17 Aircraft assembly jig constructed of room-temperature epoxy laminating compound and no. 1500 fiber glass cloth. Assembly jig is mounted on a base constructed of metal tubing. Note numerous drill bushings potted into laminated tool. (*Furane Plastics, Inc.*)

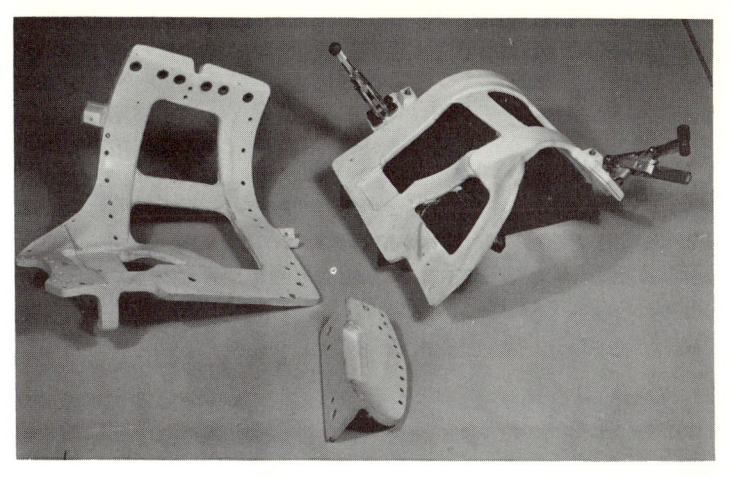

Fig. 3-18 Aircraft drill jig and scribe template constructed of room-temperature epoxy laminating compound and fiber glass fabric. Note drill bushings set in laminated facing. (*Ren Plastics, Inc.*)

bination tools, particularly as combination drill and router fixtures (see Figure 3-19). When a drill jig is also intended for use as a router fixture, an abrasion-resistant epoxy gel coat is usually used to provide wear-resistant edges to the router openings. Bushings may be potted into laminated tools either during the laminating of the tool or after the laminate has been cured.

It is generally agreed that the best method is to allow the laminate

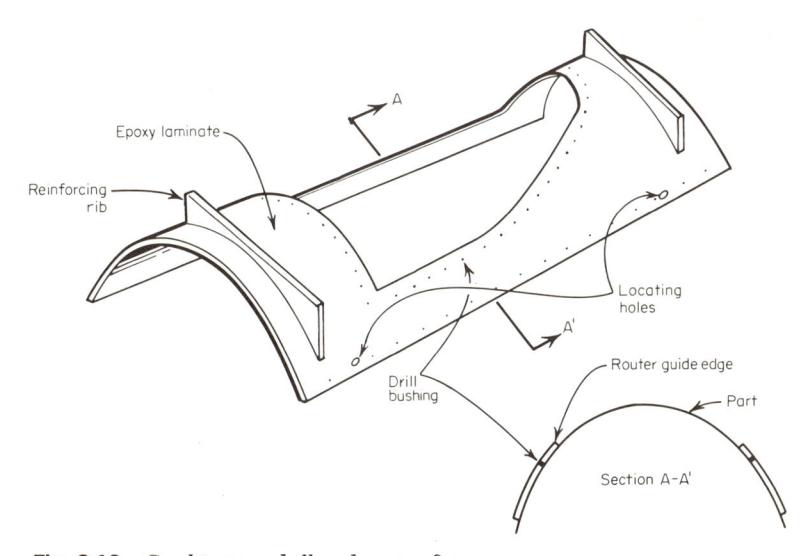

Fig. 3-19 Combination drill and router fixture.

94   Plastic Tooling

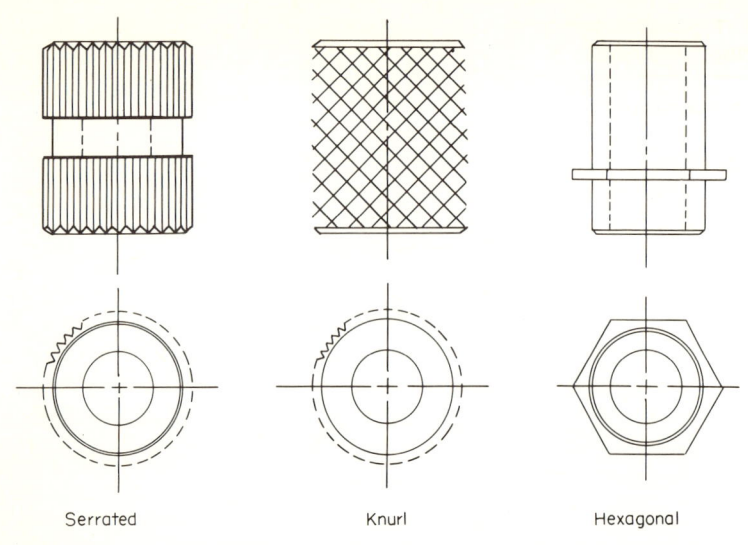

Serrated   Knurl   Hexagonal

Fig. 3-20 Types of bushings used with epoxy potting compounds.

to cure, drill oversize holes, and pot the bushings in with an appropriate epoxy potting resin. This provides maximum accuracy of bushing location, since it eliminates any errors which might be caused by shrinkage of the resin during the cure cycle. This method also requires less skill on the part of the worker. Figure 3-21 illustrates the technique for potting bushings into tools after the laminate has cured.

(a) Drill oversize hole

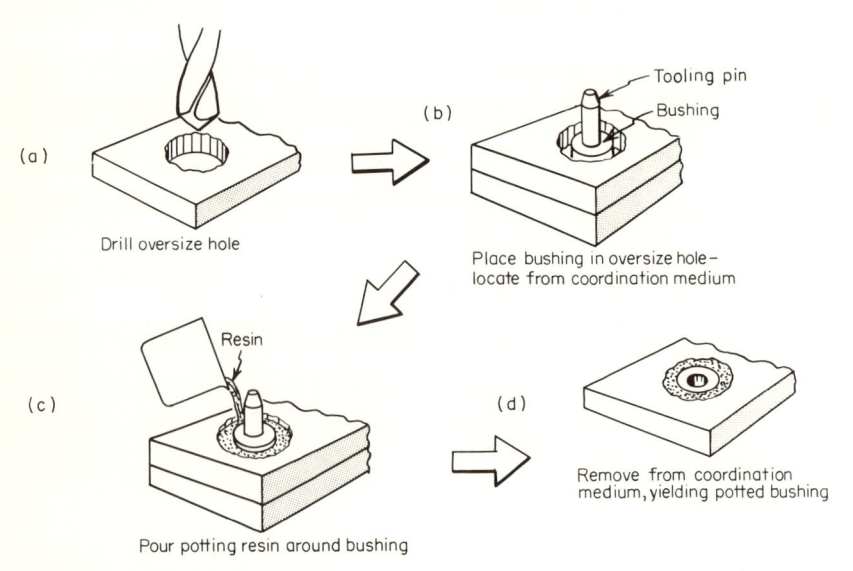

(b) Place bushing in oversize hole — locate from coordination medium

(c) Pour potting resin around bushing

(d) Remove from coordination medium, yielding potted bushing

Fig. 3-21 Procedure for potting bushings into laminated tools.

TABLE 3-7 Typical Properties* of Epoxy Potting Compounds

Deflection temperature, °F	140–150
Hardness, Shore D	85–90
Bond strength, psi	2,000–2,500
Compressive strength, psi	12,000–14,000
Shrinkage, inches/inch	0.003

* At room temperature (72°F ± 5°F).

Epoxy resins, with various fillers, form the basis for most potting compounds. Such materials must be capable of withstanding heat, working stress, vibration, and shock. The main consideration in selecting potting materials is the compound's resistance to heat generated through the use of dull drills; drill misalignment; drilling into hard, tough materials; or combinations of these three. The heat thus generated is transferred through the bushing to the epoxy potting compound. This can cause the potting compound to soften, allowing the bushings to creep or work themselves loose. Resins with a high heat-distortion point are recommended for potting bushings into laminated tools.

Bushings can also be installed during the laminating process of the tool. In such cases, the locating pin is generously coated with parting agent at the same time that the model surface is being prepared with parting agent. A gel coat is applied and allowed to become tack-free. Following the procedure described earlier in this chapter, one or two layers of style no. 7500 tooling cloth and laminating resin are applied. The bushings are then slid onto the locating pins and pressed down until they are firmly in place. Great care should be taken not to get any parting agent on the outer surface of the bushing during this operation. The remaining 14 layers of laminate are then applied. Care must be exercised so as not to unseat the bushings. Also, holes must be cut in the fiber glass cloth in order that the cloth can slide down over the bushings and locating pins.

In the event that bushings become loose or worn, they can be removed and new bushings potted into the tool using the procedure outlined previously. Carelessness on the part of the production worker can make the replacement of drill bushings an expensive proposition for any company. It should be kept in mind that even the best-made tool, fabricated with the best materials available, is prone to damage by a careless worker with a drill in his hand.

Checking Fixtures

A *checking fixture* is an inspection aid which is used to check production parts for dimensions and configuration. Normally a checking fixture is a transfer of a dimensionally approved coordination medium made directly from the master model of the part or assembly to be checked.

Epoxy laminates have proved to be ideal for use as checking fixtures. They are extremely accurate, lightweight and easy to handle, durable, and inexpensive to fabricate. In many cases, checking fixtures serve the dual role of being a trim tool as well as a checking fixture. In such cases, the tool will contain the entire peripheral outline of the part of assembly. Checking fixtures have numerous cutouts or access holes for the purpose of checking the fit of the part to the tool in critical areas (see Figures 3-9 and 3-22). These holes are normally cut out after the laminate has cured.

Normally, the following criteria should be taken into consideration when designing and fabricating an epoxy laminated checking fixture:

1. A bushed attach-hole pattern which has been coordinated to the part model, either directly or indirectly through appropriate coordination media.

2. Provisions for adequate check pins to check the complete attach-hole pattern of the part.

3. The surfaces of the checking fixture representing the surface of the part should be clearly identified.

Fig. 3-22 Large laminated aircraft master gauge, used to check contour and location of drill bushings. Note lightening and access holes in tool face. (*Furane Plastics, Inc.*)

It should be pointed out that a plastic checking fixture is only as good as the design of the tool and the quality of the materials in it. The strength of the materials being used should be of paramount consideration in the design of the tool. Epoxy laminated tools have a relatively low modulus of elasticity and will consequently deflect under loads unless properly designed. Therefore, it is essential that the design of checking fixtures be such that they will not deflect under normal operating loads. It is recommended that particular attention be given to the design of the reinforcement and to the design of the base on all checking fixtures, since the accuracy of the tool is dependent on the stability of these two items.

Weld Fixtures

A weld fixture (see Figure 3-23) is a tool which is used to hold parts of an assembly in proper alignment during a welding operation. The use of epoxy laminates for weld fixtures provides cost savings through elimination of expensive machining and reduction in tool fabrication flow time.

In fabricating plastic weld fixtures, certain factors determine the method of construction. Heat is an especially important consideration. In many cases, the weld fixture is not exposed to heat because the weld is made away from the supporting members of the fixture. When it is obvious that the fixture will be exposed to heat, a high-temperature laminate should be used.

Many spot-weld fixtures are made of epoxy laminates because of the ease of fabricating odd shapes and the dimensional stability of the epoxy

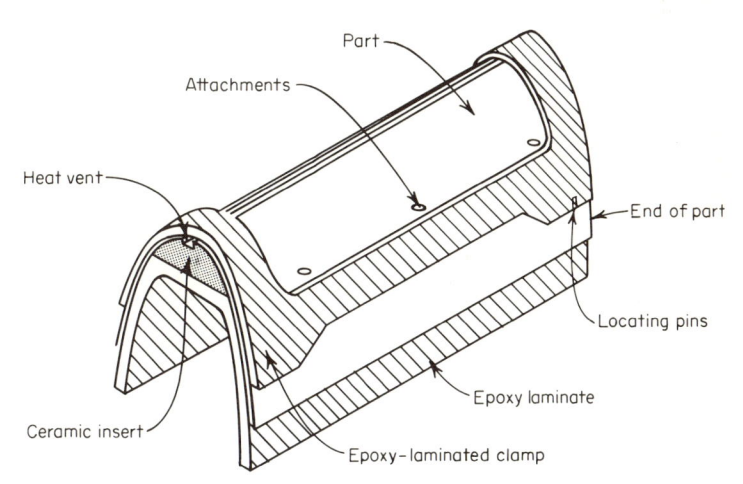

Fig. 3-23 Epoxy laminated weld fixture. Note that the parts to be welded are clamped between the two-piece tool.

98 Plastic Tooling

laminate. In many cases, weld fixtures are constructed as combination tools. For example, it may serve as a drill and scribe fixture as well as a weld fixture.

Diesinking Patterns

A diesinking pattern is used to guide the tracer and consequently the metal cutter in the machining of metal dies. A diesinking pattern is sometimes referred to as a "Keller pattern" or a "duplicator model." Regardless of what it is called, its function is the same: to provide a surface for the tracer or stylus to pass over. Guided by the path of the tracer, the die cutter machines the metal die to the exact configuration of the pattern (see Figure 3-24).

Epoxy laminates satisfy the three basic requirements for a diesinking pattern: (1) accuracy, (2) surface hardness, and (3) surface smoothness. Since the completed metal die will be the exact configuration and dimensions of the diesinking pattern, it is important that the pattern be constructed to extremely close tolerances. An epoxy laminate also

Fig. 3-24 Photograph illustrating sequence from master pattern to steel die. Right is mahogany master pattern made per the engineering drawing. Left is epoxy–fiber glass laminated diesinking pattern. Center is production die machined from forged steel. The laminated plastic diesinking pattern provides a hard surface for guiding the tracing stylus and die cutting mechanism. (*Hysol Division, The Dexter Corp.*)

has a surface hardness sufficient to withstand the pressure of the stylus. When softer materials are used for diesinking patterns, the pressure of the stylus can cause a little furrow along the pattern surface. This furrow is reflected as a defect in the metal die, since the cutter machines the exact pattern the stylus traces.

There are other considerations which indicate that laminated tools are an ideal choice for diesinking patterns. First, they can be made inexpensively and in a short flow time. Second, they lend themselves to the accurate reproduction of complex shapes. Third, they can be modified easily and quickly.

REFERENCES

Industrial Glass Fabrics, J. P. Stevens & Co., Inc.
A Review of Plastics for Tooling, Plastics Technical Evaluation Center, Picatinny Arsenal, Dover, N.J., March 1964.
The Techniques of Using Epoxy Plastic Tooling Materials, Ren Plastics, Inc., Lansing, Mich.

CHAPTER FOUR
Cast Plastic Tools

INTRODUCTION

Epoxy casting compounds are most commonly used to make tools used in the forming of metal and to make foundry patterns and coreboxes. Inasmuch as the next chapter deals with foundry tooling, the emphasis in this chapter will be placed on cast epoxy metal-forming tools. This chapter is intended to cover the materials, tools fabrication techniques, and typical designs of tools made with epoxy casting compounds.

It should be recognized immediately that plastic metal-forming tools are best suited for making low volume production parts or prototype parts. As a general rule, plastic tooling cannot compete with steel tooling where high production rates and quantities are required. For example, the cost of steel dies is justified in the automotive industry where production runs of 100,000 parts are not uncommon. In the aircraft industry, where the total number of parts required may be less than 200, plastic dies have been used to great advantage.

The basic procedure for constructing a cast epoxy tool involves preparing a model with parting agent, constructing a framework around the model, mixing the two components in their proper ratio, and pouring the mixture into the mold cavity. After the casting has cured sufficiently at room temperature, it is removed from the model. The result is a casting that is a mirror image of the model. Tools of this type will be accurate to within 0.002 inch per inch, have a compressive strength of approximately 12,000 psi, and be capable of use at temperatures up to 125°F. While this fabrication sequence is somewhat simplified, it serves to accurately and briefly describe the basic procedure. Specific techniques of making various tools are described later in this chapter.

Cast epoxy tools are the least-expensive and most easily fabricated type of plastic tool. The prime advantages are the low labor costs and the short flow time required to fabricate a tool. These two factors often make them the choice for dies for producing prototype parts.

The advantages of cast epoxy tools can be listed as follows:

1. They can be fabricated with a low expenditure of man-hours.
2. They can be cast to close tolerances, without the need for subsequent machining or hand-finishing.
3. They are dimensionally stable.
4. Tool faces are tough and durable.
5. Complex configurations can be made at low cost.
6. Tool fabrication does not require a high skill level.
7. The tool fabrication flow time is much shorter than in other forms of tooling, both metal and plastic.
8. Cores can be used to reduce material costs as well as to reduce shrinkage.
9. They can be easily and quickly repaired.

There are two main disadvantages of cast epoxy tooling that deserve mention at this point. First, because the resin system is usually heavily filled, it is prone to entrapment of air during pouring. If this is allowed to occur, the result will be defects in the face of the tool. This normally results in expensive rework and/or repair. Second, the exothermic heat generated during the cure can result in excessive shrinkage, causing an inaccurate tool. Normally, both of these objections can be overcome by using good judgment and following good shop practices. For example, shrinkage can be minimized by selecting the proper resin for the application and by using of cores. These topics are discussed later in this chapter. Air voids can be eliminated by the use of several techniques during the actual pouring of the liquid casting compound.

Cast epoxy tools should not be looked upon as a panacea for all tooling problems. They can be used to greatest advantage on smaller complex configurations. Obviously it is easier to pour a liquid into a cavity with many complexities than it would be to machine the shape out of metal or to cut and fit glass cloth and laminate. Conversely, it would be better to laminate a tool with a large, simple shape in order to reduce tool shrinkage, decrease the tool weight, minimize material costs, and obtain a tool with a greater strength-to-weight ratio. The configuration, size, and type of tool must all be considered when deciding what method should be used to construct a particular tool.

The Materials

Epoxy casting compounds are two component systems that have been formulated specifically for making plastic tools. They usually contain fillers such as aluminum or steel to impart certain characteristics such as impact strength, wear resistance, and hardness to a tool. Fillers also help to reduce the amount of exothermic heat generated during cure, thereby reducing shrinkage.

There are basically two different types of epoxy casting compounds: *surface casting compounds* and *mass casting compounds*. Surface casting compounds are used in applications where only up to ½-inch thickness is required. Mass casting compounds are capable of being cast up to 5 inches in thickness in a single pour. The techniques for the use of these materials are given in detail later in this chapter. At this point, it is sufficient to say that it is extremely important to use the proper material for each application. For example, if a surface casting compound is used to make a casting 2 inches thick, excessive exothermic heat will be generated and the casting will shrink or warp out of proper configuration. Conversely, a mass casting system used to make a casting less than ½ inch thick will not cure to the desired hardness in the normal cure time prescribed for that particular resin system. It is important to choose the proper type of casting resin in order to achieve the desired results.

METHODS OF CASTING EPOXY TOOLS

The basic techniques for casting epoxy tools fall into two categories: open-face casting and surface casting. There are variations of these methods, but all casting of plastic tools can be said to fall into one of the two basic methods. In this section, we intend to discuss the basic techniques in detail; later in the chapter we cover specific applications and designs.

Open-face Casting (or Mass Casting)

Open-face casting is the simplest method of making a cast epoxy tool. This method is used to most economical advantage on tools of low relief, i.e., small shallow tools, or on tools having intricate detail. A mass casting resin system should be used to make a cast epoxy tool by the open-face casting method, since very few tools have a relief of less than ½ inch. Typical physical properties of epoxy mass casting compounds are given in Table 4-1. In order to determine whether a tool should be made by the mass cast method or by some other means, it is necessary to consider the tool area, the thickness of the casting, and the labor required. Oftentimes, the tool designer will elect to mass-cast an epoxy tool, expending more money in materials in order to achieve a drastic savings in labor. In some cases, material costs can be reduced by mixing a low-cost aggregate into the mass casting compound. The techniques of adding various fillers are discussed in detail later in this chapter.

In making a cast epoxy tool by the open-face casting method, the following steps are recommended:

1. The pattern or model should be inspected to ensure that it is accurate and free of surface defects. Time spent putting the model in perfect condition at this point will save time reworking the newly completed tool.

2. Dike boards are constructed around the area to be cast, and sealed with wax or clay.

3. A suitable parting agent is applied to the pattern. The selection of parting agent and application method should be made in accordance with the criteria given in Chapter 1.

4. The area to be cast is measured, and the exact amount of resin and hardener required is calculated. Add 3 to 5 percent to the total amount required to allow for error in calculation and the amount of material that will adhere to the sides of the container after pouring.

5. Before weighing the resin, inspect the material to ensure that the filler is evenly distributed throughout the compound and that the filler

TABLE 4-1 Typical Physical Properties of Epoxy Mass Casting Resin Compounds*

Shrinkage, inches/inch	0.002
Compressive strength, psi	12,500
Flexural strength, psi	8,500
Modulus of elasticity in flex, psi $\times 10^6$	0.9–1.3
Bond strength, psi	1,500
Deflection temperature, °F	150
Hardness, Shore D	85
Pot life, minutes	140
Viscosity, centipoises	10,000–12,000
Coefficient of thermal expansion, inches/inch/°F $\times 10^{-5}$	2.5

* Epoxy resin systems capable of being cast to 5 inches maximum thickness and cured at room temperature.

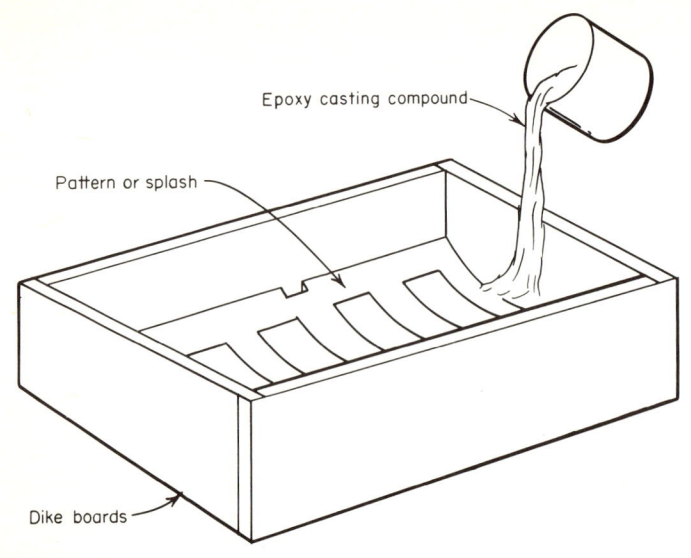

Fig. 4-1 Open-face casting method.

has not settled to the bottom of the container. If the filler has settled, the resin should be mixed until it is homogeneous throughout.

6. The two components are accurately weighed and mixed together. Mixing by hand for 5 to 7 minutes is acceptable on batches of less than 2,000 grams. However, since the casting resin usually has a high amount of filler and the percentage of hardener is usually small, the use of a mechanical mixer is highly recommended. Quantities up to 10 kilograms can be satisfactorily mixed with a propeller mounted on a $\frac{1}{4}$-inch drill motor with a speed of less than 1800 rpm. Mixes over 10 kilograms require a $\frac{1}{2}$-horsepower mixer. Mixers that do an excellent job of mixing 5-gallon batches are commercially available in both gas- and electric-powered models. Mixing by mechanical means should require from 2 to 5 minutes.

7. The casting compound is then poured over the model. There are two techniques that can be employed at this point that will ensure a void-free casting. First, the material should be poured slowly into the lowest corner of the mold cavity (see Figure 4-1). As the resin is poured, the material rises slowly and flows over the face of the model. The use of this technique will eliminate turbulence that results in entrapment of air. Air entrapment causes small pinholes or voids at the interface between the model and the casting compound, resulting in defects on the tool face.

An additional precaution that will result in good fidelity in cast tools is as follows: When pouring, the container is held 18 to 24 inches above the model and tilted just enough to allow the resin to flow over the lip of the container. In this manner, a very thin stream of resin breaks over the lip of the container and entrapped air bubbles burst as they flow over the lip. Every bubble eliminated in this manner is one less potential defect on the tool.

As an extreme measure, entrapped air can be removed by placing the container and the mixed components into a vacuum chamber and evacuating the air. This serves to remove from the compound any air that was entrapped during mixing. However, the use of vacuum does not ensure that air will not be introduced during the pouring operation. Turbulence in the resin, caused by pouring too quickly, can cause air entrapment and consequent surface defects. The author feels that by observing the proper techniques of mixing and pouring, the use of vacuum is unnecessary for most casting operations.

8. The casting is then cured in accordance with the schedule given in Figure 4-2. This figure is designed to indicate the optimum cure cycle for a given tool by using the average thickness and average ambient room temperature as a base line. For example, a casting having an average thickness of 3 inches would require 16 hours to cure in a shop having an average temperature between 65 to 70°F.

When production schedules do not permit long cure times at room temperature, some tooling shops accelerate the cure by placing the cast-

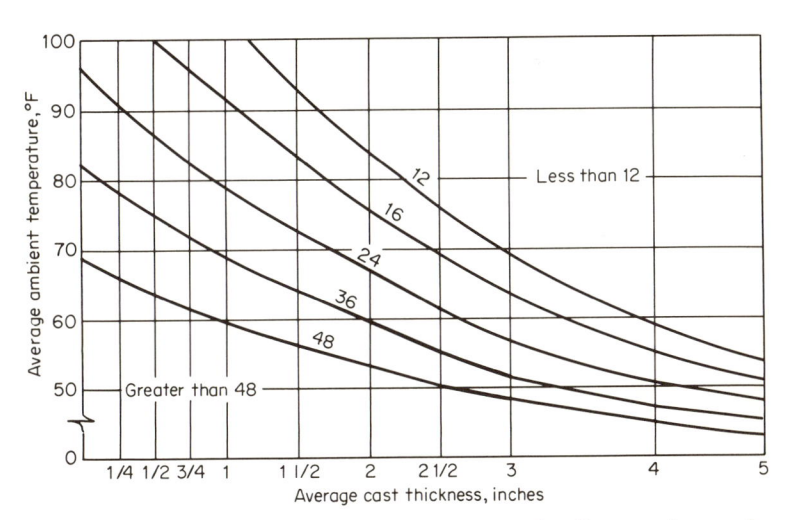

Fig. 4-2 Cure of epoxy mass casting compounds (hours prior to demolding). This chart provides guidelines for curing epoxy mass castings prior to demolding. For example, a casting 4 inches thick may be demolded in less than 12 hours, while a 1½-inch casting should be allowed to cure 36 hours at the same temperature before demolding. (*Rezolin, Inc.*)

ing in an oven at elevated temperatures. This practice is not normally a good one, since there is the possibility that excessive heat will be generated within the casting and will cause the casting to either shrink excessively, warp, or both. As a general rule, the cure of an epoxy casting resin compound should not be accelerated by application of heat, particularly if the resin system is a mass casting compound. If heat must be used, the casting should be allowed to cure a minimum of 12 hours at room temperature, and then the temperature of the oven should not exceed 125°F.

The Addition of Low-cost Aggregates to Mass Casting Resins Low-cost aggregates can be added to an epoxy casting compound to reduce material costs, since the aggregate material costs less per pound than the epoxy casting compound. Materials commonly used for this purpose are aluminum granules, walnut shells, expanded volcanic lava, sand, and in some cases vermiculite. In most cases, up to 60 percent of the total weight of the casting will be the aggregate material.

If aggregates are to be added to an epoxy mass casting compound, it is advisable to use a gel coat in conjunction with the casting. This ensures that the surface finish will be homogeneous. A homogeneous tool surface is particularly important on a metal-forming tool, for example, where differential wear of unlike materials in the tool face may result in the formation of striations in the metal part being produced. The use of an epoxy gel coat will ensure that at least the outer $\frac{1}{16}$ inch of the tool surface is homogeneous.

Normally, a cast epoxy tool incorporating the use of aggregates will be fabricated by first applying an abrasion-resistant gel coat to the model, which has already been prepared with release agent. The gel coat is allowed to set for approximately 30 minutes or until it is tacky. One-half of the volume of resin and hardener estimated to be required to pour the casting is calculated and weighed out in four equal increments. The container used to weigh out the resin should be of such size that the actual amount of resin and hardener in the container takes up only about 40 percent of the container's total capacity.

The components of the first increment are mixed as described earlier in the chapter. The compound is then poured slowly into one corner of the mold cavity. When this pour is completed, the area representing the tool face will be covered with approximately 1 to $1\frac{1}{2}$ inches of casting compound.

The second increment is now ready for use. The resin portion of the second increment has been weighed out in a container with a capacity approximately three times the volume of the resin. The hardener is added to the resin and mixed thoroughly with a mechanical mixer. The compound is then placed onto a scale, and the selected aggregate is added. The mixture should be constantly stirred to ensure that all surfaces of the aggregate are thoroughly wetted. Aggregate is added until the weight of the aggregate equals the weight of the resin and hardener combined. If the compound appears capable of taking more aggregate, more can be added until the mixture is the consistency of wet concrete. The amount of aggregate is recorded, and each subsequent increment is given the same amount of aggregate.

The second increment is now poured slowly into the mold cavity. The aggregate mixture will "float" in the first increment, preventing aggregate particles from penetrating all the way to the tool face. The third and fourth increments are prepared in the same manner and poured into the mold cavity.

Surface Casting

Material costs can be substantially reduced on large tools by using a solid core to take up most of the volume. The core is made roughly to the shape of the tool and is suspended in the mold cavity with a uniform spacing of $3/8$ to $1/2$ inch between the pattern and the core. The surface casting compound is then poured into the space between the pattern and the core. When demolded, the surface cast epoxy face provides the accurate tool face. The core is bonded to the epoxy face and becomes an integral part of the tool. This technique is used principally to fabricate drop-hammer dies, stretch dies, hydropress dies, and draw dies.

Many different materials are employed as cores for tools made by the surface casting method. Some of the most commonly used materials are kirksite, aluminum, sheet steel, wood, masonite, and epoxy–fiber glass laminates. These materials are used for various other reasons, in addition to the obvious intent of reducing costs by reducing the amount of casting resin required. The cores are used to impart structural rigidity to the tool, to reduce the weight (in some cases), and to minimize the chance of excessive shrinkage due to exothermic heat buildup in a large mass.

Kirksite is perhaps the most commonly used material for cores. In addition to its low cost, its mass is very beneficial in impact tools like drop-hammer dies and hammer forms. Cores of materials other than metal are generally used in tools for nonimpact operations such as stretch forming, vacuum forming, spin blocks, and foundry patterns.

Epoxy Surface Casting Compounds A surface casting compound is a resin system designed to be cast in maximum thicknesses of $1/2$ inch. Most surface casting compounds incorporate metallic fillers, such as steel or iron powders. These fillers impart good impact strength and abrasion resistance to the tool face. Aluminum powders, calcium carbonate, and glass fibers are also used as fillers in surface casting resins, but they have neither the strength nor the durability of steel or iron powders.

A surface casting resin is required to flow over large surface areas while traveling between a pattern and a core that are a maximum of ½ inch from one another. Because of this requirement, it is desirable to have a surface casting compound with a low viscosity. A good surface casting compound will have a mixed viscosity of 10,000 centipoises or less. Experience has indicated that casting compounds with viscosities of 10,000 centipoises or less have much less tendency to entrap air during the casting operation. The lower viscosity materials are also more capable of deaerating themselves during the casting operation, since the entrapped air will more readily rise to the surface of a low-viscosity material. Entrapped air usually manifests itself in the form of numerous voids and defects in the cast tool surface. From the foregoing, it should be obvious that close attention should be given to the selection of the proper resin system. Table 4-2 provides typical physical properties for epoxy surface casting compounds. These properties should be considered as minimum requirements for surface casting systems, since materials that do meet these requirements are readily available on the market.

Positioning of Cores One of the keys to success in the surface casting method is having the core positioned over the pattern in such a manner that the thickness between the two is uniform throughout. Uniform spacing helps the resin flow and permits the cavity to be filled with a minimum of air entrapment. In some instances, improperly positioned cores have caused thin sections in the cast tool face that result in tool failure during production usage.

There are two basic techniques for positioning cores. One method

TABLE 4-2 Typical Physical Properties of Epoxy Surface Casting Compounds*

Shrinkage, inches/inch	0.002
Compressive strength, psi	14,200
Flexural strength, psi	8,000
Modulus of elasticity in flex, psi $\times 10^6$	0.8–1.0
Bond strength, psi	1,800
Deflection temperature, °F	150
Hardness, Shore D	85
Pot life, minutes	100
Viscosity, centipoises	7,000–10,000
Coefficient of thermal expansion, inches/inch/°F $\times 10^{-5}$	2.6

* Epoxy resin systems capable of being cast to ½ inch maximum thickness and cured at room temperature.

is to attach supporting frames to the bottom of the core and then to suspend the core over the pattern by allowing the frames to rest on the dike boards surrounding the pattern. The other technique involves the placement of plastic shims between the pattern and the core. The plastic shims are usually precast to the thickness of the tool face, using the same resin system that will be used to cast the tool face. Figure 4-3 illustrates the two methods of positioning cores prior to surface casting.

Surface Casting Methods Surface casting is a method by which epoxy casting compound is poured into a cavity separating the model and the core. In this method, the core adheres to the epoxy casting compound and becomes an integral part of the tool. This technique is widely used to make tools for metal-forming.

The three basic techniques employed to make tools by the surface casting method are: (1) straight casting, (2) sprue-and-vent casting, and (3) pressure casting. The tool configuration is usually the factor

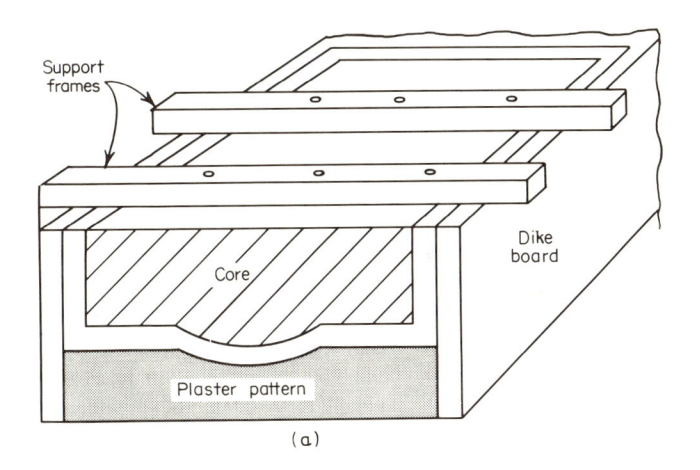

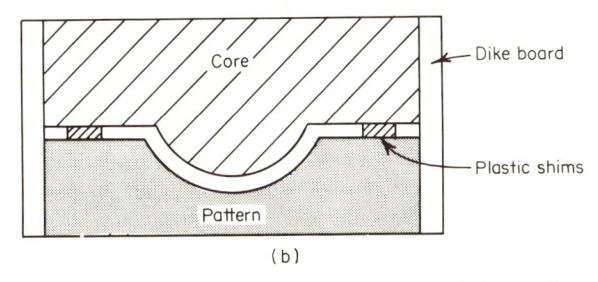

Fig. 4-3 Methods of positioning cores. (*a*) Attaching support frames to bottom of core. (*b*) Use of plastic shims.

which determines the best casting technique to employ. Therefore, it is important to understand each of the three methods and when each method can be used to its greatest advantage. This knowledge will ensure consistently good results in making cast epoxy tools.

Straight Casting Method: The straight casting method is used to advantage on tools having deep draw, no intricate detail, no undercuts, and no high spots which are likely to entrap air during the casting operation. In addition, the cavity into which the resin is poured must be readily accessible.

In the straight casting method, the resin and hardener are mixed in the proper ratio and slowly poured directly into the cavity separating the pattern and the core. This technique is illustrated in Figure 4-4, which shows the sequence of fabricating a plastic-faced stretch form die for an airplane wing leading edge.

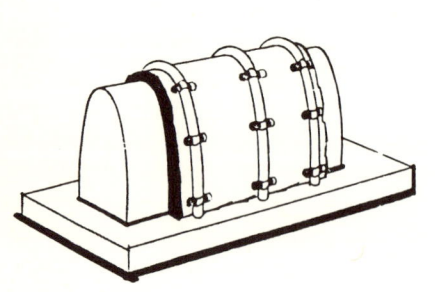

(a) Plaster mold made on model of wing leading edge

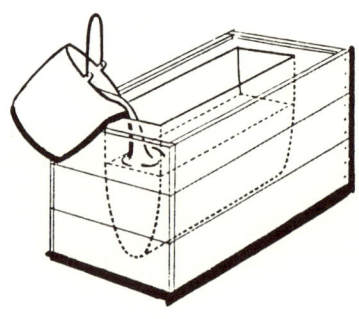

(b) Molten metal cast into sand mold to make the core

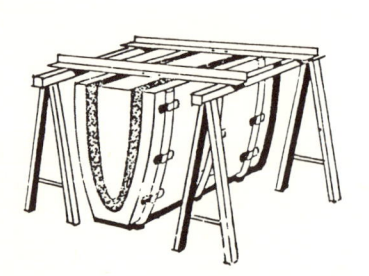

(c) Metal core suspended for setup prior to plastic cast

(d) Epoxy surface casting compound is poured between metal core and plaster mold. Ends are sealed to retain casting compound

Fig. 4-4 Fabrication sequence for plastic-faced die using straight casting method. (*Ren Plastics, Inc.*)

Fig. 4-5 Stretch form block made by straight casting method. The tool face is an epoxy surface casting compound reinforced with a kirksite core. The tool is ready to be mounted on a stretch press for forming an airplane wing leading edge. (*Ren Plastics, Inc.*)

Sprue-and-Vent Casting: The sprue-and-vent casting method is normally used for casting faces on cored tools having compound contours and/or intricate detail. This method has been widely used to cast plastic faces on hydropress dies, drop-hammer dies, and stretch form blocks.

In this method, the core is positioned over the pattern with uniform spacing (usually ⅜ to ½ inch) between the core and the pattern. Vent holes are made in the core at the location of all high spots where air could be entrapped. The resin is poured through sprues leading to the lowest points in the cavity. The sprues should be ¾ to 1 inch in diameter and rise 6 to 8 inches above the high spot in the casting. If the mold cavity is very small, a single sprue is usually adequate. On larger tools, it is advisable to use several sprues located at low points over the total tool area.

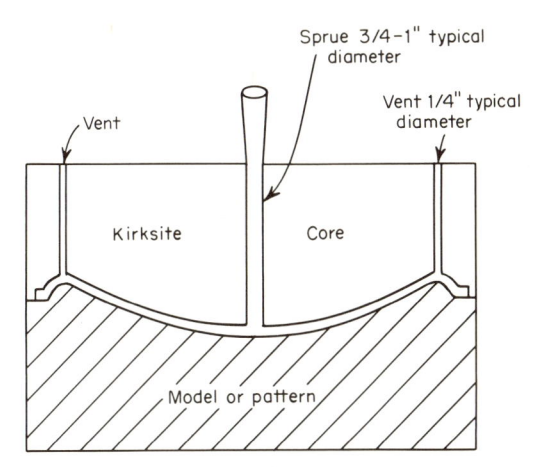

Fig. 4-6 Sectional view of typical setup for sprue-and-vent casting.

During pouring, the resin compound rises to the highest point in the cavity and forces the air out through the vent holes. The sprues should be nearly filled with the casting compound upon completion of the pouring. This creates hydrostatic pressure on the casting and ensures a resin supply to feed into the casting during the slight volume shrinkage that takes place during the resin gel period.

Pressure Casting: The pressure casting method is used on tools having intricate detail that might not be filled or reproduced by gravity feeding alone. This method involves mixing the resin and hardener; placing the mixture in a pressure pot; and applying pressure to the pot, thereby forcing the casting compound into the mold cavity. This method assures void-free castings. Figure 4-7 shows a typical arrangement for pressure casting.

In order to achieve good castings by the pressure casting method, several precautions must be observed. First, the pot and the hose should be checked to ensure that they are free of contaminants before the casting compound is put into the pressure pot. The pressure pot should be placed as close as practical to the inlet of the tool. This will minimize resin wastage and the amount of hose to be cleaned after pouring. Do not use excessive pressure. Three pounds pressure will suffice for most castings. The pessure pot and hose should be thoroughly cleaned as soon as the casting operation has been completed.

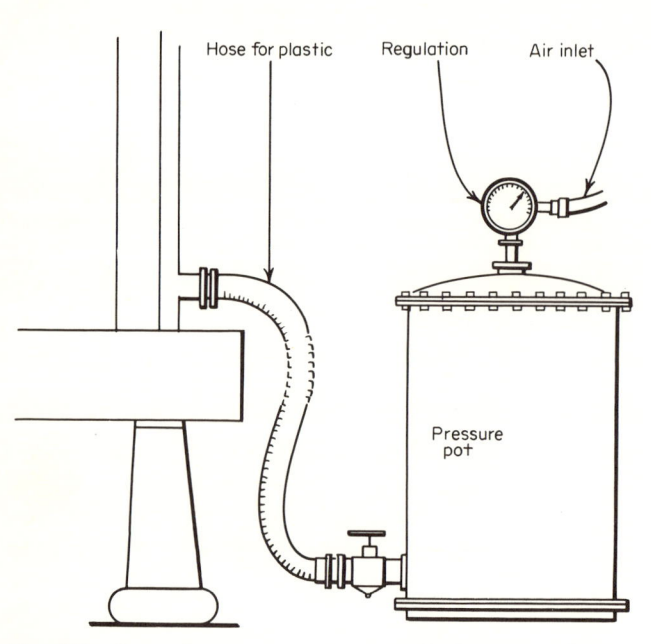

Fig. 4-7 Setup for pressure casting method. (*Ren Plastics, Inc.*)

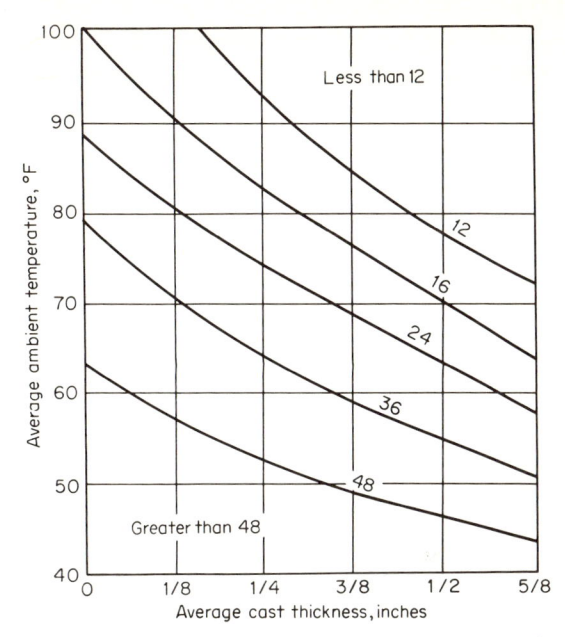

Fig. 4-8 Cure for epoxy surface casting compounds (hours prior to demolding). This chart provides guidelines for curing epoxy surface casting compounds. For example, a ½-inch-thick casting should be allowed to cure for 16 to 24 hours at 70°F, while a ¼-inch-thick casting would require 36 hours at 70°F prior to demolding.

METAL-FORMING TOOLS

The use of plastic tooling materials to make dies for forming metal parts originated in the aircraft industry. There were two main reasons why the aircraft industry pioneered this new tooling concept. One, the aircraft industry normally requires very low production quantities. Two, most aircraft-forming operations are for aluminum sheet. It became apparent that the short production runs coupled with an easily formed material greatly reduced their requirements for durable, wear-resistant die materials. It was therefore natural that the aircraft industry, after assessing its tooling requirements, turned to plastic for its metal-forming dies.

One only has to compare the fabrication methods of metal dies and plastic dies to conclude that plastic dies are much less expensive to make. Consequently, on low production volumes the tooling cost per part is substantially less when plastic dies are used. However, the use of plastic dies is not necessarily restricted to producing small quantities of parts. Parts which are easily formed can be produced in very large quantities on plastic dies. As the state of the art in plastic tooling materials progresses, plastics can be expected to make even greater progress in replacing steel as die materials.

There are certain limitations of plastic dies that the tool designer should be aware of. One big disadvantage of plastic dies is that their surfaces are not as durable as steel die surfaces. This means that the part being formed must be handled more carefully when a plastic die is used in order to avoid damage to the work surface. Another deterrent to the use of plastic metal-forming dies is their inability to produce sharp corners. As a general rule, generous radii should be used on plastic dies, particularly on parts requiring deep draw. If the part cannot be designed with a generous radius, a steel die should be used.

It is obvious from the foregoing that there are disadvantages as well as advantages to the use of plastic dies for metal forming. To use plastic dies effectively, the tool designer must know the limitations of plastic dies, be familiar with the proven die designs, specify the proper resin compounds, and ensure that good shop practices are followed during tool fabrication. If these items are observed, the result will be low-cost tooling that provides trouble-free performance in production usage.

The next section discusses various types of metal-forming tools and provides sketches and photographs of various proven plastic die designs.

Hydroform Dies

Hydroforming is a method of forming sheet metal in a press, using hydraulic pressure to form the part. The pressure is developed by pumping hydraulic fluid into an enclosed rubber bladder. A blank of sheet metal is placed on a male tool, referred to as a *hydroform die* or a *hydropress block.* The tool has locating pins, and the blank has index holes to ensure proper alignment. Flexible pads, referred to as *assist forming pads,* are placed in local areas to assure good forming of the part and protect the rubber bladder. The hydraulic pressure is applied and the part is formed over the male hydroform die. The hydroforming process is illustrated in Figure 4-9.

Hydroforming is a popular process because (1) inexpensive tooling can be used, (2) forming cycles are relatively short compared to other forming processes, and (3) a number of different parts can be formed in the same operation by simply placing the tools on the platen. The number of parts that can be formed in a single cycle is only limited by the size of the platen and the size of the parts to be formed.

Plastic-faced tools have been used very successfully as hydroform dies. Although some mass cast plastic dies have been used, surface cast tools with either a metal core or a metal base are far more common.

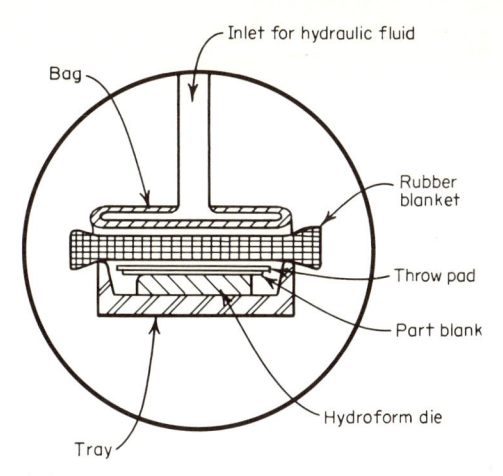

Cast Plastic Tools 115

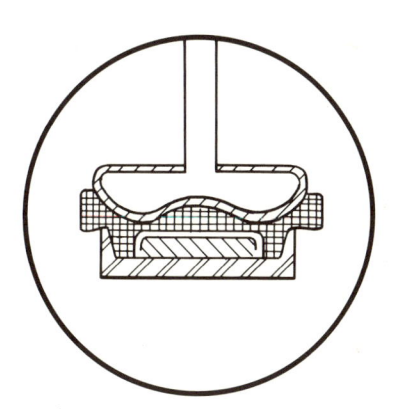

Fig. 4-9 The hydroforming process. (*a*) Beginning of forming cycle. (*b*) Maximum forming pressure.

(a) Beginning of forming cycle

(b) Maximum forming pressure

Occasionally, it is more economical to machine a hydroform die from either aluminum or pressed phenolic blocks. The choice between machining or casting with epoxy is largely determined by the configuration of the part. A die with a complex configuration can be made more economically by casting with plastic; a straight or simple shape can usually be made more economically by machining.

Drop-hammer Dies

Drop-hammer forming is used when intricate parts need to be formed under greater pressure than available with hydroforming. A two-piece tool is required for drop-hammer forming. The lower half of the tool is referred to as the die and is usually a female configuration. The upper half of the tool is referred to as the punch, and is fastened to the "ram," or hammer, of the drop-hammer press. In drop-hammer forming, the piece to be formed is positioned over the die, and the punch is brought down with great force to form the part. In cases where the part cannot be formed with a single blow with the punch, it is accomplished by a series of controlled blows. This practice is referred to as *staging*. Staging requires the use of rings encircling the part, which are stacked in layers. The staging is removed one layer at a time until the part is completely formed.

When plastics are used, the die half of a drop-hammer die is usually constructed of an abrasion-resistant, rigid, cast epoxy face supported by a kirksite core. The punch is cast with either a flexible epoxy or a urethane elastomer. Because of the tendency of flexible epoxy compounds to become brittle with age, the urethane elastomers are becoming more and more popular for the punch of drop-hammer dies. Sometimes it is found that a particular part can be better formed by using a rigid punch and a resilient die. The determination of die design is too complex a subject to be undertaken in this text. Occasionally, all-plastic drop-hammer dies are constructed by reinforcing a ½-inch-thick epoxy–fiber glass laminate with mass casting resin. However, this type of construction is not common.

Prior to the use of plastics in drop-hammer dies, the dies were made of kirksite and lead, the die being kirksite and the punch being lead. This involved hand grinding and matching of the male and female die halves. The use of cast epoxy faces on drop-hammer dies has virtually eliminated this expensive handwork. In addition, the plastic punch has proved to be superior to the lead punch in many instances, inasmuch as the plastic punch does not become flattened or misformed after repeated usage as the lead punch frequently does.

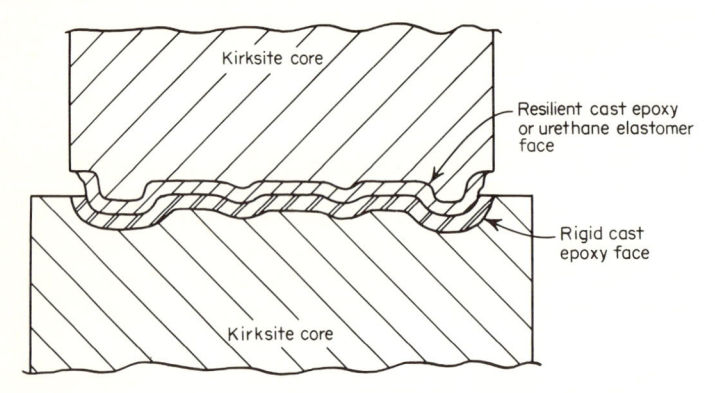

Fig. 4-10 Cross section of plastic-faced drop-hammer die.

Fig. 4-11 (*a*) Plastic-faced drop-hammer die fabricated at Lockheed Aircraft Corporation. (*Furane Plastics, Inc.*)

Another advantage of plastic-faced drop-hammer dies is that they can easily be repaired. If the die face is damaged to the extent that it needs to be replaced, a new epoxy face can easily and inexpensively be cast. A kirksite die would normally be scrapped and new dies made.

Stretch Form Blocks

Stretch forming is a method of forming sheet metal that involves applying tension to the material, and at the same time, drawing it over the configuration of a male plug referred to as a *stretch form block*. The sheet metal is stretched beyond its yield strength, causing it to permanently retain the shape of the stretch form block. Figure 4-11 (*b*) illustrates the stretch forming process. Figure 4-13 is a photograph of a plastic-faced stretch form block mounted and ready for use in a stretch press.

Stretch forming is usually used to form parts with extremely large radii such as fuselage sections for large aircraft. Stretch forming is not recommended for forming parts with intricate shapes. However, parts with reverse curvatures can be stretch-formed in a press having a ram to which a mating stretch block can be mounted (see Figure 4-14).

Plastic-faced stretch form blocks are usually fabricated by the surface casting method. Depending on the configuration, either the straight

118 Plastic Tooling

Fig. 4-11 (*b*) Plastic-faced drop-hammer die. The die face is cast with an abrasion-resistant surface casting compound. The resilient urethane-faced punch eliminates the need for metal thickness clearance allowance. (*Ren Plastics, Inc.*)

casting method or the sprue-and-vent method is most commonly used. The part configuration is obtained by taking a splash directly from the master model, allowing approximately 6 inches excess beyond the edge of the part. Patternmaking wax is built up on the splash to a thickness of ⅜ inch, and another splash is taken from it. The male splash is

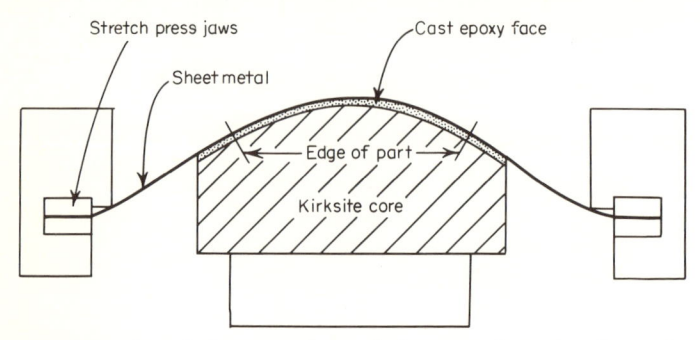

Fig. 4-12 Stretch forming of metal sheet on plastic-faced stretch form block.

Fig. 4-13 Plastic-faced stretch form block. Stretch form block is constructed of surface cast epoxy face supported by kirksite core. Tool has been mounted in stretch press and is ready to form aluminum sheet stock. (*Ren Plastics, Inc.*)

used as a foundry pattern to make the core for the stretch form block. After the core has been cast, it is sandblasted and positioned over the female splash. Epoxy casting compound is then poured into the cavity between the splash and the core. When it has cured, the epoxy compound provides the face of the stretch form block. In this manner, the tool can be cast net, with no subsequent finishing operations required.

Draw Dies

Draw forming is a method of forming complex shapes and/or deep draws in a press. Matched dies, referred to as *draw dies*, are used for this type of forming. A die set consists of a female die, a male plug or punch, and a draw ring. During the forming operation, the

Fig. 4-14 Stretch forming reverse curvature using two plastic-faced stretch form blocks.

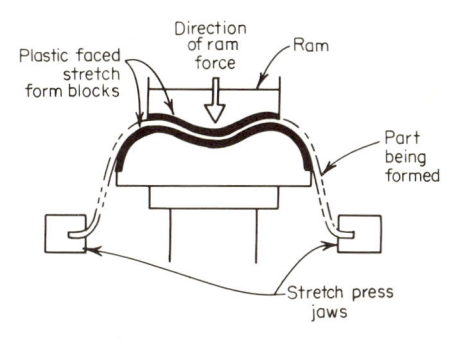

120   Plastic Tooling

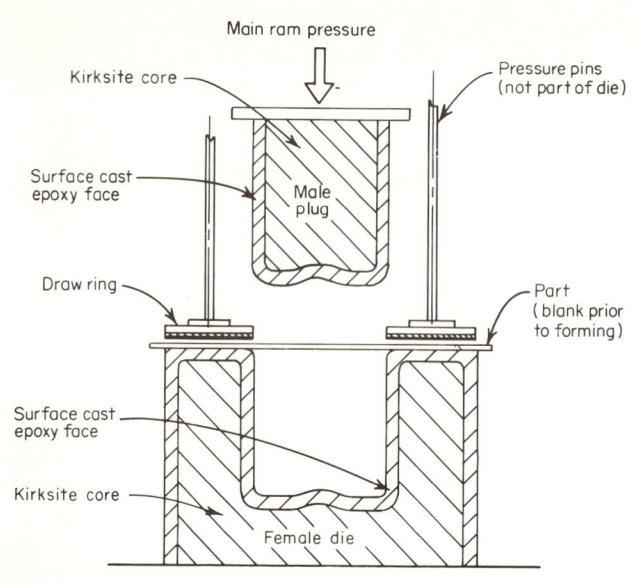

Fig. 4-15 Cross section of a bottoming-type draw die with surface cast epoxy face.

Fig. 4-16 Typical plastic-faced draw die. (*Ren Plastics, Inc.*)

Fig. 4-17 Upper left—epoxy plastic punch with 1¼-inch-thick mild steel draw ring resting on top. Upper right—epoxy plastic die. Dark areas are epoxy. Shiny areas are hardened steel inserts (for wear resistance). Bottom left—finished, trimmed aluminum part. Bottom right—aluminum part as it comes from the press. (*Ren Plastics, Inc.*)

plug is pressed into the die to form the metal. The draw ring exerts pressure on the metal blank to prevent it from wrinkling during forming.

Because draw forming requires matched dies, all-metal tooling is very expensive. Plastic-faced draw dies are highly desirable, inasmuch as an inexpensive plastic casting operation replaces expensive machining and hand matching of the die set.

The basic procedure for constructing a plastic-faced draw die is as follows:

1. A plaster mold is made from the master model.
2. The mold is then used to make a foundry pattern for casting a kirksite core.
3. The kirksite core is cast and sandblasted.
4. The core is positioned over the mold fabricated in step no. 1.
5. Epoxy surface casting compound is poured into the cavity separating the mold and the core.
6. After the epoxy casting compound has been allowed to cure sufficiently at room temperature, it is removed from the mold.

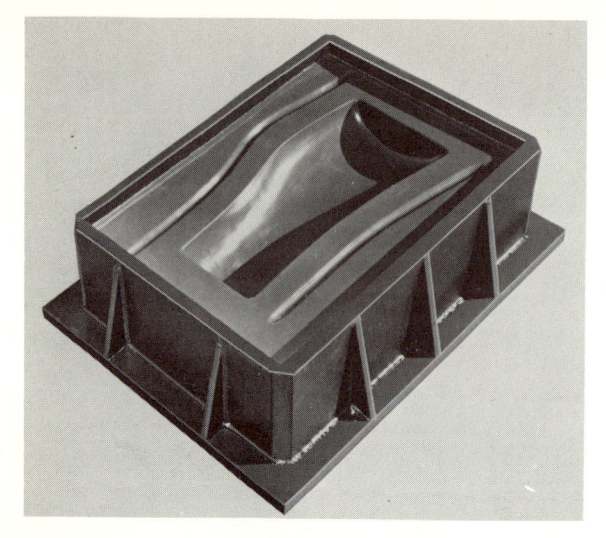

Fig. 4-18 Female half of metal forming die. Die face is flexible urethane, 60 Shore D hardness. (*Rezolin, Inc.*)

Fig. 4-19 Plastic-faced draw die. This photograph illustrates that plastic draw dies are not restricted to small parts. Press operators removing formed sheet metal panel with 12-inch depth of draw on right side of panel. These plastic dies were used to make 20 prototype parts. (*Ren Plastics, Inc.*)

Fig. 4-20 Typical forming die set used to make part of a duct system. Die faces are surface cast epoxy. (*Rezolin, Inc.*)

Fig. 4-21 (*a*) Punch press die in the open position. Dies are surface cast epoxy face with metal core. (*Furane Plastics, Inc.*)

7. The epoxy-faced die half is then used as a pattern for casting the mating die.

CONCLUSIONS

Cast epoxy tools can prove to be very effective and economical. The degree of success of this form of tooling depends on the proper selection

Fig. 4-21 (*b*) Punch press die in the open position with blank in place. (*Furane Plastics, Inc.*)

Fig. 4-21 (*c*) Punch press die in the closed position forming metal blank. (*Furane Plastics, Inc.*)

of the application, the correct resin systems, and good design and fabrication procedures. The series of photographs at the end of this chapter show many varied applications of cast plastic tools for metal-forming operations.

CHAPTER FIVE

Foundry Applications for Plastic Tooling

INTRODUCTION

The use of plastics in foundry pattern equipment has experienced tremendous growth and acceptance by patternmakers in recent years. In many pattern shops, plastic tooling compounds have become as important as wood, metal, and plaster as patternmaking materials. This wide acceptance of plastics is largely based on economics. The foundry industry has recognized that labor time, flow time, and cost of producing foundry pattern equipment can be significantly reduced through the use of plastics. Plastic pattern equipment is especially economical when multiple sets of patterns are required.

Because of the nature of their usage, foundry patterns must be capable of withstanding great abuse. The pattern is subjected to abrasion by sand, severe impact on automated equipment, and damage by rough handling. Patterns must also remain dimensionally stable under various sand-compaction operations. For these reasons, foundry pattern equipment used in long production runs has customarily been made out of metal. However, tooling resin formulators, aware of these requirements, have successfully developed tooling resin compounds with greatly improved abrasion resistance and impact strength. This has led an increasing number of foundries and pattern shops to implement the use of these new materials for producing their pattern equipment. Plastic tooling compounds are being used to construct coreboxes, cope-and-drag equipment, matchplates, and some shell coreboxes.

Although, as a general rule, plastic pattern equipment will not last as long as metal equipment, it is capable of long production runs. Comparative wear tests have shown that cast iron or bronze will outlast plastic patterns. However, the wear characteristics of plastic patterns are about the same as aluminum and far superior to wood. Actual experience has shown that over 100,000 castings can be made from a single plastic pattern.

After the durability of plastic patterns has been evaluated and compared with other types of pattern equipment, cost becomes an important consideration. It has been estimated that plastic foundry pattern equipment costs less than one-third the cost of equivalent metal equipment. Therefore, if a foundry had a requirement for 100,000 castings, they could achieve substantial savings by using plastic pattern equipment. However, if a requirement for 300,000 castings existed, the foundry would find that the savings were neutralized by the need for three sets of pattern equipment. On longer runs, it would obviously be advisable for the foundry to invest in metal equipment.

What the preceding paragraph is intended to point out is that the initial fabrication cost is only one of a number of considerations that must be made when deciding which type of pattern equipment to use for a specific job. The limitations of plastic pattern equipment must be recognized. If the foundryman logically "picks his spots" for the use of plastic equipment, he can effectively save money on his pattern equipment. The overly enthusiastic, across-the-board use of plastic pattern equipment will surely lead to difficulties.

This chapter is intended to provide the reader with a basic understanding of the foundry industry: how metal is cast, what types of pattern equipment are used, when and where it is advantageous to use plastic pattern equipment, what types of materials to select, and how to design and fabricate plastic pattern equipment.

FOUNDRY PATTERN EQUIPMENT

A metal casting is made by pouring molten metal into a cavity that is usually made in sand. The configuration of the cavity is established by a foundry pattern, around which the sand is packed. When the foundry pattern is withdrawn from the sand, the cavity into which the metal is poured remains. After the molten metal has cooled and solidified, the sand is removed from around the solid casting. The casting is then trimmed, machined, or drilled as required by the engineering drawing. This basic sequence is followed, with minor variations, on all metal castings.

It quickly becomes apparent that the first key to good-quality castings is the pattern equipment. The pattern equipment determines the configuration, and consequently the accuracy of the metal casting to a large extent. Other variables in the process of casting the metal can result in a rejected part, but initially the pattern equipment is the most significant factor in producing a good-quality, accurate casting. If the foundry pattern is inaccurate, has a poor surface finish, or flexes out of proper configuration when the sand is rammed, there is nothing that can be done during the subsequent operations to correct the problem, short of expensive machining of the completed casting.

Frequently, more than one pattern is required to produce a single casting. The casting may be hollow or have cavities that require the use of cores. For example, 11 coreboxes and 2 patterns were required to produce the casting shown in Figure 5-1. Great skill is required on the part of the patternmaker to make equipment of this type. Each part must be individually made to within very close tolerances so that they all will coordinate properly when used to make a metal casting.

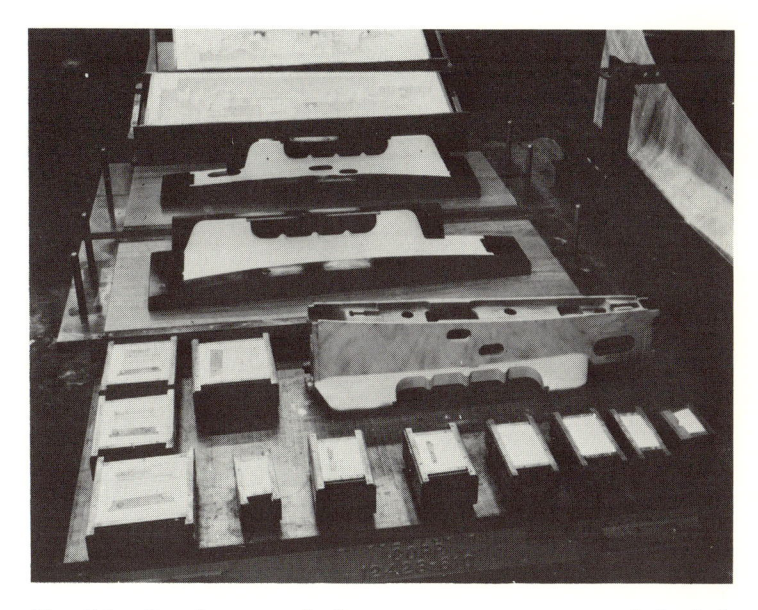

Fig. 5-1 Complete set of plastic pattern equipment and finished metal casting. Pattern equipment is constructed of epoxy laminate reinforced with lightweight aggregate and laminating resin. (*Furane Plastics, Inc.*)

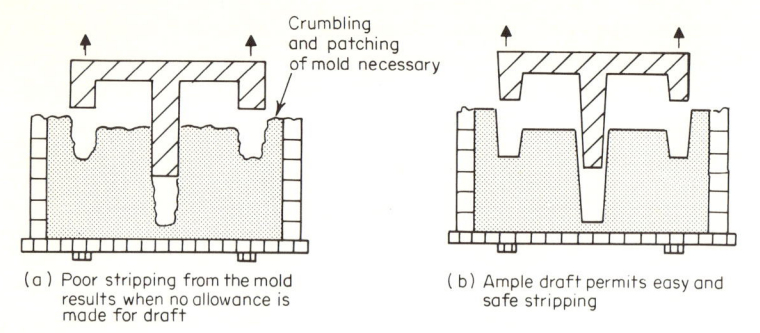

Fig. 5-2 Design with adequate draft. (*a*) Poor stripping from the mold results when no allowance is made for draft. (*b*) Ample draft permits easy and safe stripping.

In making the casting, the pattern is embedded into the sand to form the impression into which the molten metal is poured. Since the pattern is repeatedly embedded into and withdrawn from foundry sand, it is susceptible to abrasion. Abrasion of the foundry pattern can result in rejected castings because of inaccuracy. It quickly becomes obvious that the two prime requirements of foundry pattern equipment are that they be durable and accurate. As is the case with tooling in every other industry, it is important that it be capable of being constructed as inexpensively as possible. Plastic pattern equipment has proved itself capable of meeting these requirements.

A discussion of the terminology associated with the foundry industry follows.

Foundry Patterns

A *foundry pattern* is a model of the part. The pattern is used to make the sand mold into which the molten metal is poured. The pattern may be made of wood, plaster, metal, plastic, or other materials; the selection depends on a number of considerations which will be discussed in this chapter. All patterns must have *draft* and *shrinkage allowances.*

Draft is the taper allowed on the vertical faces of a pattern to facilitate easy removal of the pattern from the sand mold. It is important that a pattern be capable of being neatly withdrawn from a sand mold. A pattern with inadequate draft will cause tearing of the mold walls when it is removed from the sand. This condition will necessitate costly repair of the mold wall or will produce poor-quality castings. Usually a taper of $\frac{1}{8}$ inch per foot is considered "good draft."

Shrinkage allowances are made on all patterns to compensate for the contraction of the metal as it cools and solidifies in the sand mold. In other words, the pattern is made oversize. Each metal shrinks at a different rate. Consequently, in order to provide a pattern that will produce accurate castings, the patternmaker must know what type of metal will be used. Special shrinkage rulers are made for each common cast metal. By using one of these rulers, the patternmaker avoids the need to calculate the shrinkage allowance for each dimension in the pattern.

Some castings are hollow or have various-shaped openings and/or cavities. These cavities are molded by the use of *cores*. A core is a separable part of the sand mold (see Figure 5-3). It is usually made separately and placed in the sand mold after the pattern has been withdrawn. Cores are generally made of sand and are made in pattern equipment called *coreboxes*. The core is suspended in the sand mold by a continuation of the core beyond the casting dimensions, referred to as a *core print*. The pattern halves are constructed so as to accommodate the core print, which also serves to position the core properly in relation to the other mold components.

All patterns are molded in a metal framework known as a *flask*. The flask is made up of two parts. The upper half is called the *cope*, and the lower half is designated as the *drag*. The cope and drag are accurately indexed by means of flask pins which are located on the outside of the flask. The flasks are positioned to the pattern, and sand is packed or rammed around the pattern in both the cope-and-drag halves of the flask. The cope and drag are then separated and the pattern is withdrawn. The cope and drag are then placed against one another and indexed by means of the flask pins.

Frequently the foundry is faced with a requirement for a large quantity of a specific small casting. In instances such as this, it is economical to produce them by using a matchplate. A *matchplate* is a plate on which patterns are split along the parting line and mounted back-to-back. The plate separates the patterns and serves as a parting plane. The use of matchplates bearing multiple patterns enables the foundry

Fig. 5-3 Core is suspended in between the cope-and-drag halves of a sand mold to make a hollow casting. The core print (the extreme end or continuation of the core) positions the core in its proper location.

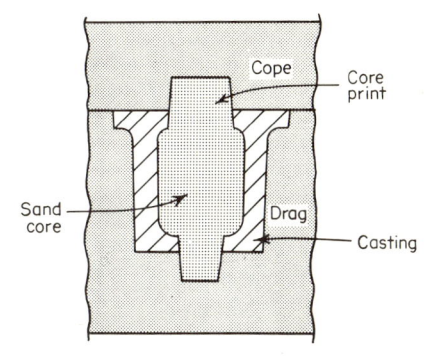

Fig. 5-4 Matchplate pattern consisting of four patterns of epoxy casting compound mounted on an aluminum matchplate. (*Hysol Division, The Dexter Corp.*)

to increase production rates substantially by casting a number of castings in the same mold.

The critical aspect of fabricating a matchplate is ensuring that the parts on each side of the plate "match up" to one another. This is essential, since a good casting cannot be produced unless the two sand impressions mate precisely when they are brought together.

Matchplates are commonly made from cast aluminum. Over the years, aluminum has proved itself to be durable enough to resist the mechanical jarring of jolt–roll-over equipment and to provide long service life at a low cost. However, matchplates are now being made of plastic. Although the initial cost of plastic matchplates is higher, this cost is offset by the fact that flow time is frequently less than one-third that of an aluminum matchplate, and that plastic matchplates do not require the cleanup after being demolded that is needed by aluminum patterns.

Frequently a pattern is too large and/or bulky to be mounted on a matchplate. In these instances, the pattern is split on its parting line and each half is mounted on a separate base. The top half of the pattern is called the cope and the bottom half is called the drag. This type of pattern equipment is referred to as *cope*-and-*drag* equipment. They are each positioned in a flask, and sand is rammed around the pattern. When the patterns are removed, the flasks are coordinated to one another and the molten metal is poured into the cavity created by the patterns. When made in plastic, this type of equipment is usually constructed of epoxy–fiber glass laminate reinforced with either laminated eggcrate, aggregate core, or urethane foam.

Patternmaker's Sheet Wax

Sheet wax is frequently used in the production of patterns and coreboxes. The material is a specially formulated product available in thicknesses from $\frac{1}{64}$ to $\frac{3}{8}$ inch. The sheets are usually sold in two standard sizes, 8 by 12 inches and 12 by 24 inches. This material is different from normal wax in that it will not soften or distort under heat produced by normal exothermic reaction. Patternmaker's sheet wax is produced to tolerances of $\pm$ 0.001 inch.

Patternmaker's sheet wax is used in a variety of applications. Sheet wax is used to simulate metal thickness in the fabrication of forming dies. This is accomplished by laminating the female die half over a master pattern. The master pattern is then removed, and a layer of sheet wax the thickness of the metal to be formed is placed inside the female die. The male die half is then laminated directly over the sheet wax. When the die halves are completely cured, they are sepa-

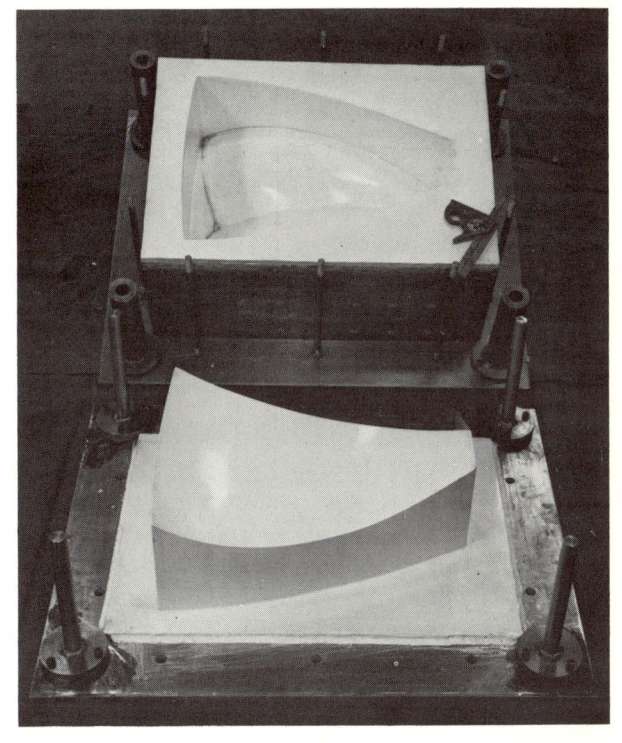

Fig. 5-5 Plastic cope-and-drag equipment, constructed of $\frac{3}{8}$-inch laminate reinforced with lightweight aggregate coated with laminating resin. (*Hysol Division, The Dexter Corp.*)

rated, and the wax is then removed. In the closed position, the thickness of the metal to be formed separates the two die halves.

Sheet wax is also used to expand patterns for shrink allowance and to compensate for part thickness on a variety of other tooling applications.

FABRICATION PROCEDURES FOR PLASTIC PATTERN EQUIPMENT

This section provides detailed information on procedures and techniques for fabricating various types of foundry pattern equipment. The author is aware that some foundries and pattern shops have developed specialized techniques that they consider improvements over the basic methods discussed here. The author recognizes that the companies concerned consider these special techniques to provide them with certain competitive advantages, and has therefore restricted this section to fundamental procedures. It is felt that as the reader becomes familiar with plastic tooling compounds and their handling characteristics, his natural creativity will lead him to the development of his own special techniques which further reduce costs or increase the life of pattern equipment. The novice will soon discover that plastics are versatile materials capable of being used to repair worn patterns and to make production pattern equipment. And he will later develop his own repair techniques and material preferences.

Duplicate Patterns

One of the most outstanding advantages of plastics as foundry pattern materials is the ease and economy with which duplicate patterns can be made. Duplicate patterns made of plastic are frequently mounted on matchplate patterns. By this means, a matchplate with several patterns mounted on it can easily be made at only a fraction of the cost of a matchplate requiring the individual machining or carving of each pattern. Duplicate cope-and-drag equipment is also frequently made using the method outlined here.

Making duplicate patterns with plastic tooling compounds requires that a master pattern be constructed first. Normally, the master pattern is constructed of wood, plaster, or plastics, using techniques described in Chapter 2 of this text.

The master pattern is then mounted on a machined metal plate. Dike boards are constructed around the pattern. The pattern, base plate, and inner surfaces of the dike boards are all sealed and coated with an appropriate parting agent. Information on proper selection of sealers and parting agents is provided in Chapter 1.

Fig. 5-6 Unique application for laminated foundry patterns consisting of 32 vane blades made from 3 identical molds. (*U.S. Gypsum Co.*)

The next step is the fabrication of a plastic-faced plaster transfer. This consists of a hydrophobic epoxy gel coat backed up or reinforced with gypsum cement. The step-by-step procedure for making a plastic-faced plaster transfer medium is given in Chapter 7. Bushings are embedded in the plastic-faced plaster transfer medium and are used in subsequent operations to hold the base plate and the mold together during the casting of the duplicate pattern.

After the plastic-faced transfer medium has cured, the master pattern

Fig. 5-7 Left—wood master pattern, center—transfer mold, right—cast epoxy duplicate pattern. (*Rezolin, Inc.*)

Fig. 5-8 Cutaway view of foundry pattern constructed of epoxy surface casting compound reinforced with rough-cast aluminum. (*Rezolin, Inc.*)

is removed. The mold cavity is inspected for defects. Any defects or surface imperfections are repaired at this time with an appropriate epoxy paste patching compound. A pouring sprue and riser holes are drilled in the base plate. The surfaces of the plastic-faced plaster transfer and the base plate are coated with parting agent.

The plastic-faced plaster and the base plate are positioned together. Next they are attached to one another by means of bolts running through the bushings. The duplicate pattern is then poured using a mass casting compound and casting procedures outlined in Chapter 4, and cured according to Table 4-2. After the duplicate pattern has cured, it is

Fig. 5-9 Duplicate matchplate pattern made of metallic-filled epoxy casting compound. Note fineness of detail accurately reproduced by casting and curing at room temperature. (*Hysol Division, The Dexter Corp.*)

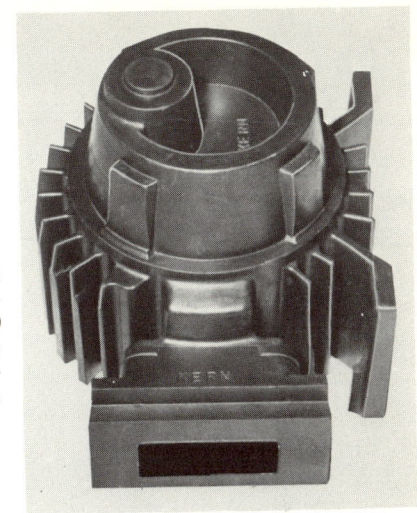

Fig. 5-10 Duplicate pattern made of urethane casting compound. Urethane with 60 Shore D hardness provides toughness and abrasion resistance for slinger application. (*Rezolin, Inc.*)

removed from the mold. The use of lag screws to remove the pattern is recommended. If care is taken not to damage the plastic-faced plaster mold, as many duplicate patterns as required can be cast.

It is possible to cast duplicate patterns using a urethane casting compound with a Shore D hardness of 60 to 65. However, it should be kept in mind that the present urethane casting compounds are most accurate when cast in thicknesses of less than ½ inch. When cast in thicknesses of less than ½ inch, urethane casting compounds will produce patterns with a shrinkage of less than 0.001 inch per inch. If greater thicknesses are required, it is recommended that the urethane be cast in ½-inch stages or a core be used to keep the thickness of the urethane casting compound to ⅜ inch nominal.

Coreboxes

Coreboxes may be either one- or two-piece, depending on the configuration of the core. When the corebox consists of more than one section, it should be designed so that the corebox sections can be stripped away from the core rather than having to remove the core from the box.

Plastic coreboxes are most frequently laminated, although some of the smaller ones are cast using epoxy casting resin. The laminated coreboxes are normally lighter in weight than an equivalent wood or cast epoxy corebox. This is a significant advantage that makes easier and less costly handling of coreboxes.

The manner in which coreboxes are used calls for rigid construction. Cores may be made either by hand or by machine. In the hand method, the sand is placed into the corebox by hand and compacted with pneu-

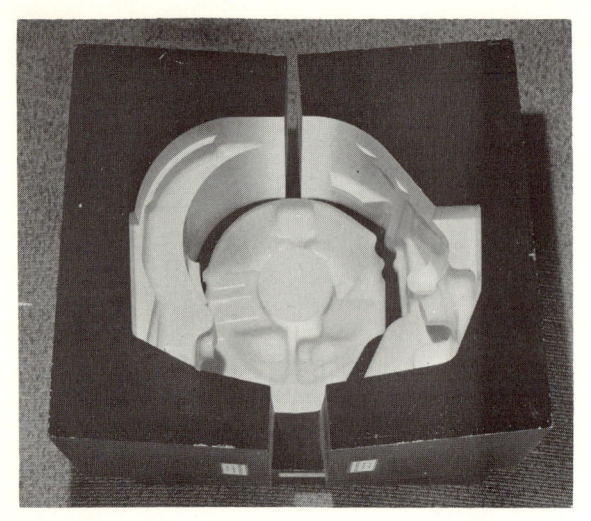

Fig. 5-11 Epoxy laminated corebox. (*Rezolin, Inc.*)

matic hammers. Machines are also used to make cores. The most common is a core-blowing machine which forces sand into the corebox cavity by air pressure. The air pressure within the box is relieved by vent holes located in the corebox. Experience has shown that machine methods of core making require a much stronger laminate to resist pressure and shock loads. In the case of a laminated corebox, a thickness of ⅜ to ½ inch is recommended. It may, in many cases, be adequate to use a ¼-inch laminate reinforced with urethane foam or aggregate filler.

Laminated Coreboxes The initial step in fabricating a laminated corebox is to construct a wood pattern of the shape of the core. The surface of the pattern is sealed and positioned on a metal surface plate. Match-buttons or alignment pins are then positioned on the surface plate if the corebox is to consist of more than one section. All surfaces which will be exposed to resin are then coated with an appropriate parting agent. Techniques for applying sealers and parting agents are discussed in detail in Chapter 1 and will not be repeated here.

An abrasion-resistant gel coat is then applied and allowed to reach a tack-free stage. At this point, epoxy resin and fiber glass cloth are laminated onto the model to a thickness of ¼ inch. Since most coreboxes have complex shapes, it is recommended that small pieces of fiber glass cloth be used. The use of 6-inch squares of fiber glass cloth will make the task of laminating much easier. It will also minimize potential voids caused by the bridging of layers of the laminate in corners or in areas having small radii.

Oftentimes a framework is applied to the corebox at this point. The framework may be constructed of wood or precast aluminum. The common procedure is to press the framework against the laminate and allow it to cure overnight. After a 16-hour cure, strips of fiber glass cloth wetted with epoxy resin are applied where the laminate and the framework meet to provide additional reinforcement.

At this point in time, the corebox may be completed in one of three ways:

1. An additional $1/8$ to $1/4$ inch of laminate may be applied.
2. The cavity between the framework and the laminate may be filled with urethane foam.
3. The cavity may be filled with lightweight aggregate which has been coated with epoxy laminating resin as described in Chapter 3.

The corebox should be given an appropriate cure at room temperature before it is removed from the model and trimmed.

Cast Coreboxes As stated earlier, coreboxes can also be cast, using either an epoxy casting system or a polyurethane casting system. The epoxy casting system will have a Shore D hardness in the 85 to 92 range. Success has been achieved with polyurethane casting compounds in the 60 to 65 Shore D hardness range.

Cast coreboxes are made over a pattern of the core in the same fashion as laminated coreboxes. Once the pattern has been sealed, coated with release agent, and mounted on a surface plate, dike boards are positioned around the pattern. The dike boards should be sealed appropriately

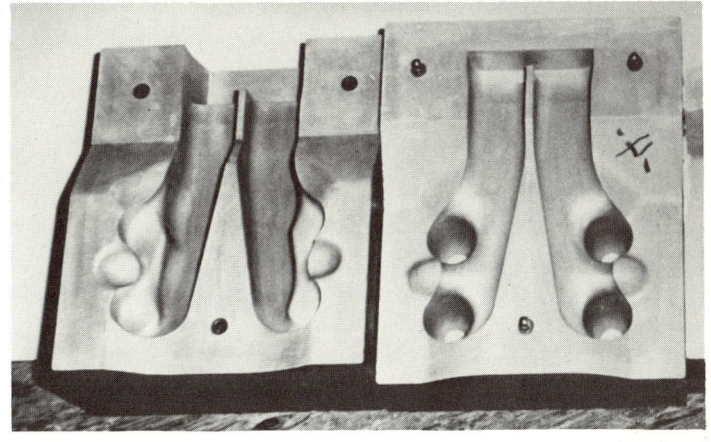

Fig. 5-12 Laminated epoxy cylinder head port corebox for diesel engine. (*Nelson Pattern Co.*)

Fig. 5-13 Urethane corebox of Pontiac cylinder, cast in an aluminum frame. Urethane casting compound was 60 Shore D hardness for optimum wear characteristics. (*Hysol Division, The Dexter Corp.*)

prior to this step. The edges and joints of the dike boards must then be sealed with modeling clay to prevent leakage of the casting resin.

To conserve on material and to decrease the weight of the corebox, it is common practice to use cores made of either wood or foam. The core is precut and positioned in the mold cavity, so that a uniform spacing of $3/8$ to $1/2$ inch exists between the core and the pattern. An epoxy surface casting compound is selected, and cast between the pattern and the core, using the techniques described in Chapter 4.

Fig. 5-14 CO_2 corebox and sand core. Corebox is constructed of epoxy mass casting compound. (*Hysol Division, The Dexter Corp.*)

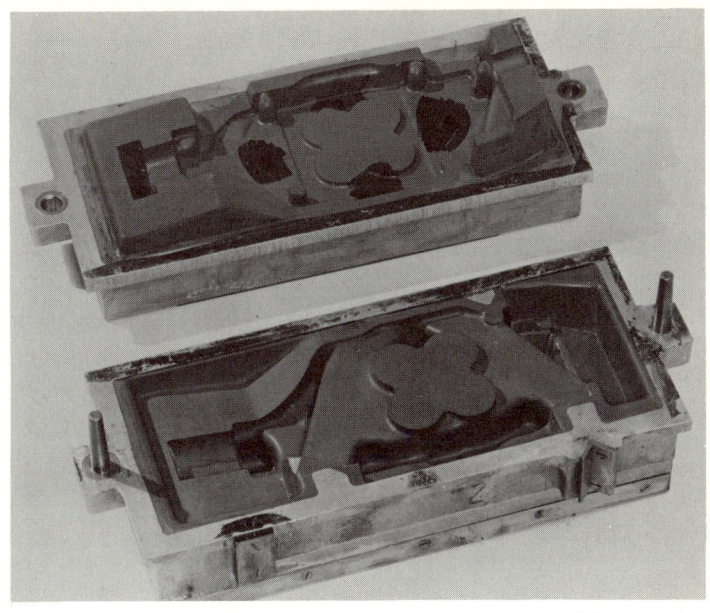

Fig. 5-15 Blow corebox fabricated by a major automobile manufacturer. Corebox is abrasion-resistant epoxy casting compound in metal framework. (*Furane Plastics, Inc.*)

If a gel coat is to be used, the following sequence should be used: cut and position the core; remove the core; apply the gel coat; reposition the core; and pour the casting resin when the gel coat has become tacky. The cast epoxy corebox should be cured in accordance with the schedule shown in Figure 4-8, Chapter 4.

Coreboxes can also be cast using a polyurethane casting system. The procedure is basically the same as for casting coreboxes with an epoxy system. However, it should be kept in mind that polyurethane systems are very sensitive to moisture. Techniques for achieving optimum results with polyurethane casting systems are discussed in Chapter 7.

Cope-and-drag Equipment

The ease with which duplicate patterns can be made has contributed greatly to the increased use of plastic cope-and-drag equipment. It has been estimated that as much as three months flow time can be saved by reproducing a pattern in plastic instead of metal.

Cope-and-drag equipment is usually of laminated construction. The most common method of reinforcement is the use of a lightweight aggregate coated with epoxy laminating resin. The use of this type of reinforcement produces a good cost savings because it drastically reduces

Fig. 5-16 Epoxy paste compound used to make checking slugs in cast-iron foundry shell coreboxes. (*Nelson Pattern Co.*)

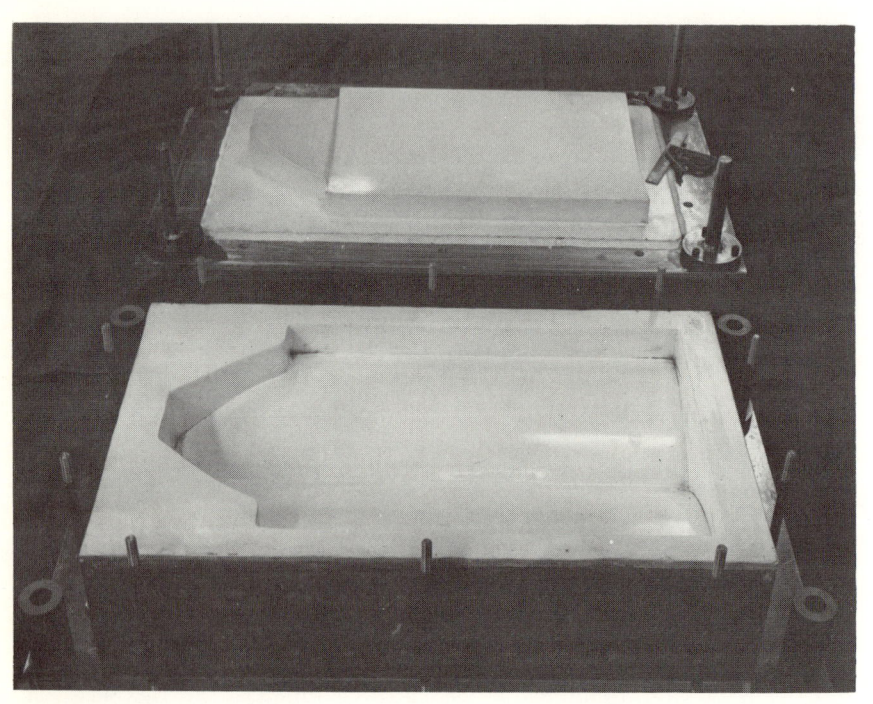

Fig. 5-17 Plastic cope-and-drag equipment constructed of epoxy–fiber glass laminate mounted on metal framework. Laminate is reinforced with mixture of lightweight aggregate coated with epoxy laminating resin. (*Hysol Division, The Dexter Corp.*)

labor time. For example, the use of this type of reinforcement in cope-and-drag equipment made it possible for one manufacturer to reduce his laminated pattern thickness from $3/8$ inch when reinforced with an eggcrate structure to $1/8$ inch when reinforced with aggregate.

The sequence for making laminated cope-and-drag equipment is relatively straightforward. As in all plastic tooling work, a master pattern is required. The master pattern may be new, or it may be an existing production pattern. If an existing pattern is used, it should be carefully checked, and worn areas should be restored to the proper configuration. Worn or damaged patterns may be easily restored with an epoxy paste patching compound. When it has been determined that the master pattern is accurate, the surface is sealed and prepared with parting agent. The method of sealing and the choice of parting agent will be determined by the type of surface of the master pattern, i.e., wood, plaster, or metal. The guidelines for this method can be found in Chapter 1 of this text.

The next step is to make a transfer from the master pattern. If only one duplicate pattern is to be made, the transfer can be made of gypsum cement or a plastic-faced plaster. If more than one duplicate pattern is to be made, a plastic-faced plaster transfer is recommended. A detailed procedure for making plastic-faced plaster transfers is provided in Chapter 6 of this text. Because of the complexity of most foundry patterns, it is advisable, when making the transfer, to position blow-off diaphragms around the pattern. This will enable compressed air to be used literally to blow the transfer apart from the master pattern and to make the task of separating the two a much easier one.

After the transfer mold has been removed from the master pattern, it is inverted and inspected. Any defects or surface imperfections should be repaired at this point with an epoxy paste patching compound. Upon completion of the repair, the surface is coated with parting agent.

An epoxy gel coat is then applied to the surface of the transfer mold. A metallic-filled abrasion-resistant gel coat is recommended for this application. The surface coat is allowed to set for 30 to 40 minutes or until it has become tack-free.

Using the laminating procedures described in Chapter 3, several layers of 1500 tooling cloth are applied. Because many foundry patterns have complex shapes, the use of small pieces (6- or 8-inch squares) of cloth usually will make the laminating easier and allow it to proceed more quickly. The laminate should be built up to at least a thickness of $1/8$ inch if aggregate is to be used as reinforcement. A $1/4$-inch-thick laminate reinforced with aggregate produces extremely rigid and almost indestructible pattern equipment.

The optimum laminate thickness for the individual user can be determined by starting off with a ⅜-inch laminate on the first pattern, and decreasing the laminate thickness by $\frac{1}{16}$ inch on subsequent pattern equipment. The performance of the equipment can be observed in production usage over a period of time. This will provide the patternmaker with a realistic picture of performance versus laminate thickness.

If we assume that the desired laminate thickness has been predetermined and that the last layer of fiber glass cloth has just been applied, the next step is to immediately fill the cavity behind the laminate with lightweight aggregate coated with epoxy laminating resin.

The procedure for mixing the lightweight aggregate and laminating resin is as follows: A predetermined amount of laminating resin and hardener are weighed in the proper ratio and thoroughly mixed. The lightweight aggregate is then slowly added to the mixture and stirred in until the surfaces of the aggregate are thoroughly coated with the resin mixture. Actual tests have shown that a mixture of 5 parts by weight of aggregate and 1 part by weight of resin mixture will produce a core with a compressive strength of approximately 4,000 psi.

After the aggregate and laminating resin have been mixed, the mixture is poured into the laminated cavity and tamped into place. The working time for the mixture is approximately 30 minutes after the resin and hardener are combined. Therefore, it is advisable only to mix batches of a size that can be easily handled within that time period. If additional material is required, subsequent batches can be mixed and tamped into place. The aggregate can be used to fill a cavity of any thickness without fear of exothermic heat causing warpage.

The foundry pattern should then be allowed to cure for a minimum of 24 hours before it is removed from the transfer mold.

Short-run Shell Coreboxes

For many years, the use of plastic to make shell coreboxes was thought to be beyond the capabilities of plastic tooling materials. However, recently it has been discovered that the use of epoxy–aluminum needle compounds makes shell coreboxes for producing prototype shell cores. Plastic shell coreboxes have produced up to 400 shell cores when operated at 500°F using a 30-second investment and 5½-minute cure cycles.

Although this level of performance is not sufficient to warrant consideration of plastic shell coreboxes for production runs, it does show that plastic shell coreboxes can be used to make cores for prototype parts or limited production runs. When it is taken into account that a plastic shell corebox can be made for approximately one-fourth the cost of a metal one, it becomes apparent that substantial cost savings are possible in selected instances.

The plastic tooling system used to make shell coreboxes is a dry mixture of aluminum needles and epoxy powder. It is sold under various trade names such as Fiber-Tool and Veritool. Using this system, short-run shell coreboxes can be made by using an existing corebox as a pattern or by starting from a wood pattern of the core. Figure 5-18 shows a corebox, a shell core, and a casting made by using this type of corebox.

Since the fabrication sequence for the completion of the plastic-faced plaster transfer media is straightforward and has been covered in detail

Fig. 5-18 (*a*) Shell corebox constructed of high-temperature epoxy gel coat reinforced with epoxy–aluminum needle compound. (*U.S. Gypsum Co.*)

Fig. 5-18 (*b*) Shell core made in plastic shell corebox shown above. (*U.S. Gypsum Co.*)

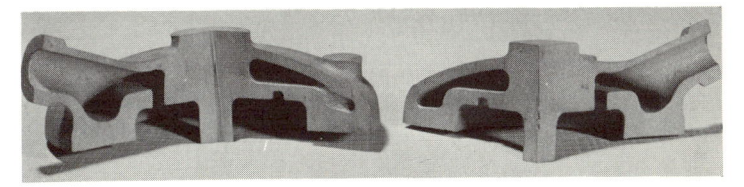

Fig. 5-18 (*c*) Cutaway view of bronze casting showing cored section made with shell core. (*U.S. Gypsum Co.*)

previously, those steps are not covered in detail here. The detailed instructions begin with the placement of aluminum dike boards on the plastic-faced plaster model. Aluminum plate stock, $\frac{1}{4}$ or $\frac{3}{8}$ inch thick, is suitable for this purpose. Alignment pins or bushings (brass master dowels or equivalent) are inserted at this time.

A high-temperature epoxy gel coat, suitable for service up to 600°F, is then weighed in the proper ratio and mixed. The gel coat is carefully applied in a $\frac{1}{32}$-inch thickness and allowed to gel for 1 hour at room temperature. A second $\frac{1}{32}$-inch layer of gel coat is then applied.

The epoxy–aluminum needle compound is applied directly over the second gel coat. The material is preproportioned in a plastic bag. The bag should be tumbled to ensure that the epoxy and aluminum needles are evenly distributed. The compound is then applied evenly in $\frac{1}{2}$- to 1-inch layers; each layer should be tamped before the successive layer is applied. The corebox is then given an oven cure.

The following oven cure cycle is typical for this type of plastic tooling compound: 2 hours at 250°F; 3 hours at 350°F.

The oven should then be turned off and the corebox allowed to slowly cool to room temperature inside the oven. If the cure cycle recommended by the manufacturer varies from the cure cycle described here, use the one the manufacturer recommends since his material warranty is contingent on the user following his directions.

After the cure cycle, the corebox is demolded from the plastic-faced plaster transfer medium. The corebox surfaces are cleaned as required. The corebox halves are joined together, and the backsides are machined parallel. The final step in the fabrication sequence is the attachment of the mounting hardware. Aluminum angle stock, $\frac{1}{4}$ or $\frac{5}{16}$ inch thick, is recommended for this purpose.

As stated earlier, plastic shell coreboxes made in this manner have been used successfully to make in excess of 400 shell cores. By careful selection of the proper application, plastic shell coreboxes can be used to produce savings.

CONCLUSIONS

It should be apparent from the foregoing discussions that plastic pattern equipment can be used very effectively to reduce costs in many instances. However, the use of plastic pattern equipment should not be regarded as the solution to all pattern problems.

Basically, plastic pattern equipment has the following advantages:

1. Lower cost
2. Easily and inexpensively duplicated

3. Easily repaired or changed
4. Better removal from sand
5. Lightweight
6. Longer life than wood

However, there are disadvantages to plastic pattern equipment that must also be considered.

1. Shorter production life than metal
2. More susceptible to damage than metal

It is significant to note that plastic pattern equipment has been used successfully for a variety of foundry applications. Some of these are duplicate patterns, CO_2 coreboxes, cope-and-drag equipment, matchplates, and core-dryer spotting slugs. The fact that plastics continue to be used in these applications on an increasing basis attests that their niche is taking shape.

In order to use plastics effectively in his pattern equipment program, the foundryman only needs to have a good enough knowledge of plastic tooling materials to understand their capabilities as well as their limitations. The intelligent application of this knowledge to his pattern equipment problems should enable him to select the right applications, the correct materials, and the proper methods of design and construction which will produce plastic pattern equipment to meet his requirements effectively.

Fig. 5-19 Core dryer constructed of epoxy–aluminum needle high-temperature plastic tooling compound. (*Furane Plastics, Inc.*)

CHAPTER SIX

High-temperature Plastic Tools

INTRODUCTION

The trend toward using more plastic and composite parts that require curing or processing at elevated temperatures has been evident in recent years. A large number of these parts have compound contours or complex shapes that make the cost of tooling by conventional metalworking techniques prohibitive. High-temperature plastic tools have come to be recognized as economical, reliable, and accurate tooling media for use in both autoclaves and ovens at elevated temperatures and high pressures. In this chapter, high-temperature tools will be considered to mean tooling that is subjected to service temperatures of 250°F or more.

The successful development of new epoxy tooling resin formulations and improved tool fabrication procedures has resulted in wider utilization of high-temperature plastic tooling. High-temperature plastic tools have been used successfully as replacement tooling for metal tools which proved to be unsuitable or too costly. High-temperature plastic tooling is now widely used for the following typical applications:

Bonding Assembly Jigs and Lay-up Mandrels These tools are used for the fabrication and cure of reinforced plastic parts and plastic composite structures. These parts normally require cure at temperatures in the 250 to 350°F range, with autoclave pressures as high as 80 psi.

Metal Bonding Jigs These tools are used as a form on which to lay up and cure adhesively bonded metals. The cure is usually accomplished in an autoclave at temperatures above 350°F and pressures up to 80 psi.

Thermoforming Molds A great number of thermoplastic parts are formed on thermoforming molds. The process consists of heating plastic sheet stock, draping it over a form, and drawing a vacuum, thereby using atmospheric pressure to form the plastic to the desired shape. Room-temperature-curing epoxy resin systems were formerly used for this application because forming temperatures rarely exceeded 200°F. However, the newer thermoplastics being widely used in aircraft and

Fig. 6-1 Apollo heat shield skins are fabricated on high-temperature epoxy laminated bonding assembly jigs at North American Rockwell Space and Information Division. (*Furane Plastics, Inc.*)

Fig. 6-2 High-temperature epoxy laminated lay-up mandrel used to fabricate polyester stabilizer wing tip production parts. (*Furane Plastics, Inc.*)

Fig. 6-3 Thermoforming mold made of high-temperature laminating resin and glass cloth. Production part is made of thin-gauge thermoplastic sheet. (*Hysol Division, The Dexter Corp.*)

aerospace applications (polycarbonates, polysulfones, and high-temperature acrylics) require forming temperatures in excess of 300°F. Consequently, high-temperature plastic tools are now used for this application.

Life Expectancy of High-temperature Plastic Tools

A preliminary investigation into the life expectancy of high-temperature plastic tools in relation to processing requirements has been made. The study was based on a survey of companies in the aircraft and aerospace industries that are using plastic tools for similar processing requirements. The data presented in Table 6-1 were, therefore, based on high-temperature plastic lay-up mandrels and bonding assembly jigs which were fabricated by several companies. Various resin systems and fabri-

Fig. 6-4 Thermoforming mold made of aluminum needle–epoxy binder cast tooling compound. Accurate reproduction of the most intricate details is easily achieved with this tooling material. Vacuum holes are easily drilled through thin surface layer of high-temperature epoxy gel coat. (*U.S. Gypsum Co.*)

TABLE 6-1 Life Expectancy of High-temperature Plastic Lay-up Mandrels and Bonding Assembly Jigs

Max. cure temp., °F	Max. cure pressure, psi	Min. vacuum, inches Hg	Anticipated no. of cycles
255	50	20	300–350
285	0	20	500–550
330	80	20	300–400
360	55	20	150–200
375	55	20	150–200

NOTE: Minor repair may be required during the anticipated life due to normal abuse. Assessment for major rework/rebuild should be made after anticipated number of cycles have been completed.

cation techniques were used. The information should only be regarded as a general guideline in determining the suitability of high-temperature plastic tooling for specific requirements.

Advantages and Disadvantages of High-temperature Plastic Tools

There has been a natural reluctance for some firms to accept high-temperature plastic tools as a substitute for metal tooling. The term "natural reluctance" is used because it was natural to be skeptical about a tooling media for which there was limited physical property data and very little use data on which to base a decision. In its early stages, high-temperature plastic was only utilized as a last resort when other forms of tooling had proven unsuccessful or too expensive. Consequently, high-temperature plastic tools were only used as interim or short-run tooling. This usage enabled some companies to select appropriate tooling materials, standardize their tool fabrication procedures, and generate data on the performance of high-temperature plastic tools in a variety of production processes. This has led to the recognition of some significant advantages of high-temperature plastic tooling over other types of tooling.

Lower Total Tooling Cost High-temperature plastic tools can be laminated or cast to finished dimensions, eliminating the need for expensive machining or handworking to contour. Plastic tool fabrication equipment is relatively inexpensive. Personnel in the lower pay grades can fabricate high-temperature plastic tools when properly supervised.

Shorter Lead Time High-temperature plastic tools can be laminated or cast to complex configurations in a single operation, eliminating many of the operations normally required for fabricating metal tools. This enables the complete tool to be fabricated within a single shop. Flow time on high-temperature plastic tool fabrication can be reduced to a few days.

Dimensional Stability High-temperature plastic tools remain stable after a number of cycles at elevated temperatures. They can be either laminated or cast net to close tolerances. Critical lines can be held to within a few thousandths of an inch. The ease with which plastic tools can be made directly from splashes made from master models assures excellent tool and part coordination.

It should be noted that, at this writing, high-temperature plastic tools have found only limited application in the processes usually associated with high-volume production (injection molding, compression molding, and blow molding). Because of the short cycles usually employed in these processes the low thermal conductivity of plastics has been a distinct drawback. Plastic dies have been used, however, to produce prototype parts by these processes.

Summary

High-temperature plastic tools can effectively compete with metal tooling for a variety of aircraft and aerospace applications. Until recently, high-temperature plastic tooling was used on an interim basis only for the applications described in this chapter. Through improved resin formulation and improved fabrication techniques, it is now being used as production tooling. When proper materials are selected and good fabrication techniques are employed, substantial reductions in tooling costs can be realized through the use of high-temperature plastic tools.

SELECTION OF PROPER MATERIALS

Normally, the material selected for fabrication of a high-temperature plastic tool will be an epoxy laminating or casting resin. In order to achieve optimum physical properties, these materials will require curing at elevated temperatures. Some of these materials gel, or "B stage," at room temperature and later develop heat resistance in an oven post-cure. Normal tooling procedures call for "soaking" the tool in an oven at a temperature 50°F above the intended use temperature.

The first consideration in selecting an epoxy tooling resin system should be the physical properties at elevated temperatures. Tables 6-2, 6-3, and 6-4 provide some typical physical properties of high-temperature epoxy tooling resin compounds. All the major tooling resin formulators have resin systems of these types and are able to assist in selecting the formulation most suitable to individual needs.

The second consideration should be the ease with which a tool can

TABLE 6-2 Typical Physical Properties of High-temperature Epoxy Laminates*

Shrinkage, in./in.	0.00014
Hardness, Shore D:	
75°F	93
500°F	82
Flexural strength, psi:	
75°F	44,000
500°F	6,800
Flexural modulus, psi $\times 10^6$:	
75°F	2.4
500°F	0.004
Deflection temperature, °F	578
Continuous operating temperature, °F	400
Coefficient of linear thermal expansion, in./in./°F $\times 10^{-5}$	0.592

* 12 plies 1500 glass cloth, Volan A finish, cure prescribed by the resin formulator.

be fabricated with the selected resin system. In this regard, close coordination should be maintained with tooling shop personnel. A tooling resin system may have excellent physical properties, but could have poor handling characteristics. The use of such a resin system will only increase tooling costs and will have a detrimental effect on tool quality. Again, optimum handling characteristics should be discussed with the

TABLE 6-3 Typical Physical Properties of High-temperature Epoxy Castings

Shrinkage, in./in.	0.003
Hardness, Shore D:	
75°F	85
500°F	75
Compressive strength, psi:	
75°F	25,000
500°F	8,000
Flexural strength, psi:	
75°F	8,500
500°F	5,000
Viscosity, centipoises:	
75°F	7–30,000
Coefficient of linear thermal expansion, in./in./°F $\times 10^{-5}$	2.5–2.7
Deflection temperature	400°F
Bond strength, psi, 75°F	2,000
Continuous operating temperature	325–350°F

TABLE 6-4 Typical Physical Properties of Aluminum Needle–Epoxy Binder Cast Tooling

Shrinkage, inches/inch	0.006
Compressive strength, psi:	
70°F	4,900
400°F	3,400
500°F	2,700
Maximum use temperature, °F	500
Coefficient of thermal expansion, inches/inch/°C $\times 10^{-5}$	3.0
Suitable for continuous service, °F (at pressures below 100 psi)	up to 450
Specific heat, g-cal/g/°C	0.22

tooling resin formulator. Some physical properties may have to be sacrificed in order to achieve good handling characteristics.

Generally, the size of the tool will dictate whether it should be laminated or cast. Normally, larger tools are laminated in order to minimize weight and to make the tool easier to handle during production usage (see Figure 6-5). Small tools with complex shapes or details are generally cast.

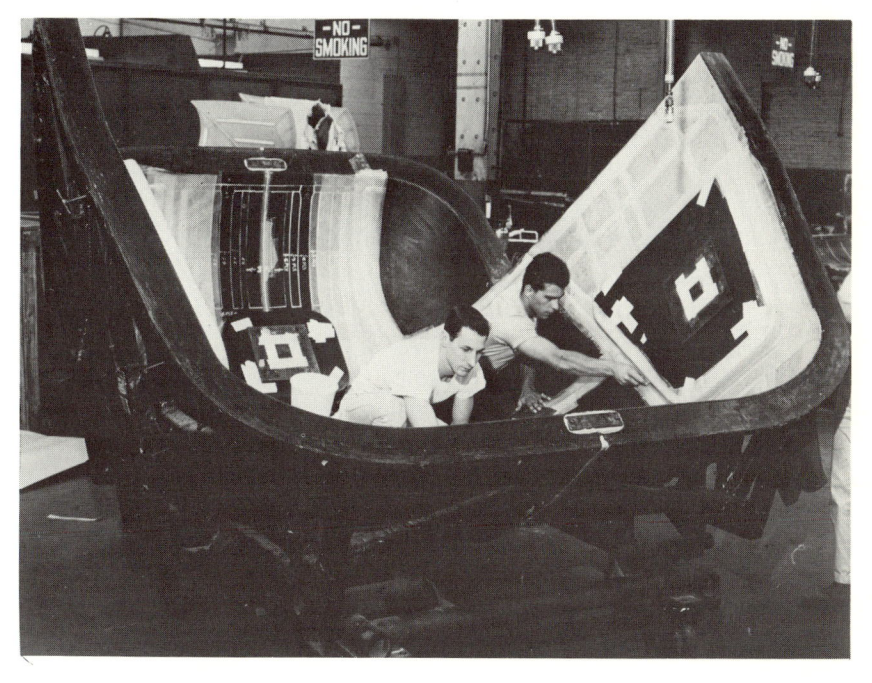

Fig. 6-5 High-temperature epoxy laminated tool used to produce fiber-glass-honeycomb helicopter canopies at Sikorsky Aircraft. (*U.S. Gypsum Co.*)

PLASTIC-FACED PLASTER PATTERNS

When high-temperature plastic tooling first began to gain acceptance as a tooling medium, one of the biggest problems encountered was surface defects and cure inhibition caused by transfer of moisture from the pattern to the tool during postcure of the tool at elevated temperatures. The large majority of high-temperature plastic tools were fabricated using plaster transfers taken from master models as patterns. It was necessary to dry the plaster splash for 2 or 3 days in an air-circulating oven prior to using it as a pattern for a high-temperature plastic tool. If the pattern was too large for any available ovens, the plaster pattern would frequently be dried at room temperature for as long as 10 days in order to allow excess moisture to evaporate. This system had two main disadvantages: (1) loss of several days flow time and (2) the possibility that residual moisture still existed in the plaster, and would have a detrimental effect on the high-temperature tool fabricated upon it.

The successful development of hydrophobic epoxy tooling compounds has virtually eliminated high-temperature tooling problems related to moisture-caused degradation. The hydrophobic epoxies are those epoxies that are capable of curing in the presence of moisture. Prior to the introduction of hydrophobic epoxies, toolmakers were limited to the use of epoxy compounds that were very sensitive to water or moisture. Contact with water generally inhibited the cure of the epoxy to such an extent that degradation of the physical properties occurred.

The hydrophobic epoxy compounds were first introduced as a thixotropic gel coat capable of withstanding exposure up to 380°F for up to 8 hours. It was found that when the hydrophobic gel coat was applied to the model and backed up with gypsum cement and hemp, it produced a pattern with a durable epoxy surface which acted as a vapor barrier between the pattern and the high-temperature plastic tool fabricated upon it. Figure 6-6 shows a cross-sectional view of a plastic-faced plaster pattern.

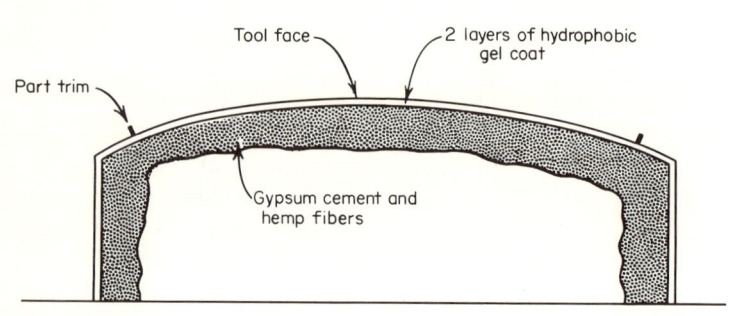

Fig. 6-6 Cross section of plastic-faced plaster pattern.

Although plastic-faced plasters have been primarily used as patterns for high-temperature plastic tools, they are now finding use as Keller models and as short-run lay-up tools for prototype part fabrication.

The advantages of plastic-faced plaster patterns can be listed as follows:

1. The epoxy face provides an effective barrier, preventing moisture or steam from emanating from the plaster pattern and ruining the high-temperature tool being fabricated upon it.
2. The epoxy face provides a more durable surface than ordinary plaster; consequently it holds sharp corners and edges better than plaster. This is a significant advantage when used as a Keller pattern.
3. The plastic surface facilitates easier release of the plastic tool or part.
4. Reduced tool fabrication flow time is possible, since a plastic-faced plaster pattern does not need to be ovendried.

Procedure for Fabricating Plastic-faced Plaster Tools

The following procedure is recommended for fabricating a plastic-faced plaster tool or pattern. It is assumed that the model surface has been properly sealed.

1. Apply parting agent to the surface of the model, in accordance with the manufacturer's instructions. The type of parting agent most suitable for the application will vary with the type of model surface material (see Chapter 1 of this text).
2. Calculate the amount of hydrophobic resin and hardener required to apply a $\frac{1}{16}$-inch coat to the model surface. As a rule of thumb, 70 grams per square foot will provide a $\frac{1}{16}$-inch gel coat.
3. The resin and hardener are weighed in the proper ratio and mixed thoroughly. Batches under 2,000 grams may be mixed by hand for 5 minutes. Larger batches should be mixed for 3 minutes with a mechanical mixer.
4. The gel coat should be brushed or squeegeed onto the model surface. It is advisable to use reusable nylon brushes with the hairs embedded in epoxy to avoid bristles pulling out and becoming a defect on the tool surface. The thickness of the gel coat should be as uniform as possible ($\frac{1}{16}$ to $\frac{1}{32}$ inch); heavy concentrations in low spots and in corners should be avoided.
5. The gel coat is allowed to cure until it has reached a tacky stage. This can be determined by pressing a finger into the resin in the excess

area beyond the part trim line. The material has reached a tacky stage when you are able to leave your fingerprint without resin sticking to your finger. Normally a hydrophobic gel coat will take approximately 45 minutes at room temperature to reach a tacky stage.

6. A second batch of hydrophobic gel coat is then weighed and mixed. The second layer should be slightly thicker than the first gel coat; consequently 90 grams per square foot should be used to calculate the amount of material required. The second batch is then buttered onto the first gel coat.

7. Gypsum cement soaked in hemp fibers is *immediately* applied to the second layer of hydrophobic gel coat. To ensure a good bond between the gypsum cement and the gel coat, this step should be carried out within 15 minutes after completion of step no. 6.

8. The gypsum cement and hemp fibers should be built up to a thickness of 1 to 2 inches, depending on the size of the tool. Generally, a thickness of 1 inch is sufficient for tools less than 4 feet in length.

9. The tool is allowed to cure at room temperature for approximately 6 hours. After that time, the tool can be removed from the model and inspected. After tool cleanup and the application of parting agent, the plastic-faced plaster tool is ready for use.

HIGH-TEMPERATURE PLASTIC TOOL FABRICATION METHODS

There are many schools of thought with regard to the best method of fabricating a high-temperature plastic tool. Many competent toolmakers who work in plastic believe, for example, that a high-temperature laminate should be made using 181-type glass cloth only; others use 1500-type cloth only; while still others use a combination of 181 cloth and 1500 cloth, backed up with a still thicker weave. There are many proponents of autoclave cure of high-temperature tools, while the large majority of toolmakers find oven postcure satisfactory for their applications.

It is not the author's intention to thrash through all the various schools of thought and try to select or to recommend the *best* or *only true* method. A survey of high-temperature tool usage throughout the United States indicates that tools made by slightly different methods are performing satisfactorily, and have produced a number of good parts. It is apparent that the end usage of the tool has a bearing on the fabrication procedure that should be employed. For example, a vacuum-forming tool being used at 200°F can be fabricated by a completely different method than a bonding tool used in an autoclave at 400°F.

With many of these variables in mind, the author has decided not to attempt to lay down an ironclad rule as to what is the only or best method of fabricating high-temperature plastic tools. Rather, the author is outlining fabrication procedures that have been successful in producing tools for aircraft and aerospace requirements. This will provide the reader with fabrication techniques which have a "good track record." As the individual or shop gains skill and experience, variations can be attempted on a limited basis.

The selection of proper materials is extremely important. It can determine whether you will be successful or unsuccessful in fabricating high-temperature plastic tools. The typical physical properties listed in this chapter should be considered as minimum requirements for your high-temperature tooling needs. You will find several resin formulators offering resin systems that easily meet these requirements. After you have found a resin system with acceptable physical properties, obtain a sample and evaluate the material's handling characteristics. The high physical properties will not be of much value to you, if you have to double your labor expenditure in order to achieve them.

Before committing a tooling program to a resin system and tool fabrication procedure, make some experimental tools. These tools should be checked for dimensional accuracy after postcure, and should then be cycled at least 50 times through simulated or actual production usage. In doing this, you will learn several things: (1) suitability of the resin system, (2) verification of the tool fabrication procedure, (3) heat-up and cool-down rates, (4) durability data on the tool based on requirements for tool repair and rework, and (5) acceptability of the tool design criteria.

Once you have settled on a tool fabrication procedure, make certain that all the shop personnel strictly adhere to the established procedure. If early experience indicates that the established procedure has certain deficiencies that need correcting, you should make the necessary revisions in the procedure and again ensure that everyone is following it. If this is not done, you will soon find that every tool fabricator is trying his own innovation designed to improve tool quality. The result will be that you will be confronted with numerous tool failures, and no record of the variations on which you can base an analysis of the problem.

The high-temperature tool fabrication procedures outlined in the following section of this chapter have been successfully used to produce literally hundreds of high-temperature plastic tools. While various companies have inserted slight variations into the procedures, the basic procedures outlined in this chapter are widely used, and should guarantee a good measure of success.

PROCEDURE FOR FABRICATING A HIGH-TEMPERATURE EPOXY LAMINATED TOOL

It is assumed in this section that a high-temperature epoxy laminated tool will be fabricated upon a plastic-faced plaster pattern. The surface of the pattern should be inspected to ensure that it is perfect and without blemish. If flaws are detected, they should be repaired. It is much easier to repair the pattern than it is to rework the completed high-temperature tool.

The surface of the pattern should be coated with at least three layers of parting agent. Be sure that the parting agent selected is suitable for use at the maximum temperature of the oven postcure.

The use of a high-temperature epoxy gel coat is recommended. The gel coat selected should be compatible with the laminating resin system to be used. A gel coat provides a hard working surface which can be sanded should any surface imperfections appear on the tool. If a gel coat is not used, any sanding will wear into the first layer of glass cloth and create burrs on the tool face. The use of a gel coat permits the tool surface to be sanded with wet-and-dry sandpaper and buffed to a high gloss finish.

The gel coat should be weighed and mixed with the hardener in the proper ratio. Brush or squeegee the gel coat onto the pattern surface. The thickness of the gel coat should be between $\frac{1}{16}$ and $\frac{1}{32}$ inch. It is advisable to work the material a second time in order to eliminate any possibility of entrapped air. The gel coat is then allowed to become tacky. The time required will vary depending on the resin system used. The material supplier will be able to tell you how long the material requires to become tacky.

While the gel coat is becoming tacky, prepare the glass cloth and laminating resin required to laminate four layers of the tool. When you have calculated the amount of glass cloth required, cut it to fit the tool. At that point, weigh the glass cloth. The weight of laminating resin and hardener used should equal the weight of the glass cloth. Normally, 1500 tooling cloth with a Volan A finish is suitable.

When the gel coat has become tacky, the high-temperature laminating resin and hardener are mixed in the proper ratio. A coat of laminating compound is then brushed onto the gel coat, and a layer of cloth applied onto the resin. With a squeegee, work the resin up through the glass cloth. Ensure that the cloth is thoroughly impregnated and tight to the surface of the tool. The first few plies of glass cloth may be put on in small pieces to reduce the possibility of bridging in corners and joggles.

Each of the three successive layers is applied in the same manner, always working the resin up through the cloth. The glass cloth weave should be rotated 45 degrees for each successive layer. A peel ply of 1528 glass cloth is applied dry to the fourth layer of the tool. A layer of silicone-impregnated glass cloth is then applied as a bleeder, and a vacuum bag applied to the tool. After vacuum has been applied, the excess air should be swept out of the laminate. This can be accomplished by applying petroleum jelly or some other lubricant to the vacuum bag surface, and sweeping the entrapped air out with a squeegee. The tool should be allowed to gel at room temperature for a minimum of 12 hours.

After the tool has gelled, the vacuum bag and peel ply are removed, and 12 layers of 1500 tooling cloth and laminating resin are applied in the same manner as described earlier. After the last layer has been applied, the peel ply, bleeder cloth, and vacuum bag are again applied to the tool. The tool is allowed to gel at room temperature and is then given the oven postcure prescribed by the resin manufacturer.

After the tool has cooled down to room temperature and the vacuum bag, bleeders, and peel ply have been removed, it is now ready to have the reinforcement structure installed. The most common method of reinforcing high-temperature epoxy laminated tools is by means of an eggcrate structure attached to the backside of the tool face (see Figure 6-7).

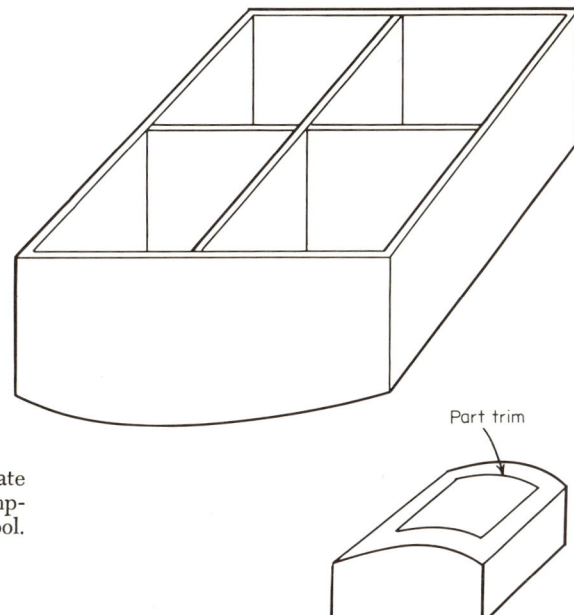

Fig. 6-7 Typical eggcrate reinforcement of high-temperature epoxy laminated tool.

160   Plastic Tooling

The eggcrate structure is normally made of ⅜-inch-thick laminate of the same materials used in the tool face, or of 1-inch-thick high-temperature honeycomb panels. Metal reinforcement is *never* used on high-temperature epoxy laminated tools. Experience has shown that the difference in the thermal coefficient of expansion of the two materials results in warpage of the tool.

The following procedure is commonly used for fabricating the eggcrate reinforcing structure for a high-temperature laminated tool. The layout of the reinforcing structure is scribed onto the back of the tool face. Depending on the tool size and configuration, the eggcrate pattern may be from 8 to 12 inches apart and a minimum of 8 inches in height. Templates are then made of either cardboard or plywood to fit to the back of the tool where the eggcrate structure is to be located. The templates are then used as patterns to cut the stiffeners. The stiffeners should be carefully cut so that they fit the back of the tool to within ⅛ inch. Gaps in excess of ⅛ inch can cause depressions on the tool face in the areas of the gaps. The eggcrate structure is bonded to the back of the tool using a paste mix of milled glass fibers and high-temperature laminating compound.

After the paste mix has gelled, two strips of 1500 tooling cloth impregnated with high-temperature laminating compound are applied over the paste mix.

The paste mix and bonding strips are allowed to cure overnight at room temperature. The tool is then cured in the oven to complete the cure of the bond between the eggcrate structure and the tool face. Normally the same oven cycle that was used to cure the tool face is used for this purpose. When the oven cycle has been completed, the oven should be turned off and the tool allowed to cool slowly in the

Fig. 6-8 Lay-up mandrel made of high-temperature epoxy laminating resin used at Goodyear Aircraft Company to make fiber glass wing tips for a jet fighter. (*Furane Plastics, Inc.*)

Fig. 6-9 Lay-up mold used at Grumman Aircraft Company to produce FRP radome housing. This high-temperature epoxy laminated tool has been used to produce over 500-piece parts. (*U.S. Gypsum Co.*)

Fig. 6-10 Thermoforming molds fabricated with high-temperature epoxy laminating compound and high-heat fiber glass tubing reinforcement. Note size and construction details. (*Ren Plastics, Inc.*)

162   Plastic Tooling

oven until it reaches room temperature. Attempts to accelerate the cooling down of the tool may result in tool warpage.

When the tool has reached room temperature, it may be removed from the model and inspected. The bottom of the tool is leveled as required. Fittings for handling and vacuum are installed per tool design or to meet requirements. Normally, if vacuum buttons are used, one vacuum button is installed for every 4 feet of tool surface area.

If the preceding procedure is followed in detail and resin systems recommended in this chapter are used, the resultant tool will be capable of repeated service in an autoclave environment at temperatures up to 400°F.

a

b

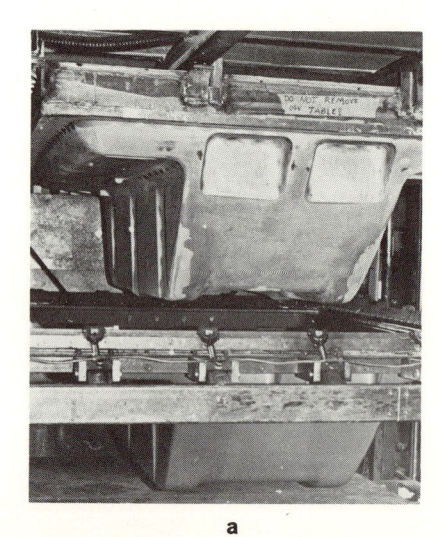

Fig. 6-11 Fabrication of an all-terrain vehicle body. (*a*) Thermoforming mold fabricated of high-temperature epoxy laminating resin is mounted in vacuum forming press. (*b*) Finished lower section of Amphicat body shell is removed from the mold. Shell is made of ABS thermoplastic sheet and is 60 inches wide and 80 inches long. (*c*) Thermoformed Amphicats parts ready for palletizing and shipment to the assembler. (*d*) Completely assembled ATV is rugged and lightweight. All-terrain vehicles are equally at home on the beach, in the water, or on a snow-covered slope. (*Ren Plastics, Inc.*)

164   Plastic Tooling

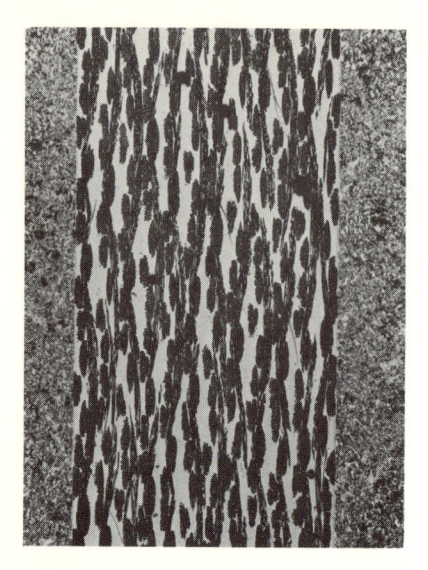

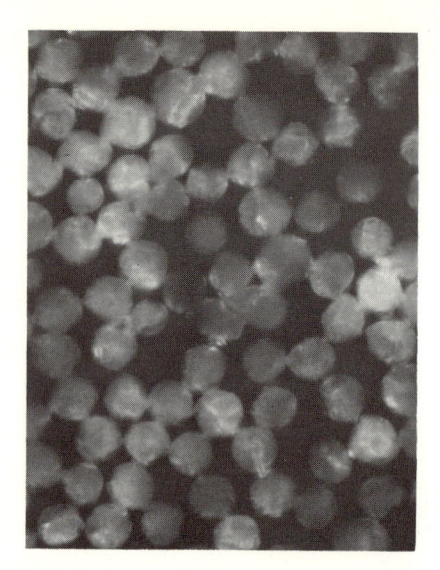

Fig. 6-12 Photomicrograph of high-temperature epoxy laminate, one at 25X and one at 1500X, illustrating complete impregnation and absence of voids in the laminate. (*Furane Plastics, Inc.*)

Procedure for Fabricating High-temperature Epoxy Cast Tools

Frequently, in the case of small tools, it is more economical to cast them than to laminate them. The procedure for casting a tool using high-temperature epoxy casting resin is quite similar to the procedures employed for making tools with room-temperature-curing casting compounds. However, there are a few techniques that have a significant effect on the quality of the high-temperature cast tool. The following brief procedure describes some of these significant points.

Firstly, plastic-faced plaster patterns should always be used when making high-temperature epoxy cast tools. The patterns should be designed so that the plastic face extends down the sides and to the bottom of the pattern (see Figure 6-13). If this is not done, steam will penetrate through the space between the dike board and the pattern and will have a detrimental effect on the cast epoxy tool.

Secondly, the dike boards should be constructed of metal, such as aluminum. This serves the dual purpose of facilitating easy release and eliminating the possibility of moisture from a wood dike board affecting the high-temperature epoxy resin.

When the metal dike boards have been positioned, the pattern and the dike boards are coated with parting agent. It is recommended that three coats of parting agent be used. The first two coats should be buffed; the third coat should be applied and not buffed.

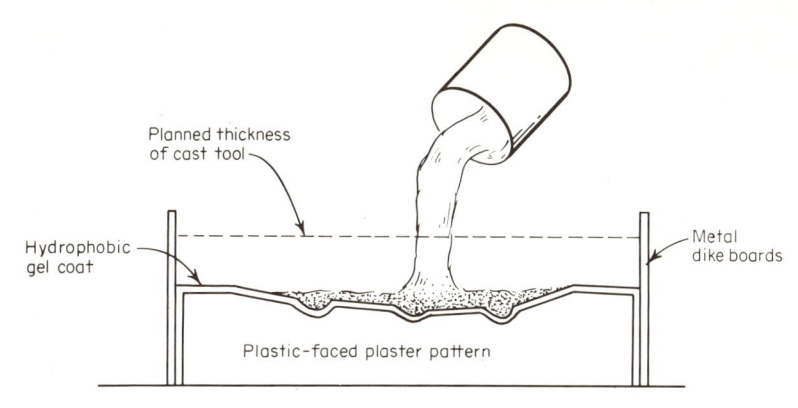

Fig. 6-13 Setup for making a high-temperature epoxy casting.

The amount of resin and hardener required is then calculated and weighed out in the correct proportions. The mixing and pouring of the high-temperature casting compound are carried out exactly the same as those operations for room-temperature mass casting compounds. It is recommended that the reader refer to Chapter 4 for mixing and pouring techniques.

After the pouring has been completed, the tool is allowed to cure overnight, or a minimum of 12 hours at room temperature. It is then placed in the oven and postcured according to the oven cycle prescribed by the resin manufacturer. When the oven cycle has been completed,

Fig. 6-14 A group of plastic injection molds and prototype parts. These molds were cast with high-temperature epoxy casting resin. (*Ren Plastics, Inc.*)

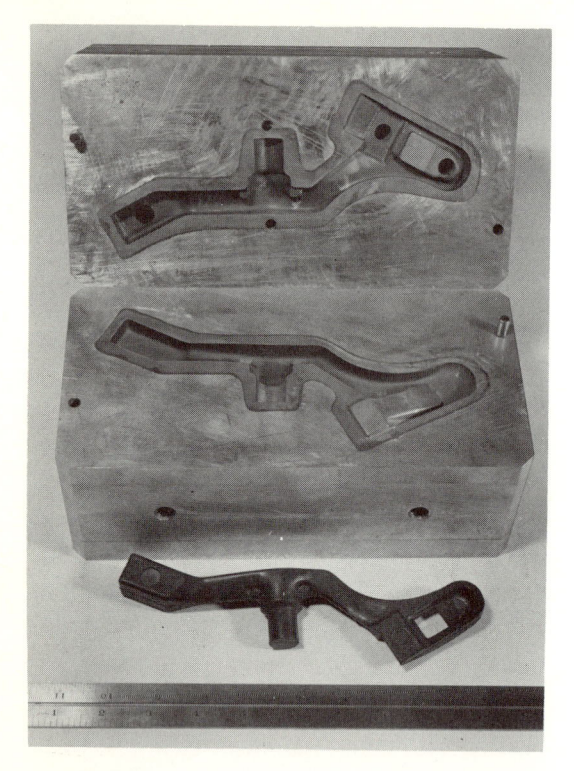

Fig. 6-15 Prototype injection mold constructed of high-temperature epoxy casting resin in an aluminum case. Note prototype part in foreground. (*Ren Plastics, Inc.*)

the oven should be turned off and the tool allowed to reach room temperature slowly, with the oven door closed. A sudden change of temperature may cause cracking due to thermal shock. This is particularly true in the case of large mass castings.

Fabrication of Aluminum Needle–Epoxy Binder Tooling

Aluminum needle–epoxy binder tooling is widely used for thermoforming molds. While the materials are more expensive than conventional high-temperature plastic tooling materials, the labor savings possible usually offset the material costs, particularly on small tools with complex configurations.

Aluminum needle–epoxy binder tooling consists of a high-temperature epoxy gel coat backed up by small aluminum needles bonded together with a high-temperature epoxy resin. The needles come in a polyethylene bag in which a predetermined amount of powdered high-temperature epoxy binder has been placed.

The tool fabrication procedure is quite simple. A plastic-faced plaster pattern is constructed in the same basic design as for a high-temperature casting. Metal dike boards are placed around the pattern, and a suitable parting agent is applied to both the pattern and the dike boards.

A high-temperature epoxy gel coat is applied to the surface of the pattern and allowed to progress just a little beyond the tacky stage. At that point in time, a second layer of gel coat is applied. *Immediately,* the bag containing the aluminum needles and the powdered epoxy binder is kneaded to ensure that the components are evenly distributed. The contents of the bag are then poured into the mold cavity and tamped into position. It is suggested that a layer of approximately ½ inch be applied over the entire bottom of the mold cavity and tamped into position. This procedure is repeated in ½-inch increments until the mold cavity is completely filled. The tool is then placed in an oven and given the cure cycle prescribed by the resin manufacturer.

In the case of a thermoforming mold, the toolmaker needs only to drill vacuum holes through the gel coat, since the aluminum needle–epoxy binder matrix is porous (see Figure 6-4).

While this high-temperature plastic tooling concept is unique and

Fig. 6-16 Left—prototype injection molded tile made in epoxy–aluminum needle high-temperature plastic tool. Right—prototype compression mold of epoxy–aluminum needle construction. (*U.S. Gypsum Co.*)

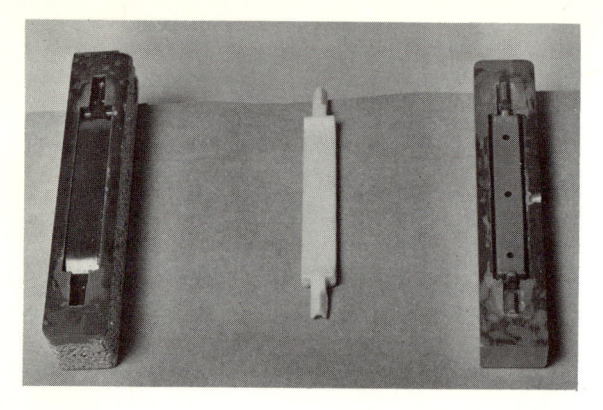

Fig. 6-17 Prototype injection mold constructed of high-temperature epoxy gel coat backed up with epoxy–aluminum needle binder. Injection molded part made in this prototype mold is in center of photo. (*U.S. Gypsum Co.*)

has been used to advantage for thermoforming molds, it has definite limitations that should be pointed out. First, a tool of this type is not durable. It is prone to damage on corners and protrusions where the epoxy binder–aluminum needles may not have been sufficiently tamped in place. Second, because the gel coat is only approximately $1/16$ inch thick, it is prone to damage by puncture. Third, a tool of any size becomes quite heavy when constructed of this material. With these thoughts in mind, it is obvious that tools made of aluminum needle–epoxy binder construction are excellent for short-run thermoforming requirements, prototype blow-molding molds and lay-up mandrels, and prototype shell coreboxes for foundry applications. Using this concept, it is possible to construct molds with complex configurations at very low cost. The tool engineer should recognize both the advantages and the limitations of this concept in order to attain the benefits and to avoid the shortcomings of aluminum needle–epoxy binder tooling.

CHAPTER SEVEN

Integrally Heated Plastic Tools

INTRODUCTION

An *integrally heated plastic tool,* as the name implies, is a plastic tool which has had a heating element embedded into it during the fabrication of the tool. When the resin has cured, the heating element becomes an integral part of the tool. High-temperature epoxy laminated tools have been the most successful to date for this application. The most successful heating methods have been electricity and steam. This chapter will discuss some of the applications of integrally heated plastic tools, as well as the materials and fabrication techniques employed.

The development of integrally heated plastic tools was stimulated by the tremendous increase in the number of plastic parts cured at elevated temperatures, accompanied by an increase in the size of the parts being made. Many manufacturers were suddenly confronted with the problem of having ovens or autoclaves with not enough capacity to cure a high volume of parts.

It became obvious that one solution to the problem would be the successful development of tooling which would provide its own heat. While this would not solve the problem with regard to autoclave-cured parts, it would have a considerable impact on tooling for parts being cured at elevated temperature under vacuum only. Consequently, techniques and materials for fabricating integrally heated plastic tools were developed. Tools of this type have been used successfully in a number of applications, including:

1. Bonding assembly tools for large fiber glass reinforced plastic radomes
2. Lay-up tools for complex-shaped plastic parts
3. Thermoforming molds
4. Mat molding dies
5. Plastisol slush molding

The utilization of integrally heated plastic tools has enabled some manufacturers to produce parts which they could not have otherwise produced with their existing equipment and facilities.

Advantages of Integrally Heated Tools

There are several advantages of integrally heated plastic tools that should be pointed out. The obvious advantage of integrally heated plastic tools is the elimination of the requirement for an oven. However, when tools of this type have been placed into production service, other unanticipated advantages have appeared.

For example, when an integrally heated plastic tool was used to produce a large FRP radome, it was discovered that the part could be laminated, vacuum bagged, cured, and removed from the mold without moving the tool. Up to that time, the manufacturer's standard procedure was to laminate the part in the lay-up area, transport the tool and the part to a bagging area where a plastic vacuum bag was applied, and move the tool to a staging area where it awaited its turn to go into the oven. After it had been cured, it was moved from the oven into another area where the vacuum bag was removed and the part separated from the mold. Consequently, the manufacturer realized that not only had he saved himself the cost of a larger oven, he had also saved the labor required to move the tool from one work area to another, and had made better utilization of floor space. Because the part could be cured on the integrally heated tool as soon as the vacuum bagging operation was completed, he found that he could almost double his production rates. While conventional tools were "logjammed" at the oven awaiting cure, the integrally heated tool was unaffected.

The use of integrally heated plastic tools frequently results in improved part quality. This is particularly true on large parts with complex configurations. It is very difficult to make tools of this type heat up and cool down uniformly in an oven because the size and shape of the part interferes with the air circulation patterns and causes unequal heat distribution within the oven.

Uniform heat distribution is particularly critical when a plastic composite structure is being cured. For example, in the case of an FRP–honeycomb sandwich part, the resin is required to flow and form a fillet, which, when cured, bonds the FRP to the honeycomb. If heat is not applied uniformly, areas of low bond strength within the part can result. Integrally heated plastic tools have been used to good advantage in instances such as this. Tools with as much as 50 square feet of tooling surface have been able to maintain a uniform temperature range of $\pm 10°F$ while operating in the 250 to 325°F range. This compares favorably with the temperature bands of large, complex-shaped tools cured in ovens.

Types of Integrally Heated Plastic Tools

An analysis of the various types of integrally heated plastic tools in service in various industries throughout the United States indicates that two types have proven most successful:

1. High-temperature epoxy laminates heated by embedded electrical elements
2. High-temperature epoxy laminates heated by embedded steam tubing

It should be noted that attempts to make integrally heated cast plastic tools have been generally unsuccessful. Cracking has been the major problem encountered with integrally heated cast epoxy tools. This has been attributed to the fact that cast epoxy tools have a high mass and a low thermal conductivity. This makes it difficult to heat the entire tool uniformly. The plastic nearest the heating elements expands, while the plastic further from the heating elements expands at a much slower rate. The stresses set up by the difference in thermal expansion cause the tool to crack. While integrally heated cast tools have been used successfully, the successes have come on relatively low-profile, low-mass tools less than 12 inches in length.

The remainder of this chapter will be devoted to discussing in detail the materials, design considerations, and fabrication techniques involved in making integrally heated high-temperature epoxy laminated tools.

LAMINATED PLASTIC TOOLS HEATED BY EMBEDDED ELECTRICAL ELEMENTS

By far the most commonly used type of integrally heated plastic tool is the high-temperature epoxy laminated tool heated by electrical elements such as Briskeat heating mesh* embedded within the laminate. In considering both electrical elements and steam as heating methods, some distinct differences become apparent. Because of the uniformity possible with layers of fiber glass, the distance of the electrical heating mesh from the tool face can be very closely controlled. This greatly contributes to the uniformity of temperature over the tool face. Electrical heating elements can be used for any tool configuration regardless of its complexity. As a general rule, the more complex the configuration, the more difficult it is to position steam tubes in a pattern that will produce a uniform temperature band over the entire tool face. Thus, electrical elements as a heating method have another distinct advantage when complex configurations are being considered. Another point which the author feels contributes to the popularity of electrical heating elements is the fact that wattages as a function of the desired operating voltage and temperature can be closely calculated. This eliminates the guesswork involved in determining the number and locations of steam tubes.

Design Considerations

Three basic considerations must be made when designing a high-temperature plastic tool heated by electrical heating mesh embedded within the laminate:

1. The design of the tool face in relationship to the reinforcing structure
2. The location of the heating mesh
3. The position of the heating mesh within the laminate

In considering the design of the tool and its reinforcing structure, it becomes apparent that the tool may become as much as 250°F hotter than the structure reinforcing it. Consequently, the tool face will expand more than its reinforcing structure. Unless the tool is properly designed, stresses will be created between the tool face and the reinforcement which could result in tool failure or warpage.

Whenever possible, the tool should consist of a laminated shell which nests in a cradle-type framework. The framework should be designed to allow for expansion of the tool face during the cure cycle without creating stresses. The configuration of most radomes and other highly contoured shapes associated with aircraft and aerospace makes the utilization of this concept possible. This is particularly true with the radome configuration shown in Figure 7-1, since the conical structure is self-

---

* A registered trademark of Briscoe Manufacturing Co., Columbus, Ohio.

reinforcing. Large tools with very little relief can be reinforced by an eggcrate structure 6 inches in height and spaced on 24-inch centers. The tool can then be nested in a metal framework similar to the one in Figure 7-1.

The location of the heating mesh is extremely important. In most tools, a uniform temperature on the tool surface is required. The standard flexible electrical elements used for this purpose consist of nickel wire wound to the desired watt density and voltage, insulated with braided fibrous glass filaments and woven into flat, open-mesh tapes approximately 2 inches wide and 0.040 inch thick. Uniform temperature is usually achieved by dividing the intended area on the tool into imaginary rectangular areas of equal width corresponding to the width of the heating tapes.

Inasmuch as these tapes provide uniform heat, the configuration of the tool must be taken into consideration when determining the location of the tapes. For example, if a tool has a 90-degree bend inside the part area, tapes placed adjacent to one another may create a "hot spot" in the tool at that location. This situation only occurs on sharply configurated tools or on 90-degree bends. Experience has indicated that the large radii on most aircraft body skins provide a gradual enough change of contour to allow heating mesh to be positioned uniformly without creating areas of high heat concentration. It should be ap-

Fig. 7-1 Typical design of laminated radome tool heated by electrical elements. Note that reinforcing structures allow the tool to expand and contract during the cure cycle. (*Briscoe Mfg. Co.*)

174   Plastic Tooling

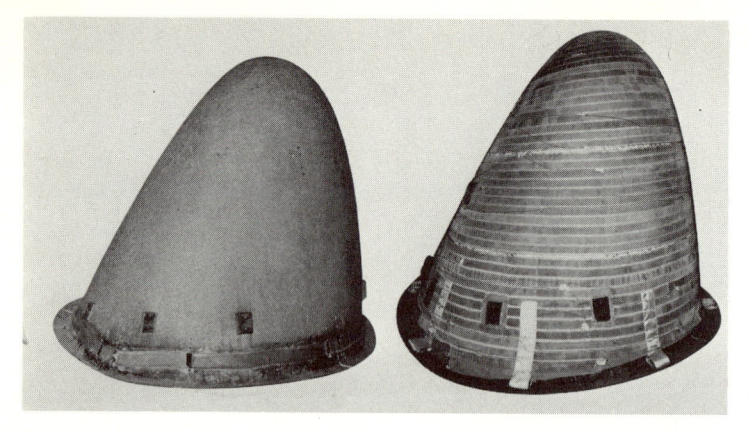

Fig. 7-2 Briskeat mesh heater for plastic mold of aircraft nose cone.

parent to the reader that the location of the heating mesh should be determined after careful consideration of the tool configuration.

When a part is being cured on an integrally heated tool located in an open bay, the dissipation of heat into the surrounding air is an important consideration. On large, low-profile tools, the periphery of the tool can be as much as 60°F cooler than the center portion of the tool unless heat dissipation is taken into account when the tool is designed.

Generally, extending the heating tapes a minimum of 8 inches beyond the part trim line will ensure that the area within the part trim is capable of being maintained at uniform temperature (see Figure 7-5). Uniform temperature is usually considered to be ±10°F, which is within

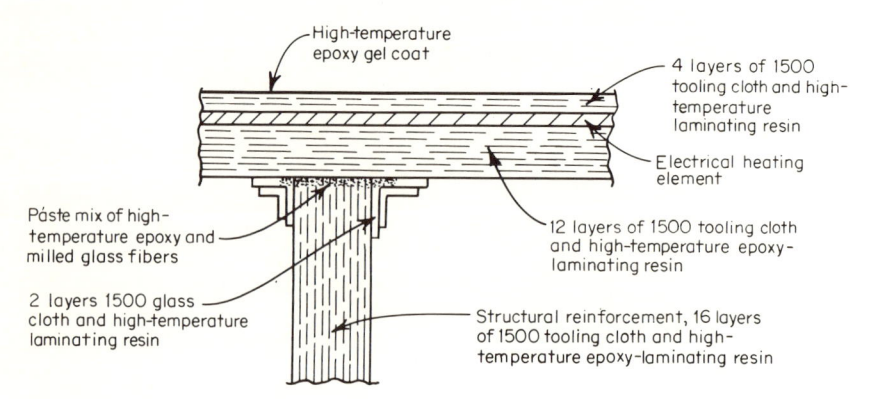

Fig. 7-3 Cross section of integrally heated high-temperature epoxy laminated tool using electrical elements as a heat source.

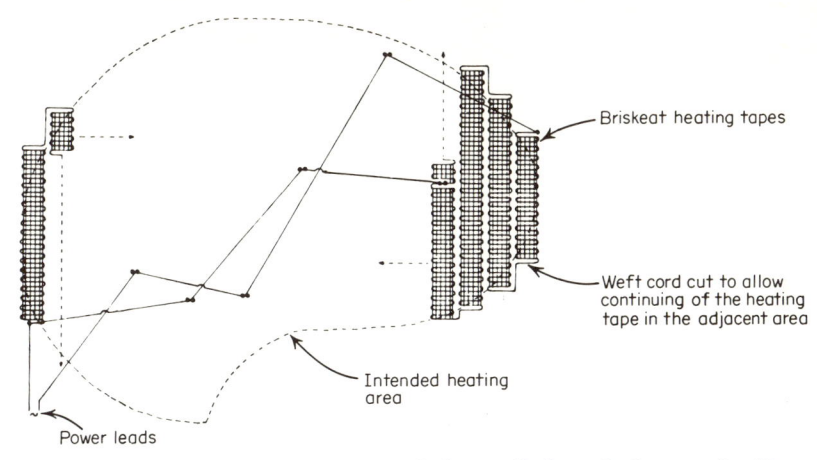

Fig. 7-4 Circuit arrangements of typical electrically heated plastic tool. Heating tapes and power leads are connected so as to effect a parallel circuit arrangement. Most of the heating tapes are purposely omitted from the sketch in order to more clearly show the connections and circuitry. (*Briscoe Mfg. Co.*)

the acceptable limits of the cure envelope for most specifications. Again, the extent to which heat dissipation must be compensated for will vary from tool to tool depending on the configuration. Until the designer becomes experienced in designing integrally heated plastic tools, it is recommended that he take advantage of the technical assistance which

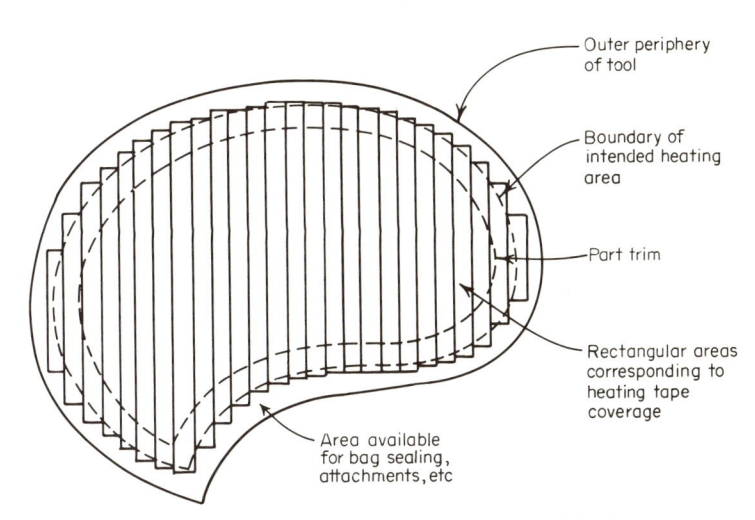

Fig. 7-5 Design considerations for integrally heated high-temperature epoxy laminated tools using electrical elements as a heat source. Tool periphery should be 12 inches beyond part trim. Heating elements should extend a minimum of 8 inches beyond part trim.

is readily available from the manufacturer of the electrical heating elements. Normally, the technical staff will provide you with assistance in:

1. Determining the most effective arrangement of heating tapes including length, width, and quantity
2. Determining the required watt density of the heating tapes to achieve the most efficient heating system
3. Selecting thermal sensing and control equipment best suited for your particular requirements
4. Providing you with recommendations on tool design based on their knowledge and experience with thermal boundary conditions and heat transfer

Tool Fabrication Procedure

The procedure for fabricating an integrally heated high-temperature epoxy laminated tool is very similar to the procedure for a conventional high-temperature laminated tool, except that the electrical elements are incorporated into the tool during the lay-up procedure. Although the technique is similar, it is appropriate to review the fabrication procedure in a general manner to ensure that the reader has a clear picture of the sequence.

The integrally heated laminated tool should be fabricated on the surface of a plastic-faced plaster transfer medium. In the interest of avoiding cumbersome detail, the author assumes that the reader is now familiar with the techniques of preparing the surface of the master model, applying parting agent, and constructing a plastic-faced plaster transfer medium. The author also assumes that the shop has a tool drawing showing the placement of the heating elements.

After the plastic-faced plaster has been checked and surface imperfections repaired as required, it is coated with a release agent capable of withstanding an elevated temperature cure. The next step is the application of a thin coat of high-temperature epoxy gel coat. The gel coat should be selected to be compatible with the high-temperature laminating resin to be used in subsequent steps. To ensure this, it is recommended that both the gel coat and the laminating resin be made by the same supplier. The gel coat should be applied evenly and thin. The thickness should be between $\frac{1}{32}$ to $\frac{1}{16}$ inch. Experience has indicated that when a high-temperature gel coat is thicker than $\frac{1}{16}$ inch, the tool surface will develop numerous cracks during production usage. Precautions taken at this point to keep the gel coat thin will pay dividends by assuring a trouble-free tooling surface in production.

After the gel coat has become tacky, four layers of 1500 fiber glass cloth and high-temperature epoxy laminating resin are applied. Care should be taken to sweep out all air bubbles and resin-rich areas. The fourth layer is followed by a generous application of high-temperature epoxy laminating resin.

At this point, the heating tapes are positioned as specified on the tool drawing. Individual heating tapes should be checked for the proper resistance before the tapes are embedded. The first heating tape is positioned so that it completely covers the first rectangular area (starting from either end). If the tape length is greater than the length of this rectangle, the weft cord is cut at the appropriate point and the heating tape is continued so that it covers the adjacent rectangular area . . . and so on, until the entire heating area is covered by heating tapes. Of course, each succeeding tape is abutted to the previous one.

Instead of this individual heating tape lay-up plan, an alternate approach is available. This entails the procurement of a heating blanket composed of the required number of heating tapes sewn together to

Fig. 7-6 Placement of heating mesh during fabrication of electrically heated laminated tool for segmented honeycomb antenna. (*Briscoe Mfg. Co.*)

form a blanket of the desired area. The embedding of such a blanket, in some instances, is quite simple and fast.

The choice of either method depends on the complexity of the heating surface. Generally for areas of complex geometry, the individual heating tape lay-up procedure is favored. On the other hand, for tools having surfaces of simple curvature, the blanket or sewn heater mesh can be incorporated. Economics enter into the choice of method since the sewn mesh is more expensive than the individual tape. Generally, the better job of uniformly covering the surface can be done by utilizing the individual tapes.

After the heating tapes have been positioned, the lead wires are allowed to protrude upward from the tool. This step is eliminated when a blanket is used because the heating tapes are already connected together electrically with the power leads sewn to the blanket and extending beyond the heating area at the desired location. Thermal sensing or control devices are sewn in at desired points with thermocouple wires sewn to the blanket and extending beyond the heating area at the desired locations. The heating tapes are then connected together at the place where they abut. In order to keep the heating tape leads free from resin during the embedding and subsequent laminating operations, it is recommended that polyethylene straws be slipped over the leads.

The next step consists of laminating two additional layers of fiber glass cloth and high-temperature laminating resin over the heating elements. A vacuum bag is then applied, and the laminate is allowed to gel overnight at room temperature.

After the tool has gelled, the vacuum bag is removed and 10 more layers of 1500 fiber glass cloth and high-temperature laminating resin are applied. This should provide a total thickness of 0.25 to 0.28 inch. The tool reinforcement is added in the same manner as indicated in the preceding chapter, and the tool is given an oven postcure in accordance with the resin manufacturer's recommendations.

The practice of using the embedded heating tapes as the heat source for the postcure cycle works very well on configurations such as radomes. It is particularly helpful when tools that are too large for existing ovens are being fabricated. If the embedded heating tapes are used to postcure the tool, it should be kept in mind that, while the embedded heating elements will adequately postcure the tool face, they do not normally effect a thorough postcure of the eggcrate reinforcing structure.

If the tool has a high-temperature epoxy laminated eggcrate structure on which it relies for support, the two components should be postcured separately before they are bonded together. This can be easily accomplished by laminating high-temperature epoxy and fiber glass cloth into

Fig. 7-7 Integrally heated tool for aircraft nose cone. Tool is high-temperature epoxy laminate and fiber glass cloth. Metal framework is designed to support the tool, but allows for unrestrained expansion and contraction during elevated-temperature cure cycle of the production part. (*Briscoe Mfg. Co.*)

$3/8$-inch by 4-foot by 8-foot sheets and postcuring the sheets in an oven. The eggcrate reinforcement is then cut out of these precured sheets. The embedded heating elements are used to cure the tool face. The reinforcement is then bonded to the tool face with high-temperature laminating resin and glass cloth. The embedded heating elements may then be used to postcure the resin bonding the two components together. The tool is then removed from the model.

LAMINATED PLASTIC TOOLS HEATED BY EMBEDDED STEAM TUBING

The use of steam heat provided by copper tubing embedded in a high-temperature plastic tool has proved effective in curing plastic parts. The tools are made by one of two methods: a completely laminated tool containing embedded copper tubing or a tool consisting of a laminated shell and copper tubing encased in a mixture of dry sand and high-temperature laminating resin. Because of the difficulty involved in bending copper tubing accurately and in laminating it into position, the latter is the preferred method of constructing tools of this type. However, the procedures involved in making tools by both methods will be discussed in a general manner.

Fabrication Procedure for Laminated Tools With Embedded Copper Tubing

As in all high-temperature plastic tool fabrication, the tool must be made directly on a model that will withstand the oven postcure temperatures and not transmit moisture to the tool surface. While metal or plastic models are sometimes used, the plastic-faced plaster transfer medium is the most commonly used for this purpose. For purposes of simplification, we will assume in this discussion that the tool is being made directly on a model that meets the above criteria and has been coated with a suitable parting agent.

The first step is to apply a thin (less than $1/16$ inch) layer of high-temperature epoxy gel coat and allow it to become tacky. The time required for the gel coat to reach a tacky stage will vary with the resin system used and the temperature of the room. Normally, a high-temperature gel coat will reach a tacky stage in 45 to 75 minutes in a room at approximately 72°F.

The next step is to laminate six layers of style 1500 fiber glass cloth and high-temperature laminating resin. The resin system should be selected using the criteria provided in Chapter 6 of this text. The laminate should be allowed to gel for at least 4 hours, preferably overnight.

The copper tubing is then bent to conform to the configuration of the tool. Normally $1/4$ to $1/2$ inch copper tubing is used for this purpose. Various types of flexible plastic tubing have been evaluated for this application, but their poor heat resistance and low thermal conductivity made them unacceptable for this purpose.

When the copper tubing has been formed, it is then tacked into position with an epoxy paste adhesive. When the adhesive has cured sufficiently to hold the tubing in place, a mixture of high-temperature epoxy laminating resin and milled glass fibers is used to make a fillet between the tubing and the six layers of laminate (see Figure 7-8). After the fillet has cured for 4 to 6 hours, an additional 10 layers of fiber glass cloth and high-temperature laminating resin are applied. Oftentimes, unless the tool is very large, the ridges created by the embedded copper tubing provide enough structural support that an eggcrate reinforcement is not required.

If a reinforcing structure is required, it should be fabricated and bonded to the backside of the tool as described in Chapter 6. The tool is postcured on the model.

Fabrication Procedure for a Laminated-Composite Tool With Embedded Copper Tubing

The initial steps of the procedure for fabricating a tool consisting of a laminated face backed up by a mixture of epoxy and dry sand in

Integrally Heated Plastic Tools 181

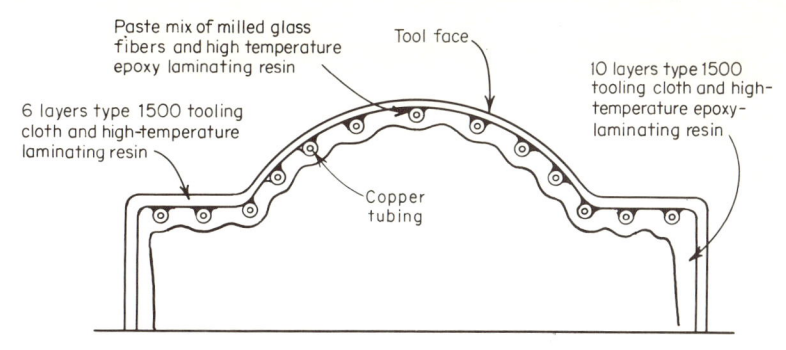

Fig. 7-8 Cross section of high-temperature epoxy laminated tool with embedded copper tubing for steam heat.

which the copper tubing is embedded are the same as for making an all-laminated tool. A high-temperature epoxy gel coat is applied and allowed to become tacky. Then, six layers of 1500 fiber glass cloth and high-temperature epoxy laminating resin are applied. Wax or some other flexible material of uniform thickness is then built up over the laminated section to a thickness of 1 inch, and a plastic-faced plaster shell is fabricated over the buildup.

When the plastic-faced plaster has cured, it is removed, and the buildup is then removed from the laminate. The backside of the laminate is sandblasted to assure good bonding of the backup structure. The copper tubing is bent to the proper shape and cleaned with solvent.

The next step is to tack the tubing to the back of the laminate with epoxy adhesive. After the adhesive has cured, the shell is positioned over the tool, and sealed where the two surfaces meet.

Fig. 7-9 Master pattern for outboard motor shroud. Pattern has been sealed and coated with release agent. (*Ren Plastics, Inc.*)

182   Plastic Tooling

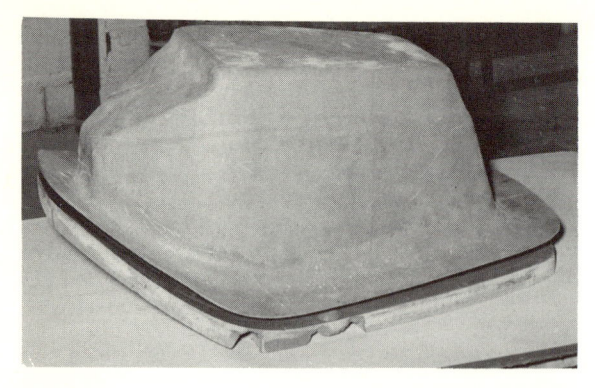

Fig. 7-10 Six layers of type 1500 fiber glass cloth and high-temperature epoxy laminating resin have been applied to master pattern. (*Ren Plastics, Inc.*)

Dry sand is then mixed with high-temperature epoxy laminating resin. The amount of sand required varies with the resin system. In some systems as much as 75 percent by weight of sand is used. The tooling resin supplier should be consulted for his recommendation. If the tool has a simple shape and the resin mixture is not required to flow into

Fig. 7-11 Copper tubing is bent to conform to the tool configuration, and tacked into position. (*Ren Plastics, Inc.*)

Integrally Heated Plastic Tools 183

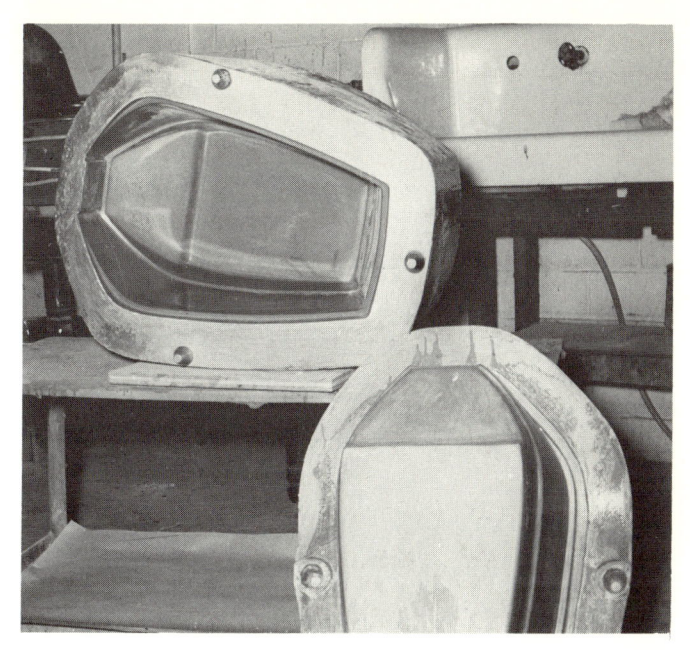

Fig. 7-12 Finished cavity mold and finished plug. This tool was used to produce over 1,000 parts. (*Ren Plastics, Inc.*)

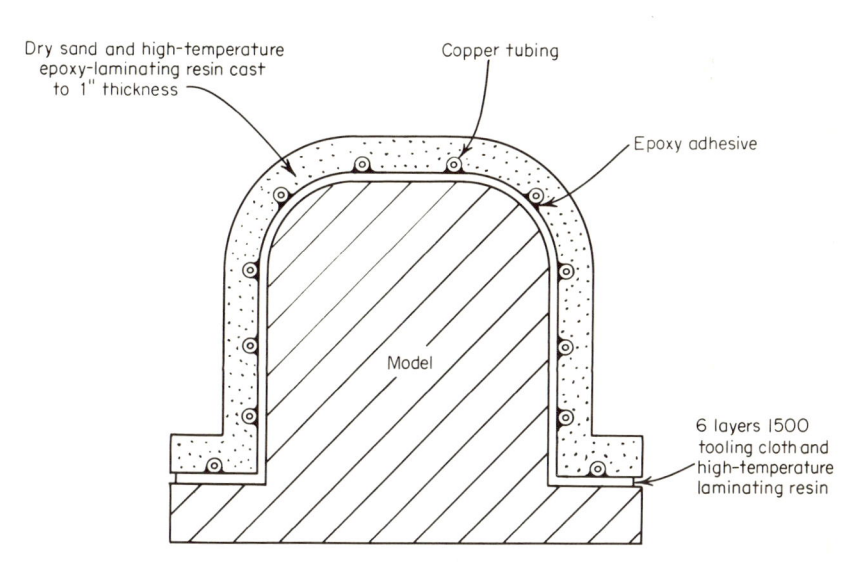

Fig. 7-13 Cross section of a laminated-composite tool with embedded copper tubing for a heat source.

small areas, more sand can be added. In order to minimize exothermic heat, as much sand as possible should be used.

The sand-resin mixture is then poured into the space between the shell and the laminate and allowed to cure for 12 hours at room temperature. The tool remains on the model throughout the oven postcure. When it has cooled to less than 85°F, it may be removed from the model.

SUMMARY

For certain applications, an integrally heated plastic tool can be extremely cost effective. Not only can cost savings be realized over other forms of tooling, but savings through elimination of requirements for ovens, decreased floor space requirements, and faster tool turnover in production are also possible. Integrally heated plastic tools, however, should not be considered as a panacea. The decision to use an integrally heated plastic tool for a particular application should only be made after a thorough analysis of available production facilities, tooling cost comparisons, availability of shop skills, and consideration of the design of the tool.

REFERENCES

Integrally Heated Reinforced Plastic Tools, Technical Bulletin 68-6, Briscoe Manufacturing Co., Columbus, Ohio.

Techni-tips/Tooling Digest, vol. 8, no. 2, Ren Plastics, Inc., Lansing, Mich., April 1966.

CHAPTER EIGHT

Flexible Plastic Tools and Molds

INTRODUCTION

Flexible plastic tooling materials play an important part in the overall tooling picture. The use of these materials permits the casting and molding of complex shaped parts that cannot be made on rigid tooling. Flexible tooling is used to greatest advantage on parts with intricate detail, undercuts, and/or deep draw with very little draft.

While flexible tooling compounds are used to make metal-forming tools and pads, the greatest usage of flexible plastic tooling materials is in the making of flexible molds. These molds can be used to cast plaster, epoxy, polyester, and foam parts. Part removal is greatly simplified through the use of flexible molds.

Flexible molds are used as production molds in the manufacture of decorative statuary, lamps, plaques, and imitation wood carvings. Inexpensive prototype parts are also made in flexible molds. This enables the part to go through the various design stages without the necessity of fabricating and modifying expensive steel dies.

This chapter deals with flexible plastic tooling materials, the techniques of using these materials, and some of the tooling applications of the various materials. In order to use flexible tooling materials effectively and economically, it is necessary that the tool engineer or moldmaker have a thorough knowledge of the variety of moldmaking materials available to him. He must have a working knowledge of the following considerations:

1. Material cost
2. Physical properties
3. Dimensional stability, shrinkage
4. Labor costs involved to make the mold
5. Compatibility with materials from which the production part will be made

With this knowledge, he will be able to choose the most economical material for the application, and design a tool that can be fabricated at the minimum cost. For example, after analyzing a particular application, the tool designer may elect to utilize a more expensive material in order to achieve superior release properties or longer production life. In other cases, the tool designer may find that the cost of the material is more than offset by the labor savings possible in the moldmaking process.

There are basically four different materials commonly used in flexible tooling applications: the room-temperature-vulcanizing (RTV) silicone rubbers, the polyurethane elastomers, the polysulfides, and the latexes. Of these four materials, the RTV silicone rubbers and the polyurethane elastomers have the most to offer as tooling materials. Each material will be discussed individually in this chapter.

ROOM-TEMPERATURE-VULCANIZING SILICONES

The room-temperature-vulcanizing silicone rubbers are a highly versatile family of elastomers. In addition to their use in tooling applications, silicone rubbers are used for a wide variety of aircraft and aerospace uses, protective coatings, and potting and encapsulation of electrical components.

Some of the significant characteristics of silicones which make them so useful as tooling materials are (1) retention of properties over a wide temperature range, (2) low compression set, (3) outstanding release properties, (4) excellent resistance to chemicals, (5) low shrinkage, (6) easy handling characteristics, and (7) the ability to be molded and cured at room temperatures. Of interest to the industrial hygienist is the fact that the silicones do not produce any toxic effects upon contact with skin.

The development of silicone rubber compounds for moldmaking applications has made rapid technological progress in recent years. At the

TABLE 8-1 Typical Cured Properties of RTV Silicone Rubber Moldmaking Materials

Tensile strength, psi	750
Elongation, %	250
Tear resistance, die B, lb/in	100
Durometer, Shore A	60
Linear shrinkage, %	< 0.2

present time, there are special moldmaking compounds that offer the moldmaker outstanding physical properties as well as easy handling characteristics. Table 8-1 provides typical physical properties of silicone rubber moldmaking compounds.

Flexible moldmaking with silicone rubbers can be classified into two categories: (1) cast molds and (2) shell molds or glove molds. Cast molds are made by pouring the RTV silicone casting compound over the model. This method provides the minimum labor costs possible in flexible moldmaking. Shell molds or glove molds are made by using another material to reinforce or "back up" a shell of RTV silicone rubber tooling compound. While this method usually incurs higher labor costs, substantial savings in material costs are frequently possible. The configuration of the master model largely determines which method to use. For example, a mold for a part having a low profile can be easily made by simply casting the RTV silicone rubber over the model. However, when a mold of a large part is required to produce parts having a flat plane or close tolerances, a backup structure is recommended.

The fabrication procedure for each type of mold is discussed in detail in the following sections. As the reader progresses through these sections, the advantages and disadvantages of the two methods will become obvious.

Open-face Casting of Silicone Rubber Molds

Flexible molds made by the simple casting method are used most frequently to produce parts having low profile. Molds of this type, for parts such as wall plaques and drawer fronts, can be made very inexpensively and in a very short flow time.

This section provides step-by-step instructions on the fabrication of RTV silicone rubber molds by the open-face casting technique. The seqeunce of photographs used to illustrate this fabrication method shows how an RTV silicone rubber mold was made to produce 100 prototype parts of a coil magazine. The molds were produced at one-third the cost and in one-tenth the time of cast metal molds which would have otherwise been required to produce the same 100 prototype epoxy parts.

188   Plastic Tooling

Fig. 8-1 Metal master pattern. Prior to use, pattern is cleaned with solvent and washed with hot water to remove possible contaminants. Master pattern is then coated with release agent. (*General Electric Co.*)

Fig. 8-2 RTV silicone rubber casting compound and curing agent are weighed in the proper proportions. Capacity of container should be four times the volume of the casting compound required. (*General Electric Co.*)

Model Preparation It is imperative that the master model or pattern be free of defects prior to the casting of a silicone rubber mold. Silicone rubber molds are very difficult to repair or "touch up." Since any defects in the model or pattern will be faithfully reproduced in the silicone mold, great care should be taken to ensure that the pattern is in perfect condition before proceeding to the next step.

The next step is to construct a framework around the pattern. The framework should be leveled on a surface table to ensure that the casting is of uniform thickness. If this precaution is not taken, difficulty in production usage will be encountered in completely filling the mold. All surfaces to be exposed to the RTV silicone rubber casting compound are then coated with a suitable release agent (Figure 8-1).

Weighing and Mixing The amount of material required to make the mold should be carefully calculated. A clean container with a capacity of approximately four times the volume of silicone rubber required to make the mold should be used. Clean containers should always be

Fig. 8-3 RTV silicone rubber casting compound and curing agent are thoroughly mixed with a spatula for 3 to 5 minutes. Larger batches should be mixed with a power tool. (*General Electric Co.*)

Fig. 8-4 After mixing, the silicone casting compound is placed under vacuum and deaerated. (*General Electric Co.*)

used so as not to introduce any contaminants that might affect the cure of the compound.

The RTV casting compound is then weighed into the container (Figure 8-2), and the catalyst is added. Unlike epoxy casting compounds, the resin-catalyst ratio of RTV silicone rubber compounds may be varied. A typical compound-to-curing-agent ratio is 10 to 1 parts by weight. However, the ratio may be varied to suit specific conditions. As a general rule, increasing the amount of catalyst will cause the material to cure slightly faster and will result in a mold with greater flexibility and less hardness. It is advisable that the ratios recommended by the manufacturer be adhered to and that the moldmaker not take it upon himself to experiment with the resin-catalyst ratio.

In order to ensure thorough cure, the casting compound should be thoroughly mixed. Mixing can be accomplished by hand or by use of a power mixer. Small batches can be adequately mixed with a spatula (see Figure 8-3) or with a paint-mixing stick. The sides of the container should be scraped clean several times during the mixing operation.

Deaeration Because the stirring action results in air entrapment in the mixed components, it is advisable to deaerate the compound prior to pouring it into the mold cavity.

Deaeration is best accomplished by placing the silicone compound in a vacuum chamber and applying vacuum. As vacuum is applied, the mixture will bubble and froth and increase in volume (see Figure 8-4). Eventually the material will return to its original volume. It is recommended that vacuum be maintained until the frothing action subsides and all the bubbles collapse. Vacuum may then be broken, and the material is ready for use. As a general rule, deaeration in a widemouthed container will require from 10 to 15 minutes.

Pouring The RTV casting compound is then slowly poured into the mold cavity with an air injection gun (see Figure 8-5) and the balance of the material poured in afterward. Enough RTV silicone should be used to fill the mold cavity to a point at least ¼ inch above the highest point of the pattern.

Curing The curing of most RTV silicone casting compounds can be accomplished in 24 hours at room temperature. However, in order

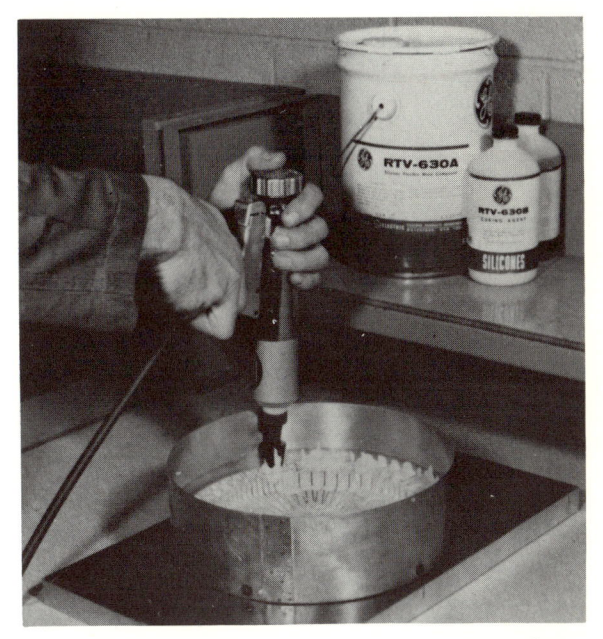

Fig. 8-5 The initial quantity of silicone is injected into the intricate detail of the pattern with an air injection gun. On less complex patterns silicone rubber is simply poured into mold cavity. (*General Electric Co.*)

192   Plastic Tooling

Fig. 8-6 After the remainder of the silicone is poured into the mold cavity, it is allowed to cure at room temperature. (*General Electric Co.*)

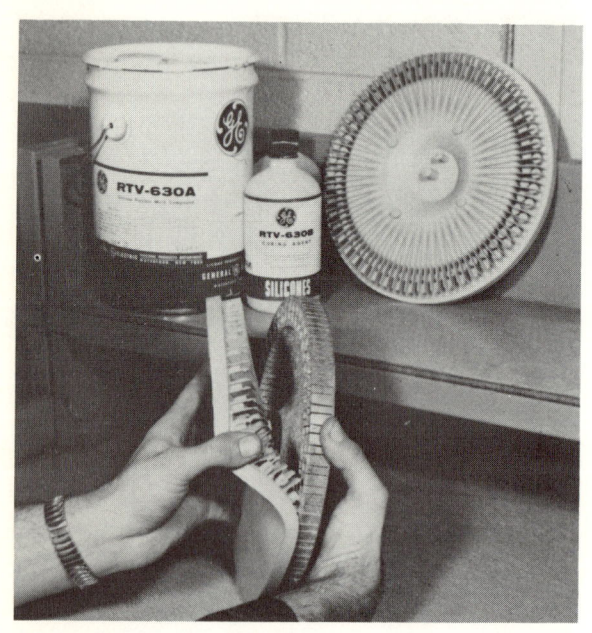

Fig. 8-7 After it has sufficiently cured, the flexible RTV silicone mold is removed from the model. (*General Electric Co.*)

to achieve optimum physical properties, a postcure at elevated temperatures (200 to 350°F) is sometimes recommended. The cure cycle recommended by the manufacturer should be followed, inasmuch as he has arrived at this cure cycle as a result of extensive testing of his product during its development stages.

Cure Inhibition *Cure inhibition* is a condition which is characterized by a gummy appearance at the interface between the pattern and the RTV silicone rubber casting. This phenomenon is usually caused by a chemical reaction between the silicone compound and either the pattern, the pattern finish, the modeling clays, or the various pattern waxes. It is advisable to ask your resin supplier which materials may create cure inhibition problems for you, and then to avoid using them.

Treatment of Molds When RTV silicone rubber molds are being used to produce parts made of plastic materials such as epoxies, polyesters, and polyurethane foam, it is advisable to condition the mold periodically. During production usage, silicone rubber molds will gradually absorb hardeners, plasticizers, accelerators, etc., from the compounds being used to make the production part. These materials build

Fig. 8-8 Prior to use, the RTV mold is immersed in release agent to ensure good release of plastic part to be cast in mold. (*General Electric Co.*)

194   Plastic Tooling

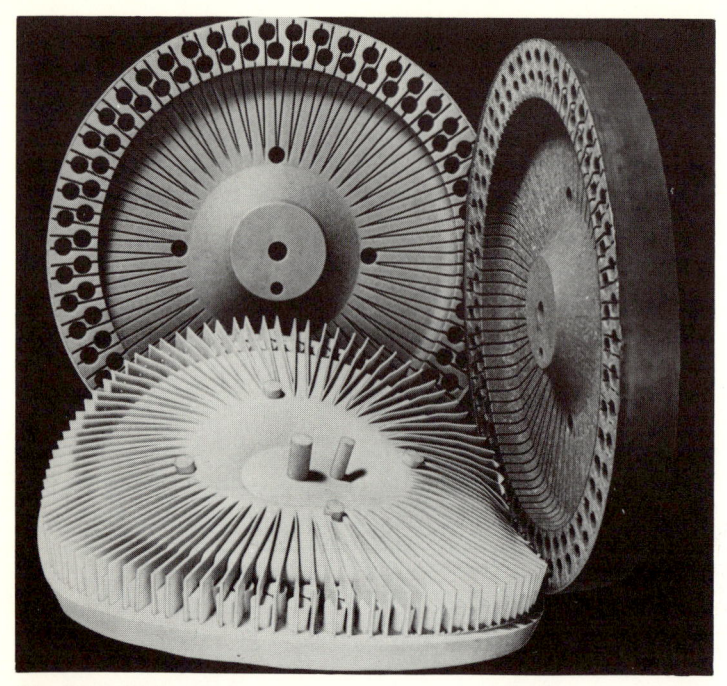

Fig. 8-9 Background—metal master pattern; left foreground—flexible RTV silicone mold; right—epoxy prototype part made in flexible mold. (*General Electric Co.*)

up a bond between the mold and the production material, until eventually it results in a torn mold.

Placing the mold in an air-circulating oven at 200°F for 8 hours will help to vaporize the contaminants. Periodic treatment of silicone rubber molds by this method helps to prolong mold life.

Silicone Rubber "Glove" Molds

An RTV silicone rubber shell mold or glove mold consists of a thin layer of silicone rubber supported by a rigid backup structure. The silicone rubber is normally approximately ¼ inch thick. Materials most commonly used for the reinforcing structure are gypsum cement, wood, epoxy resins, and rigid polyurethane foams.

Glove molds offer two advantages over open-face cast molds. First, it is possible to save substantially on material cost, since much less material is required. Second, the thin layer of silicone is more flexible than a cast mold and is therefore much easier to remove from a model or part having severe undercuts or intricate detail.

The first step in producing a flexible silicone rubber glove mold is to construct a wooden box-shaped framework around the part. In the case of a two-piece mold such as the one in the series of illustrations used here, two boxes are constructed so that they join at the parting plane of the model.

Modeling clay or sheet wax is then used to build up approximately ¼-inch layer over the part model (see Figure 8-10).

The model with the clay buildup is positioned in the wood framework. The backup material is then cast into the space between the framework and the model. Polyurethane foam is becoming widely used for this purpose because the completed mold is lighter and easier to handle than a similar mold using plaster or cast epoxy as a backup structure (see Figure 8-11). This procedure is repeated for the other mold half.

After the backup structure has cured, the mold halves are separated and the model removed. The clay is removed from the model, and it is inspected to ensure that it is completely clean of residual clay and free of defects. Each mold section is then coated with a suitable parting agent.

The model is positioned in the bottom half of the mold cavity, and the RTV silicone rubber casting compound is then poured into the area,

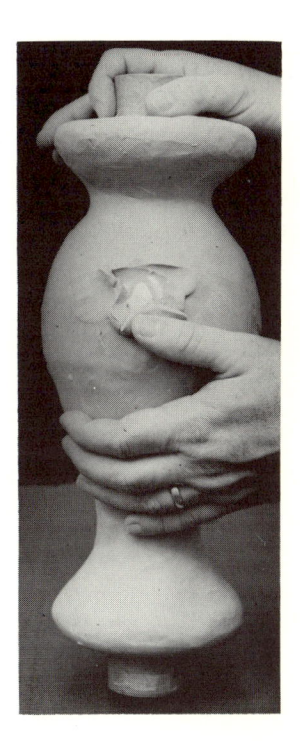

Fig. 8-10 The first step in producing a flexible glove mold is to build up clay around the model to a thickness of approximately ¼ inch. (*General Electric Co.*)

196   Plastic Tooling

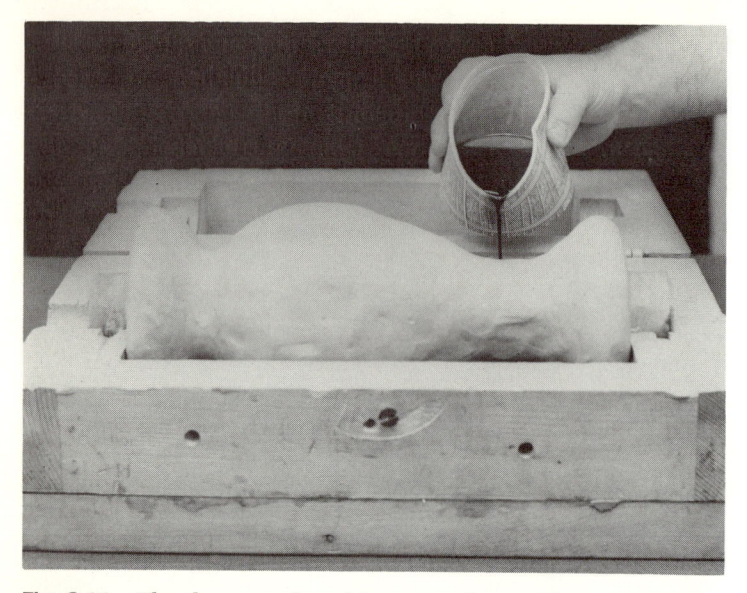

Fig. 8-11 The clay-covered model is inserted in mold box. The area between mold box and clay is filled with polyurethane foam. (*General Electric Co.*)

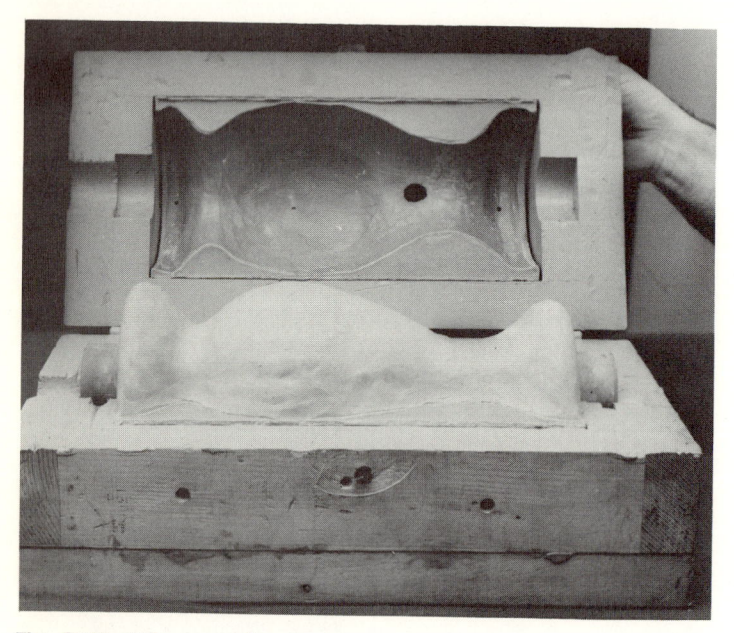

Fig. 8-12 The exposed polyurethane foam surfaces are coated with mold release, and the process is repeated for the top mold half. (*General Electric Co.*)

Flexible Plastic Tools and Molds 197

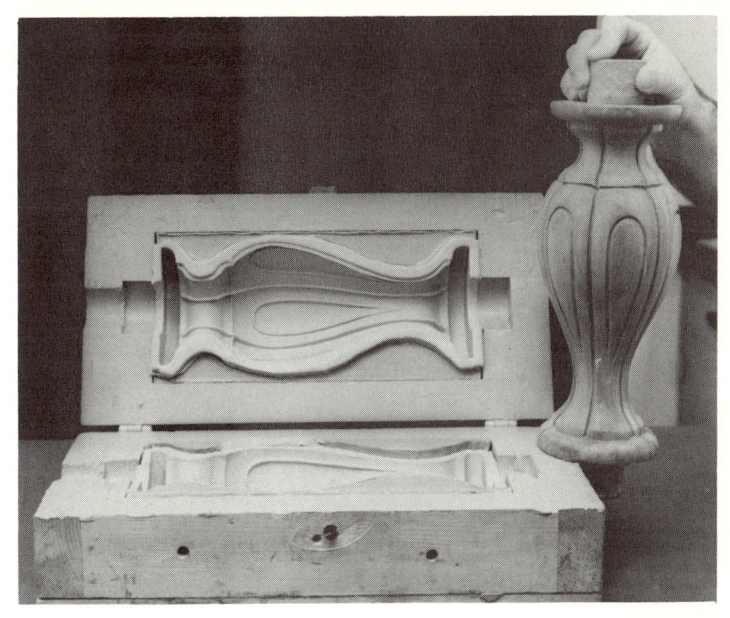

Fig. 8-13 After clay is removed, RTV silicone is poured into area between model and foam, and allowed to cure overnight. This photo shows completed flexible mold and model. Note accurate reproduction of detail. (*General Electric Co.*)

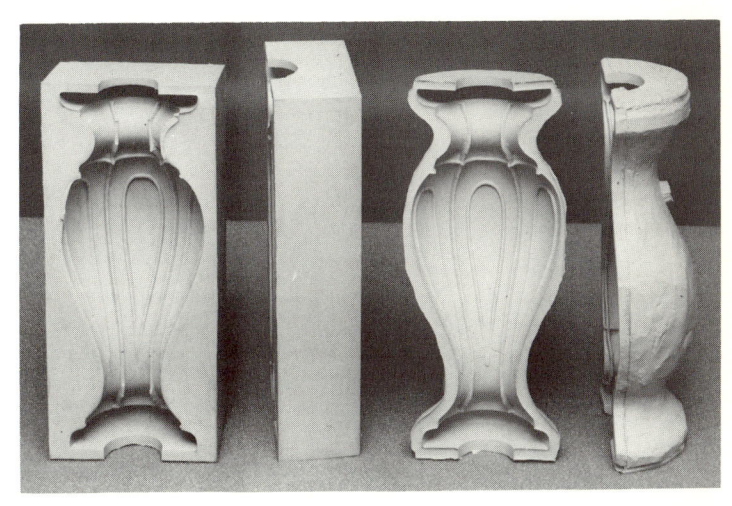

Fig. 8-14 The dramatic materials savings possible through the use of glove molds is illustrated in this photograph. Glove mold is on right; mold cast around model with no backup is on left. (*General Electric Co.*)

Fig. 8-15 Completed cast plastic lamp base (left) and original model (right). (*General Electric Co.*)

formerly occupied by the clay, between the model and the backup structure.

After the silicone rubber has been cured, the mold halves are positioned together, and the top half of the mold is poured. The top half of the mold is cast directly against the bottom half, providing a perfectly mating parting plane. After the top half of the mold has cured, the two mold halves are separated and the model is removed (see Figure 8-13). The glove mold is now ready for use in producing parts identical to the model.

FLEXIBLE POLYURETHANE MOLDS

The use of polyurethane elastomers to make flexible molds has increased sharply in the past two years. The increased usage of polyurethane elastomers can be attributed to formulation improvements which make the polyurethanes much easier to handle, and to the fact that polyurethane elastomers cost substantially less than the RTV silicones.

Polyurethane elastomers possess a combination of physical properties that make them highly desirable as flexible tooling materials. They are vastly superior to other elastomeric materials in abrasion resistance, tensile strength, elongation, tear resistance, and load-bearing properties.

Polyurethane casting compounds capable of reproducing the finest detail are now commercially available. These materials have much-improved handling characteristics, and can be mixed, poured easily, and cured at room temperature.

Fig. 8-16 This photograph illustrates the variety of sizes and shapes commonly produced with flexible urethane molds. (*Hysol Division, The Dexter Corp.*)

TABLE 8-2 Typical Physical Properties of Polyurethane Elastomers (cured and tested at 73°F ±3°)

Shore hardness	Tensile strength, psi	Elongation, %	Tear strength, lb/in.	Shrinkage in./in.
40A	500	900	90	0.07
50A	700	900	130	0.07
60A	1,100	900	185	0.07
70A	1,500	600	200	0.10
80A	1,900	600	255	0.10
50D	2,500	350	500	0.12
60D	3,000	250	550	0.15
70D	4,500	200	600	0.25

This section discusses in detail the fabrication of a flexible mold with polyurethane elastomers. Techniques which will result in improved mold quality are provided in the proper sequence.

Preparation of the Model

The most important thing to remember in using polyurethane elastomers is that they are very reactive with water. They will readily absorb moisture from the air or from any moist surface that they come in contact with. If the polyurethane elastomer is allowed to absorb moisture, the result will be reflected in the mold surface as bubblelike defects.

With the foregoing in mind, it is evident that the first step in the preparation of the model or pattern is to ensure that it is completely sealed so that it cannot transmit moisture through the parting film to the polyurethane casting compound. Methods of sealing various materials are discussed at length in Chapter 1 and will therefore not be repeated here.

After the model has been sealed, surface moisture on the model should be removed with mild heat. This can easily be accomplished by passing a hot-air gun over the surface of the model. Care should be taken not to overdo the application of heat, particularly on wood patterns. Wood patterns should not be heated over 125°F. Otherwise, moisture contained on the porous wood pattern will be released, and may cause defects in the polyurethane mold.

The model surface is then coated with a release agent. Silicone greases and spray-applied Teflon release agents have proved to be superior for use with polyurethane elastomers. After the release agent has been applied, heat should again be applied to ensure that there is no residual moisture on the model surface.

Handling and Mixing

Again, the key to success here is in keeping moisture away from the polyurethane elastomer. When you receive a polyurethane elastomer packaged in small quantities for ease of handling, the water and dissolved gases will have been removed, and the space between the elastomer and the cover of the can will have been flushed with dry nitrogen. One obvious precaution against moisture, then, is to keep the containers tightly closed until you are ready to use them.

Another precaution that is not so obvious, but is extremely important, pertains to the container used to mix the polyurethane components. The best container to use is an unlined metal can. Glass containers may also be used. The metal or glass container should be preheated in an oven for 20 to 30 minutes prior to use. Paper cups or containers must *not* be used. The paper cups will give off moisture during the degassing of the polyurethane, creating numerous surface defects on the mold. The container used should have at least twice the volume of the resin to allow for foaming without overflowing during the degassing.

The components of the polyurethane casting compound should be preheated to 125 to 130°F prior to weighing and mixing. This serves to decrease the viscosity and to greatly facilitate thorough mixing. At this point, the metal mixing container is removed from the oven, and the components are carefully weighed in the proper proportions. Variations in the proportions of individual components can greatly affect the physical properties of the cured mold. Therefore the proportions recommended by the manufacturer should be strictly adhered to. Any variations should only be done with the approval of the formulator.

The mixing of small batches of polyurethane elastomer is best accomplished by hand with a metal spatula that has been preheated. Hand-mix for at least 4 minutes. Mechanical mixing is acceptable, but usually results in air entrapment that can have an adverse effect on the compound. If a mechanical mixer is used, it should be set at a very low speed.

After the components are thoroughly mixed, they are placed in a vacuum chamber at 5 millimeters of mercury for 10 to 15 minutes. If

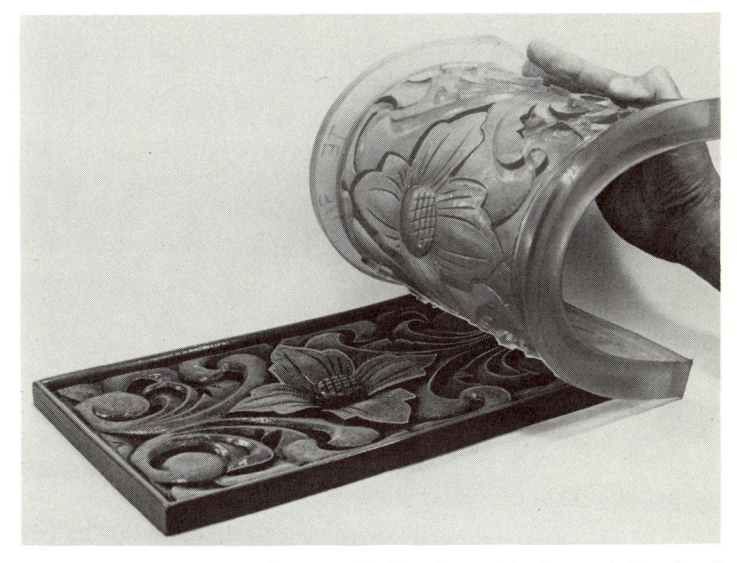

Fig. 8-17 Flexible urethane mold (hardness 45 Shore A) for detail reproductions of woodcarving. (*Rezolin, Inc.*)

the material begins to "boil over," the vacuum may be broken temporarily.

The mixed compound is then poured directly into the mold cavity. The compound should be poured at one location only. If the model surface has been preheated with a heat gun, two benefits will be acrieved; residual moisture will be eliminated, and the flow of the resin over the model will be improved. This generally results in superior reproduction of intricate surface detail. After the pouring has been completed, the surface bubbles on the back of the casting may be broken by warming gently with a heat gun.

Curing Polyurethane Elastomers

There are various cycles that can be used to cure polyurethane elastomers. The manufacturer will usually recommend that the material be cured 16 hours at room temperature, demolded, and then cured at room temperature for 5 to 6 days. With this cure cycle, shrinkage is minimized and the mold will have good tensile strength and elongation values. However, it is a rare instance when a moldmaker feels that he can enjoy the luxury of such a long cure cycle.

As an alternative to a complete cure at room temperature, an acceptable cycle that is a combination of room-temperature cure and oven cure is frequently used. This has the advantage of reducing the flow time of the cure from 1 week to 2 days. A typical cycle of this type would be a room-temperature cure for 24 hours, followed by a 4-hour oven postcure at 140°F. If this cycle is used, the shrinkage will increase slightly, the Shore hardness will increase slightly, and tensile strength and elongation will be relatively unaffected.

It is possible to accelerate the cure still further, and produce a usable mold in less flow time. This can be accomplished by curing the mold at room temperature for 2 hours, followed by an 8-hour cure at 190°F. However, accelerating the cure cycle in this manner will alter the physical properties of the mold. The shrinkage will be increased, the mold will have a higher Shore hardness reading, and the ultimate elongation will be significantly reduced.

The author wishes to point out that the foregoing cure cycles are to be considered as typical for polyurethane elastomers generally used in moldmaking. Therefore, they should not be construed as suitable for all compounds or as a substitute for a different cure cycle recommended by a resin formulator. Constant improvements are being made in polyurethane compounding. With the advances in technology, new cure cycles will be introduced by the formulator for his particular compound. The cure cycles recommended by the formulator should be followed. If it is desirable to shorten cure cycles by using the tech-

Flexible Plastic Tools and Molds 203

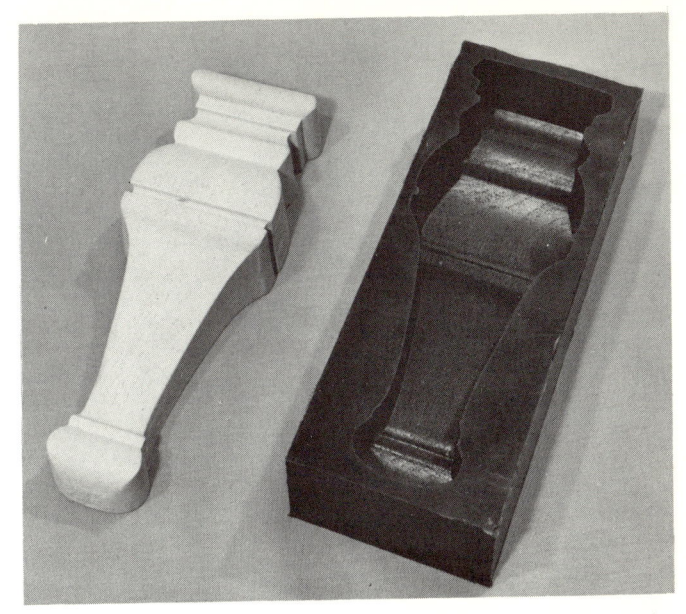

Fig. 8-18 Flexible urethane mold (hardness 35 Shore A) for producing plastic furniture leg. Note precision reproduction of woodgrain in mold face. (*Hysol Division, The Dexter Corp.*)

niques discussed in this section, the formulator should first be consulted for his concurrence.

POLYSULFIDE LIQUID POLYMERS

In selected cases, the polysulfide rubbers are an excellent choice for flexible moldmaking. Polysulfide compounds are one of the easiest elastomers to work with. They are low in viscosity, and consequently easy

Fig. 8-19 Flexible urethane mold (hardness 75 Shore A) for production mold patterns. (*Rezolin, Inc.*)

to pour. The pot life can be varied to suit the situation, the shrinkage is negligible, the material exhibits good toughness and flexibility, and the compounds cure at room temperature.

One factor that has greatly restricted the use of polysulfides, or *cold-molding compounds* as they are referred to, is their inability to withstand service temperatures in excess of 150 to 160°F. Consequently, they are not well suited for molds for casting plastic parts such as polyesters, which produce an exothermic reaction.

The softness and flexibility of polysulfide elastomers is another characteristic that has all but eliminated them from use as molds to produce parts of polyurethane foam. The pressures created by the expanding polyurethane foam are too great for the polysulfides to withstand. The resulting mold deformation makes them unacceptable for use with polyurethane foams.

One outstanding characteristic of polysulfide casting compounds is their ability to reproduce intricate detail. Further, they can be cast readily over models of clay, wax, soap, wood, plaster, or plastic. This characteristic lends itself readily to the reproduction of art objects. When service temperatures of the mold will not exceed 150°F, the polysulfides are an excellent choice for the mold material.

Procedure for Mixing and Handling Polysulfide Casting Compounds

Polysulfide casting compounds are available in both two-component and three-component systems. The three-component systems enable the patternmaker to vary the pot life and setting time. For this reason, the three-component systems are usually favored among moldmakers.

The three-component system consists of part A—the base polymer, part B—the curing agent, and part C—the additive. Normally, the portions are weighed into a container which is 50 percent greater in capacity than the volume of the material to be mixed. The additive, part C, is added to the base polymer, part A, and the two components are mixed thoroughly. The third component, part B, is then added. The mixture is stirred for 3 to 5 minutes by hand. Batches larger than 3 pounds should be blended for 2 to 3 minutes with a mechanical mixer.

After mixing, the material is poured directly onto the model. If the model has intricate surface detail, it is good practice to mix up a small batch and brush it onto the model surface, and pour the remainder of the material while the face coat is still tacky. The casting should be allowed to stand undisturbed until it has sufficiently cured. The cure times recommended by the manufacturer should be followed at all times. Normally an overnight cure is required. Premature removal from the model usually results in a distorted mold.

LATEX RUBBER MOLDS

Latex rubber molds are perhaps the oldest-known type of flexible molds. They have been used extensively for many years to produce plaster statuary and art reproductions in large quantities. While latex molds are satisfactory for art objects, they are not normally used for close tolerance tooling. Mold shrinkage up to 10 percent is common with latex molds.

The latex moldmaking compound usually is available as a natural gum rubber emulsion thinned with ammonia water. The moldmaking process consists of brushing successive coats onto the model. Each coat builds up about 3 to 5 mils, and a waiting period of 4 to 6 hours is required between coats to allow the ammonia to volatize. Consequently, moldmaking with latex is a tedious and time-consuming process.

CONCLUSIONS

There are a wide variety of flexible moldmaking materials available. No single material will be suitable for all flexible moldmaking applications. It is necessary to understand the advantages and disadvantages of each of the types of flexible moldmaking materials discussed in this chapter. If the individual understands the capabilities of the materials, and the requirements of the process, he will be able to select the type of material that is most appropriate for his particular application.

REFERENCES

Liquid Silicone Rubber for Flexible Molding Requirements, Technical Data Book S-34, General Electric Company, Silicone Products Department, Waterford, N.Y.
Ultra-high Strength RTV Silicone Rubber for Mold Making, Technical Data Book S-29C, General Electric Company, Silicone Products Department, Waterford, N.Y.

CHAPTER NINE

Rework and Repair of Plastic Tools

INTRODUCTION

As stated frequently throughout this text, one of the greatest advantages of plastic tools is the fact that they can be easily repaired or modified. On initial consideration this may not strike the reader as being particularly significant. However, it is a well-established fact that repairing and maintaining in serviceable condition those tools that are already in service is a major preoccupation of the tool engineer, the tooling personnel, and the production management.

Even though tools may be on a program of regularly scheduled maintenance, unexpected tool failures frequently occur. At these times, tool repair in a timely manner becomes the foremost objective. If tool repairs cannot be accomplished quickly, production schedules may be jeopardized and delays may result. The toolmaker frequently finds himself in the position of having to repair a tool in what he considers an insufficient amount of time. The toolmaker knows from experience that rushing a repair job frequently results in poor workmanship and an unsatisfactory repair. To compound the problem further, the repair must be accomplished as economically as possible. While this may seem to be an exaggerated state of affairs, it is a situation that happens daily in a wide variety of industries.

To this end, tooling resin formulators have developed a variety of materials to facilitate the use of plastics to make speedy repairs and alterations on a variety of tools. These plastic materials have been used successfully on a wide range of applications such as worn foundry patterns, fractured forming tools, and lay-up mandrels with surface defects.

The most commonly used plastic tool repair materials are specially compounded patching pastes. There are two types of paste patching compounds: room-temperature-curing systems capable of service temperatures up to 150°F and high-temperature paste compounds capable of service temperatures up to 380°F.

The room-temperature-curing systems are formulated to set up hard enough at room temperature to enable them to be sanded within 30 minutes. However, because of their fast setting time, the toolmaker is limited to a period of 6 to 8 minutes working time after the resin and hardener have been combined. These materials normally have the following characteristics:

- Easy to mix
- Creamy consistency enabling them to be splined or trowelled to a feather edge
- Good thixotropy
- Good strength (similar to epoxy casting compounds)
- Good dimensional stability
- Excellent bond strength
- Easy to sand

Typical properties of room-temperature-curing patching compounds are given in Table 9-1. Many of the room-temperature-curing patching compounds are available with resin-hardener ratio of 1 to 1. This is convenient for the toolmaker since it eliminates the need for carefully weighing out small quantities of material. Most manufacturers make room-temperature patching compounds available in tube kits. As illus-

TABLE 9-1 Typical Properties of Epoxy Paste Patching Compounds (for service up to 150°F)

Bond strength, psi	2,000
Compressive strength, psi	12,000
Tensile strength, psi	2,600
Shrinkage, in./in.	0.002
Hardness, Shore D	85
Gel time (pot life), min	6–8
Deflection temperature, °F	180

208   Plastic Tooling

(a) Grind through the tool face and expose the defect

(b) Wipe the repair area with a clean cloth wetted with acetone

(c) Resin and hardener are dispensed in the proper ratio

(d) The paste patching compound is thoroughly mixed

(e) The cavity is filled with the patching compound. Overfill to a height of 1/32" over the tool surface

(f) After the repair has cured, it can be sanded to match the contour of the tool

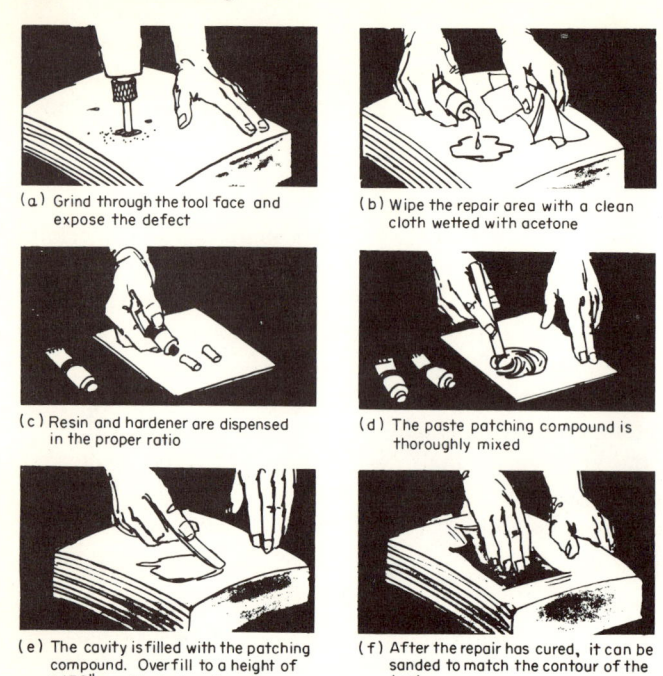

Fig. 9-1 Repair of surface defects with epoxy paste patching compounds.

trated in Figure 9-1, beads of equal length are squeezed out of the tubes, and the material is ready to mix.

The high-temperature paste patching compounds have handling properties very similar to the room-temperature systems. However, there is one exception. In order to achieve the optimum physical properties, these materials must be postcured at elevated temperatures. For small patching jobs, a 20-minute application of heat with a heat gun is sufficient to cure out the repair. Because of this, high-temperature patching systems have a much longer working time than room-temperature systems. Working times up to 30 minutes are not uncommon. On larger repairs, it is usually advisable to place the tool in an oven and give it the elevated temperature postcure recommended by the manufacturer. Table 9-2 provides typical properties of high-temperature epoxy paste patching compounds.

Normally, epoxy paste patching compounds have the excellent bond strength which is so necessary to a good repair. However, in order to achieve the optimum bond between the patching compound and the tool surface to be repaired, all surfaces must be clean and free of oil, grease, or residual parting agents. Plastic surfaces should be sanded and cleaned with acetone. When possible, metal surfaces should be degreased. If degreasing is not possible, the metal surface should be sanded and wiped with a clean cloth wetted with acetone. Adequate surface preparation is one of the most important steps in any epoxy repair.

REPAIR OF ROOM-TEMPERATURE-SERVICE PLASTIC TOOLS

Determining the Cause of Failure

Before attempting to repair a plastic tool, it is important to analyze the tool failure and determine its cause. Determining the cause of the failure or defect will make it possible, in many cases, to accomplish a repair that will prevent the same thing from happening again in the near future. For example, a foundry corebox exhibiting excessive wear on the top surface is returned to the patternmaker for buildup of the worn areas. The patternmaker determines that the wearing is caused by the coremaker when he "strikes off" the excess sand. Instead of simply building up the worn areas with epoxy paste patching compound, the patternmaker casts in metal inserts on the wearing surfaces. This action has ensured that the same corebox won't be back for a similar repair in the near future.

In studying Table 9-3, it becomes obvious that the causes of tool failures fall into three basic categories: poor tool design, improper fabrication, and misuse and mishandling. No matter how urgently the tool is required in production, the tool engineer or toolmaker should make it an established policy to analyze the cause of the tool failure and plan a repair that is designed to prevent its reoccurrence.

Surface Defects

There are two basic types of surface defects that will be considered in this section: surface pitting and defects due to handling, such as

TABLE 9-2 Typical Properties of High-temperature Epoxy Paste Patching Compounds (for service up to 380°F)

Bond strength, psi	3,000
Compressive strength, psi	12,000
Tensile stength, psi	2,600
Deflection temperature, °F	385
Shrinkage, in./in	0.003
Hardness, Shore D	
72°F	85
250°F	70
Gel time (pot life), min	40

chunks broken during removal of a part (usually due to insufficient release agent or to gouges and scratches on the tool face).

Usually, surface pitting is caused by air entrapped just below the tool face. If a gel coat has been used on the tool, the source of the problem can usually be traced to improper mixing of the resin and hardener or failure to squeegee the gel coat a second time after it had been brushed on.

There are two alternative solutions to this problem: filling and sanding the voids or resurfacing the entire surface of the tool. The extent of the surface defects should be the determining factor of which method of repair to employ. Voids under the tool surface can be detected by tapping lightly with either a ball peen hammer or a 50-cent piece.

TABLE 9-3 Typical Repairable Plastic Tooling Defects

Type	Probable causes
Surface defects (pits and voids)	Air entrapped during tool fabrication Moisture transfer from the model Rough handling of tool

Warpage	Excessive shrinkage:
	    casting—high exothermic reaction
	    laminate—resin content exceeds 50%
	Inadequate design
	Tool subjected to temperature beyond its capabilities
	Tool loaded beyond design limits
	Thermal shock

Worn areas	Normal wear in production use Abnormal wear due to rough handling or misapplication Poor choice of materials
Soft spots	Resin and hardener inadequately mixed Thermal reaction between resin compound and parting agent or other materials Gel coat too thick
Fractures (chipping, cracking, and delamination)	Inadequate design Excessively rough handling Tool loaded beyond its design limits Difference in thermal coefficient of expansion between plastic tool face and its reinforcement (thermal shock)
Loosening of components (bushings, match-buttons, tooling pins, inserts, etc.)	Normal wear during production usage Poor design Improper tool fabrication techniques Rough handling Tool used beyond its design limits

When a void is detected, its location is marked with a pencil. This process is repeated until the entire tool face has been inspected.

Once a void is located, the following procedure should be used to make the repair.

1. Using a power drill, grind through the tool face and expose the void. Do not drill beyond the void further than is absolutely necessary. Large, shallow voids are easier to fill than deep ones.

2. Remove all grinding dust from inside and around the repair area. The entire repair area should be wiped with a clean cloth wetted with acetone.

3. The required amount of room-temperature-service paste patching compound is mixed in the proper ratio. Mix only the quantity that can be used within the short working time of materials of this type.

4. Fill the cavities with the paste patching compound, taking care not to entrap any air between the patching compound and the tool. The cavities should be overfilled to a height of $\frac{1}{32}$ inch over the tool face.

5. After the patching compound has cured, it can be sanded with no. 600 wet-or-dry sandpaper until it matches the contour of the tool face.

Refacing of Plastic Tools

If the surface defects are numerous and extensive, it may be preferable to resurface the entire tool face. The following procedure should be used to reface an epoxy–fiber glass laminated tool.

1. Sandblast the entire tool face to remove the defective gel coat.

2. Inspect the model surface for defects, repair as required, and coat with release agent.

3. Using the proper techniques, apply an epoxy gel coat to the model.

4. When the gel coat is tack-free, apply two or three layers of type 1500 fiber glass cloth and epoxy laminating over the gel coat.

5. If the tool being resurfaced is a laminate, drill numerous $\frac{1}{4}$-inch holes completely through the laminate.

6. Apply a generous coating of laminating resin and press the original tool onto the new tool face. The most successful technique in this operation is to make contact at one end of the tool and lower the other end slowly, allowing the contact surface to progress slowly toward the other end. This serves to minimize air entrapment and force out excess resin.

7. Allow tool to cure for at least 24 hours before removing from the model.

In the event that a cast epoxy tool requires refacing, the procedure is quite similar. Sandblast the tool face to remove residual parting agent, open up whatever voids exist on the tool face, and provide a fresh surface to bond to. The tool is then repositioned against the model or other reference surface. A new tool face is then cast in much the same manner as outlined in Chapter 4 (in the section covering surface cast tools). This technique can be employed to cast new faces on tools with surface pitting over large areas, cast tools with fractures, or metal-forming tools exhibiting pronounced wear.

Fractures

Fractures are not a common cause of tool failure. Fractures rarely occur in epoxy–fiber glass laminated tools. Occasionally, fractures do occur in cast epoxy tools, particularly in tools with epoxy surface cast over a metal core. These fractures are usually caused by the difference in thermal expansion between the epoxy casting compound and metal core on tools stored outdoors during cold weather. Fractures are also caused by loads applied to the tool beyond its design limits and by abusive handling.

Fractures and cracks may be repaired by grinding the fractures to a width of $\frac{1}{8}$ to $\frac{1}{4}$ inch, cleaning the area with solvent, and filling the cavity with an epoxy paste patching compound.

If the fractured tool is a die used for forming metal, it may be necessary to make the repair with the same resin system as the tool face if the hardness of the paste patching compound is not the same as the material used to make the tool face. Experience has shown that if the hardness of the tool surface and the repaired area are not the same, it will cause mark-off on the metal part in the area representing the interface between the two resin systems.

Repair or Replacement of Loose Components

Metal inserts in plastic tools such as drill bushings, locating pins, mounting lugs, and routing edges frequently require repair. Drill bushings frequently become loose due to heat caused by friction from the drilling operation or from creep of the plastic due to high, uneven loading. Locating pins, because they protrude, are prone to damage by either breakage or bending.

Repair or replacement of drill bushings and locating pins is relatively simple and can be accomplished in a relatively short time period. The following procedure is used for replacing bushings and/or locating pins:

1. The bushings or pins are cut out of the tool with a hole cutter approximately $\frac{1}{8}$ inch larger than the diameter of the bushing or pin.
2. Parting agent is applied to the model or coordination medium.
3. The tool is located correctly on the model or coordination medium.

4. The bushings or pins are placed in the proper location.
5. The cavity between the bushing and the laminate is filled with an epoxy potting compound.
6. The potting compound is allowed to cure a minimum of 6 hours before the tool is removed from the coordination medium.

Repair of Worn Areas

Plastic tools that are subjected to rough usage, such as foundry patterns and metal-forming tools, usually develop worn areas that require repair. Wear resulting from this type of normal usage usually occurs in localized areas; for example, the radii in draw dies, the wrinkle areas in drop-hammer dies, and strike-off areas on coreboxes.

In cases of wear in localized areas, repairs may be accomplished as outlined in the preceding section on repair of surface defects. Where large areas are worn, it may be necessary to reface the entire tool as outlined in the preceding section on refacing of plastic tools. Metal inserts are frequently used to prevent wear in localized areas.

REPAIR OF HIGH-TEMPERATURE PLASTIC TOOLS

By high-temperature plastic tools, we mean plastic tools subjected to service temperatures between 125 and 400°F. As indicated in earlier sections of this book, these service temperatures are beyond the range of the normal room-temperature-curing epoxy resin systems. Because of the applications for which these tools are used and the temperatures at which they operate, they are subject to failures which are not normally encountered by room-temperature-service tools. Basically, failures of high-temperature plastic tools fall into three general categories: (1) surface defects, (2) delamination, and (3) vacuum leaks. This section concentrates on methods of repairing these three most common defects.

Surface Defects

Surface defects in high-temperature plastic tools are considered to be those defects in the gel coat (in the case of a laminate or epoxy–aluminum needle tool) or in the upper $\frac{1}{16}$ inch of a cast tool. Typical surface defects commonly encountered during production usage are: pitting—caused by air entrapment, cracking—caused by thermal shock or difference between thermal coefficient of expansion between the gel coat and laminate structure, and scratches and gouges—caused by metal tools used to pry plastic parts off the tools.

The repair of surface defects in high-temperature plastic tools may be easily accomplished as follows:

214   Plastic Tooling

1. Grind the surface defect with a fine tip grinder. This will provide a fresh surface to bond to, and make the cavity easier to fill.
2. Clean away all dust and loose particles formed during the grinding operation, and wipe the entire area with a clean cloth soaked in clean acetone.
3. A high-temperature paste patching compound is mixed in correct ratio and applied to the cavities. It is extremely important that no air be entrapped between the patching compound and the tool. If air *is* entrapped, it will expand during the next usage of the tool at elevated temperature and cause the repair to raise above the tool surface or pop out entirely. Some shops have developed techniques for using a syringe with a large orifice to inject the material into the defect cavity to minimize air entrapment.
4. The repair can be cured with a heat gun as prescribed by the manufacturer of the resin system. For large defects, or if there are numerous defects spread over the entire tool face, the curing of the repair should be accomplished in an oven.
5. After the repair has been cured and allowed to cool to room temperature, the area can be sanded with no. 320 wet-or-dry sandpaper and given a final finish with no. 600 wet-or-dry sandpaper, used wet.
6. Parting agent should be applied to the entire tool face before it is sent back to the production area.

This method of repairing surface defects in high-temperature epoxy tools applies to laminated and cast tools, as well as epoxy–aluminum needle tooling. It should be obvious to the reader that, since the epoxy-aluminum needle tool is in itself porous, it is not necessary to worry about air entrapment between the repair material and epoxy–aluminum needle matrix.

Delamination

Delamination in high-temperature epoxy laminates is usually caused by air entrapped between the laminate layers. When the tool is heated, the air expands and exerts tremendous force on the laminate, causing the layers adjacent to the void to separate. If the delamination is close enough to the tool face, it will create a circular, raised area (blister) on the tool face (see Figure 9-2). If the delamination is near the backside of the tool, it may not affect the tool face. However, delamination will eventually spread and result in loss of vacuum integrity for the tool. This can be a serious problem in the case of lay-up mandrels and autoclave bonding tools, since loss of vacuum integrity can result in rejection of production parts.

When the delamination is near the backside of the tool and has not

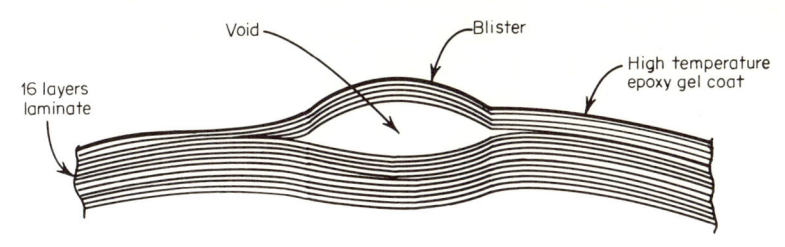

Fig. 9-2 Delamination caused by air entrapment in a high-temperature epoxy laminated tool.

caused the tool face to lose configuration, the repair can be accomplished by injecting a high-temperature patching compound or laminating resin into the void as illustrated in Figure 9-3. This will serve to stop the delaminated area from spreading and to eliminate the possibility of loss of vacuum integrity. After the repair material has been injected into the void, it should be allowed to gel at room temperature and then given an elevated-temperature postcure as recommended by the resin manufacturer. It is recommended that heat cure of repairs of this type be accomplished in an oven, since it is almost impossible to get sufficient heat to the repair material with a heat gun to effect a thorough cure of the material.

In the event that the air pocket causes blistering of the tool face, it is usually necessary to cut out the blistered area and repair it. Repair of small blisters may be accomplished with a high-temperature paste patching material. However, the difference in coefficient of thermal expansion between the paste material and laminate greatly limits the size of the blistered area that may be repaired in this manner.

The preferred method for repairing large blisters dictates the need for a plastic-faced plaster reference medium. The sequence is illustrated in Figure 9-4. A cutout is made 3 inches outside the periphery of the blister. The cutout should be made at a 45° angle. The tool

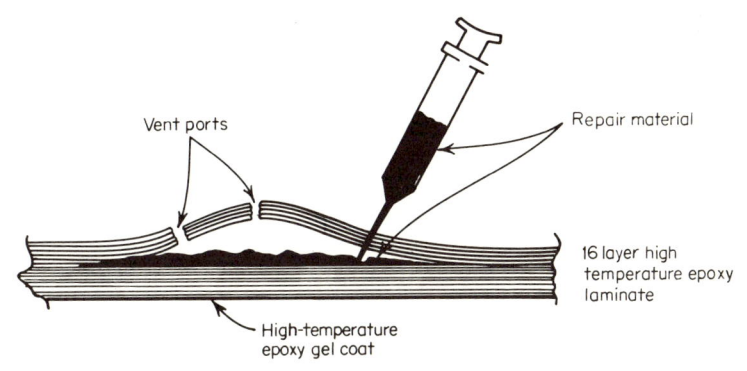

Fig. 9-3 Injecting repair material into interlaminar void.

216   Plastic Tooling

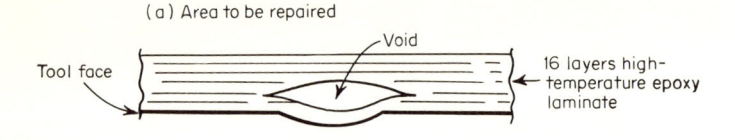

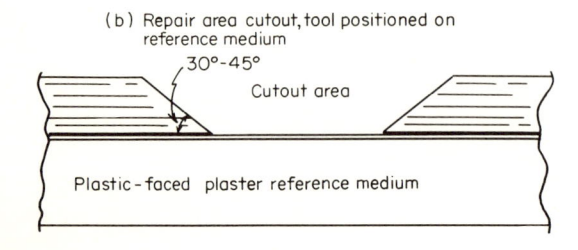

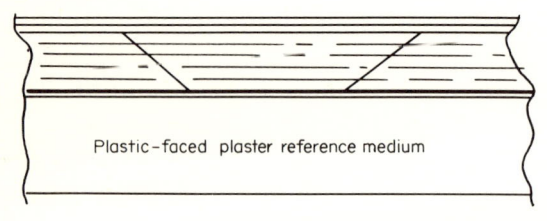

Fig. 9-4 Replacing section of a high-temperature epoxy laminated tool.

is then positioned over the plastic-faced plaster reference medium, which has already been coated with release agent. The same high-temperature gel coat used on the tool is applied to the model surface, and the 16-layer laminate is built up in the same manner as the original tool was fabricated. The repair is allowed to gel at room temperature and is then given the oven postcure recommended by the resin formulator.

Vacuum Leaks

Failure of a lay-up mandrel or a high-temperature bonding tool to maintain vacuum can result in the loss of an expensive part. It is important that these types of high-temperature plastic tools be checked for vacuum integrity at regular intervals.

If vacuum leaks are detected, the following method may be used to effectively seal the tool:

1. Sandblast the entire backside of the tool and wipe the surface clean with a clean cloth and clean acetone.
2. Apply a vacuum bag to the face of the tool.
3. Brush a low-viscosity high-temperature epoxy resin system onto the back of the tool and allow the vacuum to draw the resin into the laminate. It is also possible to use a low-viscosity urethane elastomer for this purpose.
4. Postcure the repair material according to the manufacturer's recommendations.
5. The tool is again checked for vacuum integrity. If the tool still leaks, steps 1–4 are repeated until the tool is completely sealed.

SUMMARY

Plastic tools are easily modified and repaired. The key to success is the use of good judgment, proper materials, and proper repair procedures. Before actual work on a repair is started, the cause of the tool failure should be determined. This will enable a repair to be made that will eliminate the future need for the same repair on the same tool. No matter how much pressure is exerted for a "quick and dirty" repair job, it is best to stick to proven procedures and cure cycles. Sad experience has shown many instances where attempts to circumvent accepted practices have resulted in subsequent tool failures that put the production shop in a worse predicament than it was in with the original failure. For example, an attempt to accelerate the cure of a repair of a room-temperature-service laminated tool by heating (from 12 hours to 2 hours) resulted in warpage of the tool. The tool had to be rebuilt, necessitating several days delay. The use of a "quick-set polyester" to repair a high-temperature tool resulted in the repairs falling out during the first production cycle after the repair. The tool was returned to the toolmaker, and the proper material was used on the second repair.

In conclusion, the author recognizes that most tool repairs are made under pressure. Repairs stimulate a sense of urgency that invariably leads the toolmaker to experiment on production tools with unproved materials or repair procedures. The author can cite many instances similar to the ones mentioned above where this type of action has resulted in failure. The tool engineer or tooling supervisor should be responsive to the needs of production for the particular tool in question. However, he should keep in mind that he is being paid to apply his knowledge, experience, and judgment to the situation and stick with proven practices that offer the best chance of success.

CHAPTER TEN

Safety Precautions in the Use of Plastic Tooling Materials

INTRODUCTION

The author feels that it is appropriate at this point to make recommendations related to the handling of materials used in plastic tooling. The resin and catalyst systems are reactive chemicals and, as such, can cause irritations to the skin. In addition, there is evidence that inhaling vapors emanating from these compounds can cause headaches, runny noses, sore throats, and even nausea. Therefore, the importance of taking certain precautions when handling these materials cannot be minimized. The Epoxy Resin Formulators Division of the Society of the Plastics Industry has conducted extensive research to ensure that plastic tooling materials with the minimum irritant potential be used in their products. However, although the potential hazards have been minimized, they have not been eliminated. Therefore, it is necessary for shop workers to follow certain guidelines when handling these materials. Some useful recommendations are set forth in this section.

CAUSES OF SKIN IRRITATION

Industrial hygienists agree that *the two main causes* of skin irritations or other symptoms of illness by resins are *direct contact with the skin and excessive inhalation of vapors.* It has been observed that in factories where synthetic resins are processed largely by automated processes, symptoms of illness or skin disorders have been minimal.

Plastic tooling depends largely on the individual worker and his skill in handling the various tooling compounds. Plastic tooling does not lend itself well to automation. The workers must weigh, mix, pour, and laminate with these various tooling compounds. Observations made in various shops show many shop habits that are easy to fall into that contribute largely to skin irritation. For example, what tool engineer or shop supervisor has not observed a worker spill resin on a bench during mixing, laminating, or casting; wipe it up with a cloth soaked in solvent; and later use that same solvent-soaked cloth to wipe resin from his hands and arms? The worker has just succeeded in rubbing a diluted resin-hardener mixture into the pores of his skin. What's worse, the solvents have removed the natural protective oils and fats from his skin. It is obvious that all-too-common occurrences such as this must be eliminated for the worker's own safety.

PREVENTIVE MEASURES

Preventive measures that can be taken fall into two general categories: (1) avoiding direct skin contact and (2) ensuring good ventilation in the work areas.

Protection of the Skin

1. The most effective protection of the skin is afforded by the wearing of rubber gloves. If gloves are to be worn for prolonged periods, wearing cotton gloves underneath the rubber gloves is helpful. The gloves should be washed daily, and the insides should be powdered with talcum powder.

2. Protective hand creams and ointments have proven to be very beneficial in protecting the skin. These materials should be applied before the beginning of the shift and again right after the lunch break. When the shift is finished, the worker should wash thoroughly and again apply the cream or ointment to areas that were in contact with resins. These protective creams are particularly helpful in minimizing irritations on the forehead, the face, the forearms, and the backs of the hands.

3. Maintaining cleanliness of the work areas is extremely important. Workbenches should be covered with kraft paper at the beginning of the shift. The paper should be removed and disposed of and new paper used midway through the shift. The use of solvents should be kept to a minimum. Clean cloths should be provided daily in the work areas. When a cloth becomes saturated with solvent and/or resin, it

should be removed from the work area. Resin drippings and spillages should be cleaned up immediately. Workers should wear gloves during such cleaning.

Ensuring Good Ventilation

Several measures can be taken to ensure that shop workers do not inhale the vapors from tooling resin compounds. Special precautions must be taken with the polyurethane elastomers, since their vapors can be extremely harmful to the respiratory system. Some recommended precautions are:

1. Weighing and mixing of resin compounds should be accomplished under a hood equipped with an exhaust fan. This is essential in the case of polyurethane elastomers.

2. There should be good ventilation in the work area. Ventilation should be sufficient to change the air in the work room three to four times per 8-hour shift. In shops with low ceilings, this may require installation of exhaust equipment throughout the shop. In other shops, good ventilation can be obtained simply by opening a few windows.

SUMMARY

Tooling resin compounds can cause skin irritations and other medical problems. The best way to minimize these problems is to ensure good ventilation in the work areas and minimize direct contact of tooling resin compounds with the skin.

Glossary of Tooling Terminology

A-STAGE   An early stage in the reaction of a thermosetting resin in which the material is still linear in structure, soluble in certain liquids, and fusible (see also B-stage and C-stage).

ABRASION RESISTANCE   The ability to resist surface wear; this term usually is used in reference to the ability of foundry patterns to withstand exposure to foundry sand.

ABRASIVE   Any substance used for abrading, such as grinding, polishing, or sandblasting.

ABSORPTION   The penetration into the mass of one substance by another.

ACCELERATOR   An additive used to hasten a chemical reaction. In the case of a thermosetting resin it is used to reduce curing or hardening time by entering into the reaction.

ADHESION   The state in which two surfaces are held together by interfacial forces which may consist of valence forces, interlocking action, or both.

ADHESIVE   A substance capable of holding two surfaces together. Most plastic tooling resin compounds are excellent adhesives.

AGING   The change of a material with time under defined environmental conditions that leads to improvement or deterioration of properties.

ANNEALING   A process of holding a material at an elevated temperature below its melting point, the object being to permit relieving of stresses without distortion of shape. Annealing is often used on molded or thermoformed parts.

ASSEMBLY JIG   A tool used to locate detailed parts in proper relationship to one another and hold them in a fixed position during assembly operations.

ASSEMBLY MODEL   A model used to check and/or coordinate tools, parts, or assemblies. It provides the contour, lines, and hole patterns.

AUTOCLAVE   A closed vessel for conducting chemical reactions under high pressure and temperature, frequently used for bonding reinforced plastic honeycomb parts.

B-STAGE   An intermediate stage in the reaction of a thermosetting resin in which the material softens when heated and swells in contact with certain liquids, but does not entirely fuse or dissolve.

BACKDRAFT   Taper or draft which prevents removal of plastic tool or plastic part from its mold.

BAND SAW   A saw in the form of an endless steel belt which runs over pulleys.

BEAD   A half-round cavity or protrusion in a tool or mold, depending on the application.

BLANKING DIE   A cutting die used in a power press to stamp out sheet metal blanks of predetermined size and outline.

BLEEDER CLOTH   A cloth (usually cotton or fiber glass) placed over a laminate before vacuum bagging to provide an avenue of escape for air and other gases.

BLISTER   An elevation on the surface of a laminate resembling in shape a blister on human skin. Blisters may be caused by insufficient resin; inadequate cure; or entrapped air, water, or solvent vapor.

BOND   Verb—to unite materials by means of an adhesive; noun—the union of materials by adhesives.

BOND STRENGTH   The unit load required to break an adhesive bond between two materials at or near the plane of the bond.

BOSS   Protuberance on a plastic part or plastic tool designed to add strength, to facilitate alignment during assembly, to provide for fastenings, etc.

BUSHING   A sleeve, usually metallic, which is placed in a plastic tool to provide wear resistance, i.e., drill bushings and bushings for alignment pins.

C-STAGE   The final stage in the reaction of a thermosetting resin in which the material is insoluble and infusible. Thermosetting resins in a fully cured plastic are in this stage.

CAST   Verb—to form a plastic tool or part by pouring a catalyzed resin into a mold in which it hardens; noun—the finished product of the casting operation.

CASTING RESIN   A resin compound which can be poured in liquid condition into a mold cavity to produce a plastic tool or plastic part.

CATALYST   A chemical substance which speeds up the polymerization or cure of a resin compound.

CAVITY   A depression in a mold.

CENTIPOISE   One hundredth of a poise; a unit for measuring viscosity of liquids established by the National Bureau of Standards. The viscosity of water at room temperature is one poise.

CHECKING FIXTURE   A tool used to check the contour of production parts, usually an epoxy laminated tool.

CLAMP   A device for holding parts of a mold, flask, corebox, etc., together.

COINING DIE   A tool used to make indentations on flat surfaces, such as stamped medals and emblems.

COMPRESSION MOLD   A mold which is open when the material is introduced and which shapes the material by heat and by the pressure of closing.

COMPRESSION MOLDING   A technique of thermoset molding in which the molding compound is placed in the open mold cavity, the mold is closed, and heat and pressure (the form of a downward moving ram) are applied until the material has cured.

COMPRESSIVE STRENGTH   The yield strength in compression of a material, expressed in pounds per square inch. The load is applied normal to the plane surface.

COOLING FIXTURE   A tool used to support a molded part after it is removed from the mold. The tool holds the molded part in its proper shape until it is cool enough to retain its shape without support.

COPE   The upper or topmost section of a flask, mold, or pattern.

CORE   A separable part of a foundry mold, usually made of sand, used to create openings and cavities in metal castings.

COREBOX   A box in which cores are made.

CRAZING   Fine cracks which may extend in a network on or under the surface or through a layer of a plastic tool or part. Crazing can be caused by exposure to organic liquids or vapors or by mechanical stress.

CREEP   The dimensional change with time of a material under load, following the initial instantaneous elastic deformation. Creep at room temperature is sometimes referred to as "cold flow."

CURE   The changing of the physical properties of a material by chemical reactions.

DEFLECTION TEMPERATURE   The temperature at which a plastic material deflects a given amount under a given load. In plastic tooling, it is commonly the temperature at which a material deflects 0.10 inch under 264 psi load.

224   Plastic Tooling

DELAMINATION   The separation of the layers in a laminate caused by the failure of the adhesive or laminating resin.

DENSITY   Weight per unit volume of a substance, usually expressed in grams per cubic centimeter or in pounds per cubic foot.

DRAFT   Taper given to the vertical faces of a mold or tool to facilitate removal of the part.

DRAG   The lower or bottom section of a mold or pattern.

DRAW DIE   A die used to draw form flat or preformed metal sheets into production parts. Draw dies are generally used to form shapes such as cups, boxes, hat sections, and pans.

DRILL FIXTURE   A fixture used to locate and hold production parts during the drilling operation.

ELASTICITY   The property of a material by virtue of which it tends to recover its original size and shape after deformation.

ELASTOMER   A material which at room temperature stretches at low stress to at least twice its length and snaps back to the original length upon release of stress.

ELECTROFORMED MOLD   A mold made by electroplating metal on the reverse pattern of a cavity.

ELONGATION   The fractional increase in length of a material stressed in tension, usually expressed as a percentage.

EXOTHERM   (1) The temperature/time curve of a chemical reaction giving off heat, particularly the polymerization of casting resins. (2) The amount of heat given off.

FABRICATE   To work a material into a finished form by machining, laminating, splining, casting, carving, forming, etc.

FEMALE   In molding terms, the indented half of a mold designed to receive the protruding, or male, half.

FILLER   An inexpensive, inert substance added to a plastic to make it less costly. Fillers may also improve physical properties, such as hardness, abrasion resistance, and impact strength.

FILLET   A radiused junction formed where two surfaces meet. A rounded filling of the internal angle between two molding surfaces.

FLASH   Extra plastic along the parting line of a molded part which must be removed before the part can be considered finished.

FLASK   A metal container in which a sand foundry mold is made.

FLASK PINS   Devices to assure proper alignment of cope-and-drag molds after the pattern is withdrawn.

FLEXIBLE MOLD   Molds made of rubber or elastomers used for casting plastic parts. Flexible molds can be stretched to remove cured parts with undercuts.

FLEXURAL STRENGTH   The strength of a material in bending, expressed as the tensile stress of the outermost fibers of a bent test sample at the instant of failure, measured in pounds per square inch.

FORM DIE   A die used for bending metal materials such as rods, angles, extrusions, and strips into predetermined shapes.

FRACTURE   A rupture of a surface without complete separation of the part.

GEL COAT   A specifically formulated resin compound which is applied to the surface of a model or mold. Additional resin is either cast or laminated to the gel coat. When cured, the gel coat becomes the surface of the tool or part.

GEL TIME   The time in minutes for a given amount of catalyzed resin to become unworkable at room temperature.

GLOVE MOLD   A flexible mold consisting of a thin elastomeric layer, such as silicone RTV rubber or polyurethane, supported by a rigid shell. Glove molds are used to cast plastic parts having intricate detail or undercuts.

HAMMER DIE   A punch and die combination used in a drop-hammer press for forming sheet metal parts.

HARDENER   A chemical substance added to a thermosetting resin to promote or control the curing reaction.

HARDNESS   The resistance of a plastic to compression and indentation (see Shore Hardness).

HYDRAULIC   A system in which energy is transferred from one place to another by means of compression and flow of a fluid (e.g., water, oil).

HYDROPHOBIC   Capable of curing when in contact with water.

HYDROPRESS BLOCK   A male-type tool used to locate sheet metal blanks and control their shape during hydropress forming operations.

HYGROSCOPIC   Tending to absorb moisture.

IMPACT STRENGTH   The ability of a material to withstand shock or impact, as from a sharp blow.

IMPREGNATE   To provide liquid penetration into a porous or fibrous material, as in laminating.

INJECTION MOLDING   A process whereby a specially designed machine is utilized to melt solid plastic particles and force the liquid plastic into a mold, where it assumes the shape of the mold cavity. The plastic is held under pressure until it cools and becomes solid.

INJECTION MOLDING DIES   A mold or die used in the injection molding process to establish the shape of the molded part.

INTEGRALLY HEATED TOOL   A tool or mold having embedded heating elements which provide its own heat source. Integrally heated tools are used as bonding assembly jigs, lay-up mandrels, mat molding dies, and thermoforming molds.

JOINT   The location at which two parts are held together by a layer of adhesive.

KIRKSITE An alloy of aluminum and zinc used as a core for cast epoxy metal-forming tools. It is also used for making compression molds and blow molds.

LAMINATED PLASTIC A plastic material consisting of superimposed layers of resin-impregnated fabric or fibers.

LAMINATING RESIN A liquid resin compound superficially formulated to impregnate fiber glass cloth during the process of making a laminated structure.

LAY-UP MANDREL A permanent tool which provides a contour upon which plastic parts are laminated or wrapped.

MARK-OFF An indentation or imprinting on the surface of a formed or molded part. The mark-off usually coordinates with the location of a surface defect or imperfection on the tool or die used to make the production part.

MASTER MODEL A full-scale, three-dimensional object which establishes the complete outside or inside of a part or assembly as defined by the engineering drawing. A master model usually contains all reference lines, trim lines, tooling holes, and other pertinent information.

MOCKUP Slang which, when properly used, means the same as the term master model.

MODEL A three-dimensional representation of a part or assembly, but not necessarily full-scale. Models are used for study during design evolution, market surveys, etc. This term is frequently confused with the term master model.

MOLD The cavity or form into or onto which the plastic compound is placed and from which it takes its form.

MOLD RELEASE A liquid or powdered lubricant used to prevent adhesion of a plastic part to a mold and to facilitate part removal.

NORMAL CONSISTENCY The amount of water, expressed as a whole number, required to mix 100 parts by weight of plaster to a standard degree of fluidity.

ORGANIC Designating or pertaining to the chemistry of carbon compounds, not including carbonates or the oxides of carbon.

PARTING AGENT A lubricant such as wax, silicone grease, or film used to coat a tool to prevent the plastic part from sticking to the mold and to facilitate removal of the part from the tool or mold.

PARTING LINE The mark on a molding or casting where the two halves of a mold meet in closing.

PASTE ADHESIVE An adhesive composition having a thick, thixotropic consistency.

PATTERN An exact representation, three-dimensional, of the part made to scale or to shrink-scale dimensions.

PEEL STRENGTH Bond strength in pounds per inch width, obtained by peeling two adjacent laminated layers apart and recording the adhesive strength values.

PIT   A small crater in the surface of a plastic part, usually with a width in the same order of magnitude as its depth.

PLASTER   A powdery substance derived from the mineral gypsum possessing the capability of being mixed with water and hardening into a solid, rocklike mass.

PRESSURE CASTING   A casting method whereby the liquid resin is introduced into the mold cavity under pressure. This technique is often employed to ensure complete filling of molds having intricate detail.

PROTOTYPE   A full-sized, handmade, three-dimensional representation of the final product or part. A prototype is usually a completely functional model and is constructed from the same materials that will be used to make the production item.

REINFORCEMENT   A strong inert material bonded into a plastic part to incorporate strength, stiffness, and/or impact resistance.

ROUTER FIXTURE   A tool applied to a production part which provides a guide for the router while it is being used to trim the part. The fixture locates and holds the production part as well as provides a guide for the router.

SANDWICH PANEL   A laminar construction consisting of thin facings bonded to a thick, lightweight core, resulting in a rigid and lightweight panel.

SET   To convert a thermosetting resin into a fixed or hardened state by chemical action.

SHAPER FIXTURE   A tool used to locate and hold production parts during the shaper operation.

SHRINK RULE   A patternmaker's rule graded to allow for metal contraction (foundry).

SPECIFIC GRAVITY   The density (mass per unit volume) of any material divided by that of water at a standard temperature.

SPLINE   To prepare a surface to its desired contour by working a paste resin or plaster with a flat-edged tool. The procedure is also referred to as screeding or fairing.

SPRAY LAMINATING   A mechanized process for making laminating plastics. Mechanical equipment is utilized to spray catalyzed resin and chopped fiber glass strands onto a tool or mold.

SPRAY TEMPLATE   A tool used to mask off certain sections of a part while it is being spray-painted.

SPRUE   An opening through which material is fed into a mold cavity.

SPRUE-AND-VENT CASTING   A casting method in which the liquid resin is poured through tubes (sprues) leading to the lowest point in a mold cavity. Entrapped air is allowed to escape through holes (vents) located in the core. This technique is normally used to cast a plastic surface on tools having metal or wood cores.

STEEL RULE DIE   A two-piece tool consisting of a punch with a stripper plate and a die block used for blanking and piercing thin-gauge parts.

STRETCH FORM BLOCK   A block or form over which sheet metal is formed to a desired contour on a stretch forming machine.

TACK-FREE   An intermediate stage in the curing process whereby a catalyzed resin has gelled but remains workable. Surface contact will indent the resin surface but will not cause adhesion to the contacting medium.

TENSILE STRENGTH   The stress expressed in pounds per square inch required to break a given specimen by pulling.

THERMAL CONDUCTIVITY   The ability of a material to conduct heat.

THERMAL EXPANSION (Coefficient of)   The fractional change in length of a material for unit change in temperature, expressed in inches per inch per degree Centigrade.

THERMOFORMING   A process of forming a thermoplastic sheet by heating the sheet and pulling it down onto a mold surface, usually with the aid of vacuum.

THERMOPLASTIC   Adjective—capable of being repeatedly softened by heat and hardened by cooling; noun—a material which can be softened by heat and hardened by cooling.

THERMOSETTING   Resins capable of forming solid, stable shapes through chemical reaction with a suitable catalyst or hardener.

THIXOTROPIC   Gel-like at rest but fluid when agitated. This is a desirable characteristic of gel coat compounds.

TRIM TOOL   An instrument which holds or is clamped to a part during the trimming operation.

VACUUM FORMING MOLD   A high-temperature-service mold having vacuum holes and used for thermoforming thermoplastic sheets to a desired configuration.

VISCOSITY   The resistance of a liquid to flow; thickness.

Index

Index

A-stage, 221
Abrasion, 125, 128
Abrasion resistance, 136, 221
Abrasive, 221
Absorption, 221
Accelerator, 221
Adhesion, 85, 221
Adhesive, 82, 221
   application of, 210–213
   paste, 16, 210–212
   patching, 209–213
   physical properties of, 209
Aging, 221
Annealing, 222
Assembly fixtures, 89–92, 222
Assembly jigs, 222
   bonding, 146–147
Assembly models, 69, 222
Assist forming pads, 114
Autoclave, 146, 147, 222

B-stage, 222
Backdraft, 8, 222

Bagging, 76
   high-temperature tools, 159
Band saws, 222
Beads, 222
Blanking dies, 222
Bleeder cloth, 159, 222
Blisters, 213, 215–216, 222
Bond, 74, 80, 82, 222
Bond strength, 222
   of casting resins, 17, 103, 108
   of laminating resins, 17
   of low-density compounds, 62
   of paste patching compounds, 209
   of polyester, 17
   of polyurethane, 17
   of RTV silicone, 17
   of splining compounds, 64
Bonding assembly jigs, 146–147
Bushings, 89, 94, 95, 222

C-stage, 222
Cast tools:
   advantages of, 101

232　Index

Cast tools (*Cont.*):
　coreboxes, 137
　draw dies, 119–122
　drop-hammer dies, 115, 116, 118
　duplicate patterns, 132–135
　foundary patterns, 132
　hydroform dies, 114
　matchplate patterns, 132
　stretch form blocks, 117–119
Casting:
　epoxy, 102–106, 109–112
　mass (*see* Mass casting)
　polysulfide, 204
　polyurethane, 200–203
　pressure, 112
　RTV silicone, 187–198
　sprue-and-vent, 111
　straight, 110
　surface, 107–112
Casting compounds:
　epoxy, 100–102
　polysulfide, 204
　polyurethane, 198–200
　RTV silicone, 186–187
Casting resins, 223
Catalyst, 223
Cavity, 100, 130, 223
Centipoise, 223
Checking fixtures, 69, 85, 95–97
Chemical classification of tooling materials, 16
Clamps, 223
Cleanliness:
　personal, 219
　of plaster shop, 31
Coining dies, 223
Compression molding, 223
Compression molds, 167, 223
Compressive strength, 223
　of epoxy casting compounds, 103, 108
Cooling fixtures, 223
Cope, 130, 223
Cope-and-drag equipment, 129, 131, 140
Core driers, 145
Coreboxes, 223
　foundry, 129, 135–144
　　cast, 137–139
　　laminated, 136–137
　　shell, short-run, 142–144
Cores, 223
　foundry, 129

Cores (*Cont.*):
　materials for, 129
　positioning of, 108–109, 129
Crazing, 223
Creep, 223
Cure, 223
　cast epoxy, 105, 133
　epoxy laminates, 75
　polyurethane, 202
　RTV silicone, 191–193
Cure inhibition, 193

Deflection temperature, 223
　of cast epoxy, 17, 103, 108
　of epoxy laminates, 17, 69
　of high-temperature castings, 152
　of high-temperature laminates, 152
　of low-density compounds, 62
　of paste patching compounds, 209
　of potting compounds, 95
　of splining compounds, 64
Delamination, 214–216, 224
Density, 224
Design considerations:
　for epoxy castings, 114
　for epoxy laminates, 70
　for high-temperature laminates, 160
Dies:
　blanking, 222
　coining, 223
　draw, 119–122
　drop-hammer, 91, 115–118
　forming, 123
　hydroforming, 114
　injection molding, 165–167, 225
　steel rule, 228
　stretch form, 117–119
Diesinking patterns, 98–99
Draft, 7–9, 128
　back, 8, 222
Drag, 129–131
　(*See also* Cope-and-drag equipment)
Draw dies, 119–122
Draw forming, 119, 121
Drill jigs, 92–95
Drop-hammer dies, 91, 115–118
　(*See also* Hammer dies)
Duplicate models, 81, 84

Index

Eggcrate reinforcements, 79, 160
Elasticity, 224
Elastomers, 186, 224
  latex, 205
  polysulfide, 203
  polyurethane, 198, 199
  RTV silicone, 186
Elongation, 224
Epoxy dies:
  draw dies, 119–122
  drop-hammer dies, 91, 115–118
  hydroform dies, 114
  injection molding, 165–167
  stretch form, 117–119
Epoxy resin compounds:
  casting, 15, 103, 108
  gel coats, 15
  high-temperature casting, 152
  high-temperature laminating, 152
  laminating, 16, 69, 76
Epoxy tools:
  bonding assembly fixture, 146, 147
  checking fixture, 69, 85, 95–97
  compression molds, 167
  draw dies, 119–122
  hydroform dies, 114
  injection molds, 165–167, 225
  lay-up mandrels, 146–147
  thermoforming molds, 147–149, 163
  (*See also* Laminated epoxy tools)
Epoxy tubing, 81–83, 85
  cutting of, 82–83
  physical properties of, 82
  reinforcing with, 81–83
Exotherm, 224

Fabricate, 224
Fabrication techniques:
  bonding assembly jigs, 146
  cast epoxy tools, 100
  draw dies, 119
  drop-hammer dies, 115
  flexible molds, 185
  glove molds, 194
  integrally heated tools, 171
  latex molds, 205
  lay-up mandrels, 146
  mass cast epoxy tools, 102
  polysulfide molds, 203
  polyurethane molds, 198

Fabrication techniques (*Cont.*):
  RTV silicone molds, 186
  spray-laminated tools, 75
  stretch form dies, 117
  surface cast epoxy tools, 107
Fabrics, glass fiber, 70–73
Female, 224
Fillers, 224
Fillet, 224
Fixtures:
  assembly, 89–92, 222
  checking, 69, 85, 95–97
  cooling, 223
  drill, 92–95
  router, 227
  shaper, 227
  weld, 97
Flash, 224
Flask, 129, 224
Flask pins, 129, 224
Flexible molds, 185–205, 225
  latex, 205
  polysulfide, 203–204
  polyurethane, 198–203
  RTV silicone, 186–198
Flexural strength, 69, 225
Forming:
  draw, 119–121
  drop-hammer, 115
  hydroforming, 114–115
  stretch, 118–119
Foundry patterns, 125–145
Fractures, 212, 225

Gel coats, 15–16, 225
Gel time, 225
Glass fabrics, 70–72
  physical properties of, 72
  weaving, 71
  yarn, 71
Glass paste, 73
Glove molds, silicone rubber, 194, 225
Gypsum cements:
  advantages of, 30
  handling and mixing of, 30
  physical data for, 29
  pouring, 32
  screeding with, 39
  splashing, 34

234   Index

Hammer dies, 115–117, 225
  (*See also* Drop-hammer dies)
Hand laminating, 72–75, 158–164
Hardeners, 225
Hardness, 225
High-temperature plastic tools, 146–168
  advantages and disadvantages of, 150–151
  bonding assembly jigs, 146–147
  casting procedure, 164
  injection molds, 165–167, 225
  lay-up mandrels, 146, 148, 153, 160, 161
  life expectancy of, 149–150
  physical properties of, 152–153
  thermoforming molds, 147–149, 161–163
Honeycomb sandwich panels, 84–86
Hydraulic, 225
Hydroforming dies, 114

Impact strength, 225
Impregnate, 225
Injection molding, 225
Injection molding dies, 165–167, 225
Integrally heated tools, 169–184, 225

Joints, 225

Kirksite, 226

Laminated epoxy tools:
  assembly fixtures, 89–92
  bonding assembly jigs, 146–147
  checking fixtures, 69, 85, 95–97
  elevated-temperature service, 146
  reinforcing materials, 78–88
  room-temperature service, 68
  thermoforming molds, 147
Laminating:
  hand lay-up method, 72–75
  high-temperature tools, 158
  spray-laminating method, 75–78
Latex rubber molds, 205
Lay-up mandrels, 146, 148, 153, 160, 161, 226

Life expectancy of high-temperature tools, 149–150
Low-density compounds:
  application of, 62, 63
  properties of, 62

Mass casting, 102–107
  epoxy, 103
  RTV silicone, 186
Mass casting compounds, 102–107
  cure of, 105
  physical properties of, 103
Master models, 27, 28, 226
  plaster, 28–59
  plastic, 57–67
    splined, 59–67
    skeleton of, 60–61
  templates, 39–47
  (*See also* Modelmaking)
Match-buttons, 10, 11
Matched dies:
  draw dies, 119–122
  drop-hammer dies, 91, 115–118
  injection molding dies, 165–167, 225
Matchplates, 129–130
Metal-forming tools, 113
Modelmaking, 27–67
  circular turning method, 52–53
  cylindrical turning method, 53–57
  loft template method, 39–47
  screeding method, 39
  splined plastic, 59–67
  straight run molding, 47–52
Models, 27–67
  assembly, 69, 222
  duplicate, 81, 84
  master (*see* Master models)
  splined (*see* Splined models)
  (*See also* Modelmaking)
Mold fabrication:
  alignment of, 11, 12
  core positioning of, 108
  flexible, 185–205
Mold release, 18–23, 226
Molds, 226
  flexible (*see* Flexible molds)
  hand-laminated, 68
  high-temperature, 146
  injection, 165–167, 225
  latex, 205

Index   235

Molds (*Cont.*):
  polysulfide, 203–204
  polyurethane, 198–203
  RTV silicone, 186–198
  vacuum forming, 147, 227

Normal consistency, 31, 226

Open-face casting (*see* Mass casting)
Organic, 226

Parting agents, 18–23, 226
Parting lines, 10, 226
Paste adhesive, 226
Paste patching compounds:
  application of, 207, 208
  properties of, 209
Patternmaker's sheet wax, 131
Patterns, 226
  diesinking, 98–99
  duplicate, 132–135
  foundry, 125–145
  plastic-faced plaster, 133, 154–156
Peel strength, 226
Physical properties:
  of cast epoxy, 103, 108
  of epoxy laminates, 69
  of high-temperature castings, 152
  of high-temperature laminates, 152
  of low-density compounds, 62
  of paste patching compounds, 209
  of polyurethane elastomers, 199
  of potting compounds, 95
  of RTV silicone rubber, 187
  of splining compounds, 64
  of thermosetting plastics, 17
Pits, 227
Plaster, 227
  casting, 32
  expansion of, setting, 29
  handling and storing of, 30
  mixing, 31–32
  plastic-faced, 154
  screeding, 39
  splashing, 34
Plastic dies:
  draw, 119–122
  drop-hammer, 91, 115–118

Plastic dies (*Cont.*):
  hydroform, 114
  injection molding, 165–167, 225
  stretch form, 117–119
Plastic master models (*see* Master models, plastic)
Plastic molds:
  polysulfide, 203
  polyurethane, 198
  RTV silicone, 186–194
Plastic tooling:
  advantages of, 23, 24
  disadvantages of, 25
Polycarbonate, 149
Polyester, 17
Polysulfide molds, 203–204
Polysulfone, 149
Polyurethane elastomers:
  molds, 198–203
  properties of, 199
Pressure casting, 112
Prototype model, 28
Putty mix, 73

Reinforcements, 78, 227
  epoxy tubing, 81–83
  fiber-glass-faced honeycomb, 84, 86
  laminated eggcrate, 79, 160
  lightweight aggregate, 85, 87–88
Release agents, 18–22
Repair of plastic tools, 206–217
  delamination, 214–216
  fractures, 212
  refacing, 211–212
  surface defects: high-temperature service, 213–214
    room-temperature service, 209–211
  vacuum leaks, 216–217
Router fixtures, 227

Safety precautions, 218–220
Sandwich panels, honeycomb, 84–86, 227
Screeding with gypsum cements, 39
Scrim cloth, 63
Set, 227
Shaper fixtures, 227
Sheet wax, patternmaker's, 131
Shrink rule, 227
Silicone rubber molds, 186–198

Specific gravity, 227
　of epoxy casting compounds, 103, 108
　of epoxy laminating compounds, 69
Splined models:
　gypsum cement, 39–46
　plastic, 59–67
　template setups for, 40–42, 60
Splining compounds, 63–67
Spray laminating, 75–78
Spray templates, 227
Sprue-and-vent casting, 111, 227
Steel rule dies, 228
Straight run molding, 47–52
Stretch form blocks, 117–119, 228
Supporting structures (*see* Reinforcements)
Surface casting compounds:
　application of, 102
　cure of, 113
　physical properties of, 108

Tack-free, 73, 228
Templates, 39–47
　spray, 227
Tensile strength, 228
Thermal conductivity, 228
Thermal expansion, coefficient of, 228
　　aluminum needle-epoxy binder, 153
　　epoxy castings, 152
　　epoxy laminates, 152

Thermoforming, 14, 147, 228
Thermoplastic, 12, 14, 228
Thermosetting, 12, 13, 228
Thixotropy, 15–16, 228
Tooling materials, 1–26
　chemical classification of, 16
　functional classification of, 15
　safety precautions in the use of, 218–220
Tools:
　cast (*see* Cast tools)
　epoxy (*see* Epoxy tools)
　high-temperature (*see* High-temperature plastic tools)
　integrally heated, 169–184, 225
　metal-forming, 113
　repair of (*see* Repair of plastic tools)
　trim, 228
Trim tools, 228

Vacuum forming molds, 147, 227
Vacuum leaks, 216–217
Viscosity, 227
　of epoxy casting compounds, 103, 108
　of epoxy laminating compounds, 69

Weld fixtures, 97